T0339538

Trust and Distrust in Digital Economies

In digital economies, the Internet enables the "platformisation" of everything. Big technology companies and mobile apps are running mega marketplaces, supported by seamless online payments systems. This rapidly expanding ecosystem is fuelled by data. Meanwhile, perceptions of the global financial crisis, data breaches, disinformation and the manipulation of political sentiment have combined to create a modern trust crisis. A lack of trust constrains commerce, particularly in terms of consumer protection and investment. Big data, artificial intelligence, automated algorithms and blockchain technology offer new solutions and risks.

Trust in our legal systems depends on certainty, consistency and enforceability of the law. However, regulatory and remedial gaps exist because the law has not kept up with technology. This work explores the role of competency and good faith, in the creation of social and legal relationships of trust; and the need for governance transparency and human accountability to combat distrust, particularly in digital economies.

Dr Philippa (Pip) Ryan is a barrister and a senior lecturer in the College of Law at the Australian National University in Canberra. She is a Fellow of the Australian Digital Commerce Association. Pip is Chair of the Standards Australia blockchain working group for smart contracts, and Deputy Chair of the Australian Computer Society's blockchain technical committee. In 2018, she was named an American Bar Association "Legal Rebel". Pip co-authored Van Rijmenam and Ryan, *Blockchain: Transforming Your Business and Our World* (Routledge, 2019). Her favourite place to be is with her husband at home in the Snowy Mountains, with family and friends.

Routledge Research in Finance and Banking Law

For more information about this series, please visit: www.routledge.com/Routledge-Research-in-Finance-and-Banking-Law/book-series/FINANCIALLAW

Trust and Distrust in Digital Economies

Philippa Ryan

Routledge
Taylor & Francis Group

NEW YORK AND LONDON

First published 2019
by Routledge
605 Third Avenue, New York, NY 10017

and by Routledge
2 Park Square, Milton Park, Abingdon, Oxon OX14 4RN

First issued in paperback 2021

Routledge is an imprint of the Taylor & Francis Group, an informa business

Copyright © 2019 Taylor & Francis

Publisher's Note
The publisher has gone to great lengths to ensure the quality of this reprint but points out that some imperfections in the original copies may be apparent.

Library of Congress Cataloging-in-Publication Data
A catalog record for this title has been requested

ISBN 13: 978-1-03-224100-5 (pbk)
ISBN 13: 978-1-138-47748-3 (hbk)

DOI: 10.4324/9781351104845

Typeset in Galliard
by Taylor & Francis Books

Contents

Acknowledgements

This book would not have been possible without the help of the following people who have each provided meaningful input and feedback on different topics: Samuel Brooks, Scott Farrell, Vincent Gramoli, Jamie Glister, Darryn Jensen, Barbara McDonald, Jason Potts, Pauline Ridge, Mark Staples and Mark Van Rijmenan.

I also appreciate my wonderful network of experts and enthusiasts who generously take the time to exchange ideas thoughtfully and constructively in committees and teleconferences, via social media, and at Meetups all over the world, including: Adriana Belotti, Gayan Benedict, Katrina Donaghy, Jolyon Ford, Stevie Ghiassi, Nick Giurietto, Hannah Glass, Dazza Greenwood, Rob Hanson, Kobi Leins, Steven Nam, Bridie Ohlsson, Beth Patterson, Marc Pesce, Tony Rai, Louis Ryan, Claire Warren and Emma Weston.

Special thanks to Simonna Malki and Cindy Lam for proofreading my book.

Finally, for all his love and support, my husband, Dermot Ryan.

Part I

Introduction and Classification

1 Introduction

Employers can get into legal trouble if they ask interviewees about their religion, sexual preference or political affiliation, so instead of posing these questions in an interview, an employer can simply conduct online research to filter out applicants based on their beliefs, looks and habits as disclosed by candidates via social media websites. Laws forbid lenders from discriminating on the basis of race, gender and sexuality. Yet they can refuse to give a loan to people if (for example) their LinkedIn resumés do not match their profiles on Facebook; or if a computer algorithm judges them to be socially undesirable. These regulatory gaps exist because laws have not kept up with technology and these gaps exist and are widening in every digital domain.[1] Meanwhile, using the power of this same technology can help build trust between complete strangers, because social media and the platforms upon which our digital economies run is not just efficient; it is the social glue that establishes trust.

Botsman argues that trust and efficiency have been core requisites in all marketplaces for centuries. Trust has proven to be integral to economic development and human security, because trust is central to exchange and growth.[2] It works to cross barriers and calm fears. It can therefore 'revolutionise what is possible'.[3] Reports on findings from interviews with fledgling entrepreneurs reveal that trust is a prime requisite for success, including in societies that have been culturally depraved for many years.[4]

Today, technology is developing and being adopted on an exponential curve and is impacting almost everyone everywhere. Changes at a rate that once took

1   V Wadhwa, 'Laws and Ethics Can't Keep Pace with Technology', *MIT Technology Review* (15 April 2014) <https://www.technologyreview.com/s/526401/laws-and-ethics-cant-keep-pace-with-technology/>.

2   N Gillespie and R Hurley, 'Trust and the Global Financial Crisis', in *Handbook of Advances in Trust Research* edited by R Bachmann and A Zaheer (Edward Elgar Publishing, 2013), 177.

3   R Botsman, *Who Can You Trust? How Technology Brought Us Together and Why It Might Drive Us Apart* (Penguin Books, 2017), 10–17.

4   MB Neace, 'Entrepreneurs in Emerging Economies: Creating Trust, Social Capital, and Civil Society' (1999) 565(1) *The Annals of the American Academy of Political and Social Science* 148, 148; DM Ibrahim, 'The (Not So) Puzzling Behavior of Angel Investors' (2008) 61(5) *Vanderbilt Law Review* 1405, 1440.

centuries now happen in decades, sometimes years. The processing power for computers and devices from 1956 to 2015 has experienced a one trillion-fold increase in performance over those six decades. The computer that guided Apollo 11 to the moon in 1969 has just twice the processing power of the Nintendo 64 entertainment system. A single Apple iPhone 5 has 2.7 times the processing power of the world's first 'supercomputer': the 1985 Cray-2.[5] And while processing power and speed has gone up, the price of new technology has come down. A full human genome sequence that cost $100 million in 2002 could by 2014 be done for $1,000; and will likely cost less than a cup of coffee by 2020.[6]

The law and ethics are struggling to keep up with changes in new digital economies – online platforms for marketplaces and social relationships. Consider the question of privacy. The Common Law's modern extension of the tort of breach of privacy has its origins in a suit brought by Prince Albert seeking an injunction against William Strange to stop the latter from publishing and selling a catalogue of drawings made by members of his family, including his wife – Queen Victoria.[7] The etchings had been surreptitiously removed from the royal household and fell into the hands of William Strange. The Prince claimed a personal confidence in relation to the drawings. The Court found for the Prince, holding that the jurisdiction in confidence is based not so much on property or on contract as on a duty of good faith.

The decision in *Prince Albert v Strange* established in the English legal system that confidential information of a personal and private nature may be protected by an action for breach of confidence. Corresponding United States' laws also date back to the 19th century, although bit later than the English precedent. The trigger in the United States arose when newspapers first started reporting personal information and Boston lawyer Samuel Warren objected to social gossip published about his family. This led his law partner, and future United States Supreme Court Justice, Louis Brandeis to co-author the article 'The Right of Privacy'.[8] In both cases, the printing press was enabling widespread reproduction and distribution of personal images and potentially scandalous or defamatory information.

The disruptive impact of the printing press dates back to the 1400s and publishing technology continues to be inextricably connected with the development of privacy, copyright law and free speech. Copyright law starts with early

5   WE Hilton, 'Survey of Computers, Software and Information Processing' (1990) 31(2) *IDEA: The Journal of Law and Technology* 67–84. See also, K Olsen, 'Processing Power Compared', *Experts Exchange* (2016) <https://pages.experts-exchange.com/processing-power-compared>.

6   National Human Genome Research Institute, 'The Cost of Sequencing the Human Genome' (6 July 2016) <https://www.genome.gov/27565109/the-cost-of-sequencing-a-human-genome/>.

7   *Prince Albert v Strange* (1849) 1 H and Tw 1, 2 De G and SM 293, [1849] EngR 255, (1849) 41 ER 1171, [1849] EngR 261, (1849) 47 ER 1302, (1849) 2 De Gex and Sim 652.

8   S Warren and L Brandeis, 'The Right to Privacy' (1890) 4 *Harvard Law Review* 193.

privileges and monopolies granted to printers of books.[9] The computer is the modem analogue to the printing press. Both inventions facilitate the dissemination of information, the difference being in the mechanics.

The invention of the printing press had a revolutionary impact on the value of free speech in 15th-century England by both nourishing it and threatening it. Indeed, it is fair to say that the threats to freedom of speech arose out of its nourishment, out of a fear by the British government that this new technological device, which made speech more indiscriminately accessible, required legal curbs not previously thought to be necessary.[10]

The advent of the Internet is a quantum shift in the speed with which information can be distributed. Seen in this light – after centuries of relying on manual and then automated printing presses – the invention of the personal computer was merely an incremental innovation. While the main casualties of the printing press and desktop publishing were privacy and copyright protection, the thirty years since the invention in 1989 of the World Wide Web ('the Web') by Tim Berners-Lee has seen an explosion in the generation of data and the publication of all forms of political, economic and personal expression by both individuals and organisations. And this explosion of data – in particular consumer data – has changed the way we do business.[11]

In 1994 there were just 10,000 websites globally.[12] In 2001, the launch of Google enabled fast and uncategorised searches across the entire Web. With this e-commerce took off and, in Google's first year, more than 100 million Americans made an online purchase.[13] The relationship between Google and rise of e-commerce is not to be underestimated. As well as the almost omnipresence of Google's search engine and advertising content, other major players in the online market have grown over the past ten years.

Social media has emerged as a major online presence with Facebook and Twitter, in 2004 and 2006 respectively. Smart phones (particularly Apple's iPhone) brought the Internet to mobile phones in the early 2010s and have

9 The protection of an individual's use of the printing press – free of intrusive government regulation – was a response to the repressive regime of strict regulation of the press that enabled the English Crown and later Parliament to control the production of all printed materials in England from the 1500s until the early 1700s. See, E Lee, 'Freedom of the Press 2.0' (2008) 42 *Georgia Law Review* 309, 320.

10 I Glasser, 'The Struggle for a New Paradigm: Protecting Free Speech and Privacy in the Virtual World of Cyberspace' (1999) 23 *Nova Law Review* 627, 628.

11 A Hasty, 'Treating Consumer Data like Oil: How Re-framing Digital Interactions Might Bolster the Federal Trade Commission's New Privacy Framework' (2015) 67(2) *Federal Communications Law Journal* 293, 307.

12 R Swire, 'The Evolution of Digital Media Over the Past 20 Years', *Parallax* (2014) <https://parall.ax/blog/view/3052/the-evolution-of-digital-media-over-the-past-20-years>.

13 D Mutz, 2009. 'Effects of Internet Commerce on Social Trust' (2009) *Public Opinion Quarterly* 439–461, 439. See also, P McBride, 'Digital Technologies and the Erosion of Social Trust', in *Essays* (8 November 2017) <https://paulmcbride.me/2017/11/08/essay-digital-technology-and-the-erosion-of-social-trust/>.

'completely changed the way that people consume content on a daily basis'.[14] The majority of Internet time is now spent on mobile devices worldwide, and around 50% of people get their news from a digital source, such as a website, application or notification.[15] The media's role in mediating experience by bridging the gap between events and audiences is a broad but extremely important one,[16] and media organisations now have to take into account the presentation of their news more than ever, as users of digital media place high importance on the dissemination and delivery of news.

The Modern Trust Crisis

Much has been written over the past twenty years about the erosion of trust in our institutions including government and politicians,[17] banks and financial services providers,[18] and journalists and news services. Importantly, these three great institutions are the pillars of democracy. Dissatisfaction with and lack of confidence in the functioning of the institutions of democratic government has become widespread. The narrative of this modern trust crisis probably begins with Watergate and spikes in the wake of the 2008 Global Financial Crisis.

Former United States Senator Howard Baker's most enduring moment came in the middle of the Watergate scandal, when he asked: 'What did the president know and when did he know it?' Journalism's precise role in Nixon's demise is impossible to measure definitively. To the conservative writer Paul Johnson, the 'Watergate witch-hunt' was 'run by liberals in the media', especially the *Washington Post,* and led to 'the first media Putsch in history'.[19] The television anchorman Dan Rather also viewed the media's role as pivotal – and heroic.

In their 1975 report 'The Crisis of Democracy' to the Trilateral Commission,[20] Crozier et al. set off a debate on what they called 'the increasing delegitimisation

14 R Swire, 'The Evolution of Digital Media Over the Past 20 Years', *Parallax* (2014) <https://parall.ax/blog/view/3052/the-evolution-of-digital-media-over-the-pa st-20-years>.

15 'How People Decide What News to Trust on Digital Platforms and Social Media', *American Press Institute* (2016) <https://www.americanpressinstitute.org/publica tions/reports/survey-research/news-trust-digital-social-media/>.

16 D Berry, *Ethics and Media Culture: Practices and Representations* (Taylor and Francis, 1999), 28.

17 For example, ME Warren (ed), *Democracy and Trust* (Cambridge University Press, 1999); and U Friedman, 'Trust Is Collapsing in America', *The Atlantic* (21 January 2018) <https://www.theatlantic.com/international/archive/2018/01/trust-trump -america-world/550964/>.

18 C Yeates, 'Trust in Institutions Eroded: Ken Henry', *Sydney Morning Herald* (30 August 2017) <https://www.smh.com.au/business/banking-and-finance/trust-i n-institutions-eroded-ken-henry-20170830-gy7ah8.html>.

19 P Johnson, *Modern Times: A History of the World from the 1920s to the Year 2000* (Weidenfeld & Nicolson, 1983).

20 The Trilateral Commission is a non-governmental, non-partisan discussion group founded by David Rockefeller in July 1973 to foster closer cooperation among Japan, Western Europe and North America.

of authority', describing a decline in the confidence and trust that people have in government and in their leaders.[21] The consequences of political trust are surprisingly understudied, even though the relevance of political trust to the quality of representative democracy and the stability of its institutions has been a recurrent theme in the literature since the 1970s.[22] While The Watergate scandal had a devastating effect on American politics, Baker's refrain – 'What did the president know and when did he know it?' – could be applied to every United States president since. Some argue that we (the United States and its allies) still live in the era of Watergate.[23]

Ten years on, the reverberations from the global financial crisis are still shaking up the world order. Perceptions of the global financial crisis, corporate rigging and complaints against business erode public trust. According to the *Edelman Trust Barometer*, after steady improvement between 2011 and 2017, the financial services sector has seen declines in trust among the informed public segment in the United Arab Emirates, Hong Kong, Brazil, Colombia and France, with the United States suffering the steepest decline – in the double-digits.[24] These trends are significant and important because financial services are based on trust between various parties, and trust is important in making financial decisions. A lack of trust can lead to poorer individual and societal outcomes. It also suggests that a tendency to financial self-sufficiency comes with risk that may impact well beyond monetary losses.[25]

A lack of trust in financial institutions can hamper efforts to improve financial inclusion – particularly in less developed countries and poor communities generally. Greater digital finance can lead to greater financial inclusion, but special challenges face communities where there are cultural or religious beliefs that are hostile towards embracing technology in finance.

Individuals in the informal sector (that is, the self-employed and those operating in *cash-only* markets)[26] as well as those in poor communities often do not trust bankers or bank marketers who come to their homes to persuade them to use digital finance services. Rather they are more likely to trust the

21 M Crozier, S Huntington and J Watanuki, *The Crisis of Democracy. Report on the Governability of Democracies to the Trilateral Commission* (New York University Press, 1975) 162.

22 TWG van der Meer, 'Political Trust and the "Crisis of Democracy"', *Oxford Research Encyclopedia of Politics* (January 2017) <http://politics.oxfordre.com/view/10.1093/acrefore/9780190228637.001.0001>.

23 R Perlstein, *The Invisible Bridge: The Fall of Nixon and the Rise of Regan* (Simon & Schuster, 2014).

24 Trust delivers in the financial services sector. Forty-one per cent of respondents used products/services of trusted financial services companies in the last year. Thirty-one per cent recommended them to others; per the *Edelman Trust Barometer* (2019) <https://www.edelman.com/research/trust-in-financial-services-2018>

25 A Bruhn, 'Trust In, Trust Out: A Real Cost of Sudden and Significant Financial Loss' (26 February 2018) *Accounting and Finance* 1.

26 KT Hansen, 'Informal Sector' in *International Encyclopedia of the Social & Behavioural Sciences* (2nd ed, ScienceDirect, 2015).

recommendation they receive from friends and family members who are already users of digital finance platforms. Upon persuasion, such excluded individuals will open a formal bank account to take advantage of digital financial services.[27] Trust plays a key role in ensuring that consumers have access to digital finance and digital markets. Consumers in many emerging markets are not active users of the digital channels due to lack of consumer trust and confidence in the new channels (which may including a fundamental step in digital financial inclusion, such using a mobile phone to conduct a financial transaction).[28]

Exacerbating this modern trust crisis is the rise and rise of 'fake news'. Fake news is a type of propaganda that deliberately misinforms and is spread via traditional print, broadcast news or online social media.[29] Some argue that tech giants must take the blame for any perceived erosion of trust in journalism, having failed to tackle fake news and to give trusted news sources fair treatment.[30] The rapid rise of social networking platforms has not only yielded a vast increase in information accessibility but has also accelerated the spread of fake news.[31] The corresponding rise of fake news highlights the erosion of long-standing institutional bulwarks against misinformation in the Internet age. Concern over the problem is global.[32] Fake news undermines the informing function of the press by eroding the legitimacy and credibility of traditional, reliable news outlets, creating an uninformed public unable to participate effectively in our democracy.[33] Free press plays in sustaining a democratic government by informing the public and facilitating public participation necessary for self-government.

Where does this downturn in public trust leave the economy? While the 2008 Global Financial Crisis (GFC) may have been a product of frenzied automated online trading in secondary markets that relied upon the overvaluation of assets, the infrastructure that allowed that to happen has also been

---

27 PK Ozili, 'Impact of Digital Finance on Financial Inclusion and Stability' (2016) *18(4) Borsa Istanbul Review* 329, 333.

28 PK Ozili, 'Impact of Digital Finance on Financial Inclusion and Stability' (2016) *18(4) Borsa Istanbul Review* 329, 334.

29 While the term 'fake news' has been used to describe news pranks and disinformation for more than two decades, it gained prominence during the 2016 United States Presidential Election and the United Kingdom's referendum to leave the European Union (known as *Brexit*). For early use of this term, see for example CE Baker, 'Advertising and a Democratic Press' (1992) 140(6) *University of Pennsylvania Law Review* 2097.

30 M Denholm, 'Big Tech to Blame for Erosion of Trust in Journalism', *The Weekend Australian* (20 August 2018) <https://www.theaustralian.com.au/news/>.

31 R Oshikawa, J Qian and WY Wang, 'A Survey on Natural Language Processing for Fake News Detection', *Cornell University* (2018) <https://arxiv.org/pdf/1811.00770.pdf>.

32 DMJ Lazer, et al, 'The Science of Fake News' (9 March 2018) 359 (6380) *Science* 1094.

33 A Butler, 'Protecting the Democratic Role of the Press' (2018) 96 *Washington University Law Review* 419, 421.

the platform for a movement that is pushing back against traditionally trusted centralised institutions towards disintermediation and democratisation. That platform is of course the Internet.

Botsman has spoken and written on the economic consequences of failure to appreciate the importance of the social relationship of trust in the use of technology by business.[34] Botsman's book delivers insights into social phenomena that impact on and are informed by the influence of technology on trust. She asks: why don't people trust experts?[35] In light of the way that Donald Trump ran his Presidential campaign and the tone of the arguments put by the Leave supporters in the Brexit referendum, this question has far-reaching consequences. Trump and Brexit supporters tend to prefer the opinions of 'ordinary people' over 'experts', citing inconvenient truths about climate change and the economy as examples of 'fake news' manufactured purely to promote a particular political agenda.[36] Botsman describes the Brexit and Trump wave as marking a significant shift in trust and influence from organisations to individuals.[37]

The most common fake stories we hear about revolve around politics, but we cannot undermine the impact that fake news stories have had on society in general. Fake news can polarise societies, sway public opinion, manipulate voter behaviour, undermine the validity of scientific and expert output, and thereby reinforce prejudices and superstitions. When it is hard to tell truth from fiction, it becomes even harder to know who and what to trust. For example, during the debates leading up to the Brexit referendum held in June 2016, a large majority of the 'Leave' supporters (compared to a small minority of those in favour of remaining within the European Union) said that it was wrong to rely too much on 'experts' and better to rely on the opinions of 'ordinary people'. When those opinions are about climate change, vaccinations, use of drugs or the economy, it is easy to see how readily entire constituencies can dismiss 'inconvenient truths'. Brexit and Donald Trump's successful bid for the White House were acute symptoms emerging from one of the biggest trust crises of the modern era.

Scope of This Book

Entertaining a discussion of both Trusts law and a wider moral notion of trust as a basis of social relationships is uncommon in legal enquiry, although not

34 R Botsman, *Who Can You Trust? How Technology Brought Us Together and Why It Might Drive Us Apart* (Penguin Books, 2017).

35 R Botsman, *Who Can You Trust? How Technology Brought Us Together and Why It Might Drive Us Apart* (Penguin Books, 2017), 49.

36 A Kirk and D Dunford, 'EU Referendum: Leave Supporters Trust Ordinary "Common Sense" More Than Academics and Experts', *The Telegraph* (22 June 2016) <https://www.telegraph.co.uk/news/2016/06/16/eu-referendum-leave-supporters-trust-ordinary-common-sense-than/>.

37 R Botsman, *Who Can You Trust? How Technology Brought Us Together and Why It Might Drive Us Apart* (Penguin Books, 2017), 50.

completely novel.[38] The legal institution of the Trust and social relationships of trust are cousins. At their heart is an expectation that certain behavioural norms will not be frustrated by systems, organisations and people in whom or in which we have faith. This book will explore the legal consequences of failure of both trust and Trust in the context of modern e-commerce or digital economies. For ease of reference and consistency throughout this book, trust in the context of the social relationship of trust will be written with a lower case 't', while the Trust as a legal relationship between Trustee, Trust property and a beneficiary (or beneficiaries) will be written with an upper case 'T'. In order to reinforce this distinction, the word Trustee will also begin with an upper case 'T'.

As we near the end of the second decade of the 21st century, technology is no longer an enabler but a driver in most business models. With the 'platformisation' of many fundamental financial institutions and service providers (including banking, journalism, retail, professional advice, higher education and welfare), the need to manage trust between suppliers, the suppliers' agents and the consumers of their goods and services has never been so critical. Yet, across all of these domains, trust is at an all-time low. According to the Knight Commission on Trust, Media and Democracy:

> Trust is now the deciding factor in whether a society can function. As trust in institutions erodes, the basic assumptions of fairness, shared values and equal opportunity traditionally upheld by 'the system' are no longer taken for granted.[39]

Commentators suggest that we now occupy a 'post-truth world' with eroding trust and accountability. In this trust vacuum, experts are dismissed and alternative facts flagrantly offered. This suspicion of specialists is also part of a bigger problem.[40] Whereas the telegraph, the telephone, the telex and the fax machine used to be the main technology by which we conquered the tyranny of distance, the mainstay of modern business communication is email, social media or via apps. Because so much of our social and business interaction is now conducted online, it is not unusual to interact with someone on a regular basis and either never or rarely meet with them personally. This phenomenon is the reason for writing this book. As will be explored in Part II, the main driver of trust before the Internet was the face-to-face meeting, which begins and ends with a handshake.

---

38 See for example, R Cotterell, 'Trusting in Law: Legal and Moral Concepts of Trust' (1993) 46(2) *Current Legal Problems* 75.

39 Knight Commission on Trust, Media and Democracy, 'DRAFT Chapter 2: What Happened to Trust?', *Medium* (28 Jun 2018) <https://medium.com/trust-media-and-democracy/draft-chapter-2-what-happened-to-trust-efb4f52a87c8>.

40 N Enfield, 'We're in a Post-truth World with Eroding Trust and Accountability. It Can't End Well', *The Guardian* (17 November 2017) <https://www.theguardian.com/commentisfree/2017/nov/17/were-in-a-post-truth-world-with-eroding-trust-and-accountability-it-cant-end-well>.

The power of the handshake in building trust is so significant that robots have been designed to manage this step in negotiations. A recent scientific study found that when two people who may be located thousands of miles apart communicate through a robot, shaking hands with the machine and communicating the physical act still encouraged co-operation and mutual understanding.[41] However, in the absence of real humans and their alter-ego robots, the Internet has – with varying degrees of success – devised new ways to establish trust in business. This book will explore these trust mechanisms and examine the legal consequences of their success and failure.

The particular domain of activity that this book will explore is online marketplaces and business affairs: in other words, digital economies. Economics has long been concerned with the behaviour of humans in business.[42] In this book, 'business' is to be understood in a wide sense. When we go into a shop to buy groceries, the resulting transaction is no doubt a business transaction for the shopkeeper. The same applies to online purchases and the business of the retailer or service provider. It may not seem like a business transaction from the purchaser's point of view, but this book is just as concerned with the study of the buyer's behaviour as it is the vendor's.

Structure of This Book

This book is divided into four parts. Part I (this Part) introduces the two types of *trust* to be explored in the book. It also sets out some key definitions and useful classifications. Part II explores social relationships of trust in digital economies. This part includes a discussion of the role played by cryptography in the automation of trust in distributed ledger technologies. While social relationships support trust, the particular meaning intended here is trust as a social relationship. In its verbal form, Alice trusts Bob. This distinguishes a social relationships of trust (written throughout this book with a lower case 't') from its legal cousin the Trust. The noun 'Trust' (with an upper case 'T') is a legal relationship between Trent as Trustee of Trust property for Bob (the beneficiary of the Trust).[43]

Part III of this book examines the way that Trusts operate in digital economies. For the purposes of this part, fiduciaries will be included to the extent that where they control the assets or property of their principal, their duties in

---

41 C Hayhurst, 'Handshakes So Effective at Building Trust During Business Negotiations That They Work Even When One Of The Parties Is a Robot', *The Independent* (11 May 2015) <https://www.independent.co.uk/news/science/handshakes-so-effective-at-building-trust-during-business-negotiations-that-they-work-even-when-one-10240161.html>.

42 S Macaulay, 'Elegant Models, Empirical Pictures, and the Complexities of Contract' (1977) 11(3) *Law & Society Review* 507–528; S Macaulay and WC Whitford, 'The Development of Contracts: The Law in Action' (2015) 87 *Temple Law Review* 793.

43 See, M Leeming, 'What Is a Trust?' (2008) 31 *Australian Bar Review* 211.

relation to those assets can be regarded as 'trust-like'.[44] Part III will also discuss the particular issues impacting the management of Trusts where the corpus of the Trust includes crypto-assets on blockchain networks.

The definitions and classifications that underpin this structure are explained in further detail later in this Part.

This book focuses on the way that the law is responding to the consequences of failure of (social) trust and breach of (legal) Trust in digital economies, with particular focus on Australian and other Common Law jurisdictions. However, many examples will also reference trends and legislative developments in the United States.

Part IV poses and describes some key challenges that may hamper future efforts to ensure that trust features in both social relationships in business and in the legal institution of Trusts. Importantly, the power of trust in society is regarded as fundamental to ensuring economic efficiency. In a time of automation and algorithms, the role of the human remains central in this endeavour.

---

44 See, Pauline Ridge, 'Constructive Trusts, Accessorial Liability and Judicial Discretion', in E Bant and M Bryan (eds) *Principles of Proprietary Remedies* (Thomson Reuters, 2013).

2   The Cost of Trust

There are a number of approaches that may be adopted when attempting to measure the true cost of trust. For example, economists look to the risk of betrayal by agents employed to manage interactions between exchanging counterparties. In an effort to encourage and support trustworthy behaviour and conduct, there are organisation institutions and practices imposed on the roles undertaken by the various players in modern marketplaces.[1] The sorts of activities that contribute – to varying degrees – towards building trust include auditing, accounting, compliance, defined values, marketing, reputation and transparency.[2]

Botsman argues that in this new era of trust, its true measure is reputation capital. A shift in trust from institutions back to individuals reverses an historical trend and has profound implications for society and business. Back when we all lived in small communities, individuals were known and trusted based on their reputation and behaviour. To scale trust and to make it something that can be labelled and standardised, we invented institutions, regulations and risk mechanisms (such as insurance).[3]

Botsman defines trust from a business perspective as 'a confident relationship to the unknown'. It gives people confidence to place their faith in strangers and systems. Trust is the currency for interactions.[4]

Meanwhile, from a legal perspective, an understanding of the attitude of trust begins with an account of the optimism that characterises trust: an optimism that depends in part on beliefs, commitments and background attitudes. In some sense, this attitude is a response to risk.[5] Breach of the social

1   S Davidson, M Novak and J Potts, 'The Cost of Trust: A Pilot Study', *SSRN* (24 July 2018) <https://papers.ssrn.com/sol3/papers.cfm?abstractid=3218761>.
2   C Hansen, '5 Key Lessons on Building Trust in Business', *World Economic Forum* (7 October 2015) <https://www.weforum.org/agenda/2015/10/5-key-lessons-on-building-trust-in-business/>.
3   J Gray, 'Three Reasons Why the Trust Shift Threatens All Institutions', *AFR.com* (6 June 2017) <https://www.afr.com/brand/boss/three-reasons-why-the-trust-shift-thr eatens-all-institutions-rachel-botsman-20170507-gvzsc4>.
4   R Botsman, *Who Can You Trust? How Technology Brought Us Together and Why It Might Drive Us Apart* (Penguin Books, 2017).
5   See, M Harding, 'Trust and Fiduciary Law' (2013) 33(1) *Oxford Journal of Legal Studies* 81.

relationship in trust can happen in non-digital and digital economies. Examples include misleading and deceptive conduct,[6] collusion,[7] breach of contractual obligation of fidelity,[8] breach of confidence,[9] inducing breach of contract,[10] breach of privacy[11] and breaches of statutory duty (for example, directors' duties).[12]

The records of Medieval England reveal the litigiousness of Englishmen of all classes.[13] Their complaints to the courts are well documented. The lesson that has been learned from centuries of protracted hearings and interlocutory applications is that the most-costly (and arguably the worst) of all possible outcomes in the socio-legal domain of dispute resolution will be the need for arbitration or fully contested litigation of a dispute arising from a breach of Trust. Some of the longest running, most complex and most expensive disputes in Australia and the United Kingdom have arisen from liability for breach of Trust or breach of fiduciary duty.[14] Sometimes referred to as 'mega-litigation', hearing these big disputes consumes disproportionately vast court time and public costs. Mega-litigation is a product of the increasing sophistication and complexity of commercial transactions. In the wake of the C7 'mega-litigation', Justice Sackville cautioned:

---

6   For example, *Yorke v Lucas* (1985) 158 CLR 661.
7   See, E Green and R Porter, 'Non-cooperative Collusion under Imperfect Price Information' (1984) 52(1) *Econometrica* 87; and M Ivaldi et al., 'The Economics of Tacit Collusion', *European Commission Final Report for DG Competition* (2003) <http://ec.europa.eu/competition/mergers/studiesreports/theeconomicsoftacit collusionen.pdf>.
8   For example, *Manildra Laboratories v Campbell* [2009] NSWSC 987.
9   For example, *Prince Albert v Strange* (1849) ChD 8 Feb; and *Coco v AN Clark (Engineers) Ltd* [1969] RPC 41.
10   For example, *Spotwire Pty Ltd v Visa International Service Association Inc & Anor* [2003] FCA 762 (23 July 2003).
11   For example, *Victoria Park Racing and Recreation Grounds Co Ltd v Taylor* (1937) 58 CLR 479.
12   *Fiduciary Ltd & Ors v Morningstar Research Pty Ltd & Ors* [2004] NSWSC 664 (27 July 2004).
13   DM Kerly, *An Historical Sketch of the Equitable Jurisdiction of the Court of Chancery* (Cambridge University Press, 1890), 7.
14   For example, in Australia, *Beach Petroleum Nl v Abbott Tout Russell Kennedy Matter No 50030a/96* [1997] NSWSC 655 (17 December 1997); *Duke Group Limited (In liq) v Pilmer & Ors No. SCGRG-92–1874 Judgment No. S97* [1999] SASC 97 (20 May 1999); *Youyang Pty Ltd v Minter Ellison Morris Fletcher* [2003] HCA 15; (2003) 212 CLR 484; *The Bell Group Ltd (in Liq) v Westpac Banking Corporation (No 9)* [2008] WASC 239 (28 October 208); *Grimaldi v Chameleon Mining NL (No 2)* [2012] FCAFC 6 (21 February 2012); and *Ancient Order of Foresters in Victoria Friendly Society Limited v Lifeplan Australia Friendly Society Limited* [2018] HCA 43 (10 October 2018). And in the United Kingdom: *Target Holdings v Redferns* [1995] UKHL 10; [1996] 1 AC 421; *Williams v Central Bank of Nigeria* [2013] EWCA Civ 785; and *AIB v Mark Redler & Co Solicitors* [2014] UKSC 58 (5 November 2014).

Globalisation, privatisation of public enterprises and technological and financial innovations have created fertile opportunities for disputes which involve very large amounts of money or are likely to have a major impact on the profitability or even viability of large corporations.[15]

The Australian record for a lengthy civil trial appears to be the 471 hearing days taken up by the *Duke* litigation in South Australia,[16] followed closely by the *Bell Group* in Western Australia, which ran for 404 days and at AU$263 million in legal fees and charges is (to date) Australia's most expensive litigation.[17] The disastrous *BCCI* litigation in the United Kingdom, which was abandoned by the claimants on the 256th day of the trial, serves as a reminder that mega-litigation is not a phenomenon unique to Australia.[18]

Courts have frequently lamented the burdens imposed on them by mega-litigation and have complained of their powerlessness in the face of litigants who, for whatever reason, decide to press on notwithstanding huge and often disproportionate costs burdens. As well as the private and public cost of the litigation in these cases, dishonest breach of fiduciary duty may disentitle a fiduciary from claiming due allowance for the skill and expertise they exerted in making a secret profit or unauthorised gain. This rule applies equally to solicitors in breach of their fiduciary duties owed to their clients and to those who are directors in breach of statutory duties.[19] The rules are designed to dissuade fiduciaries from being swayed by considerations of personal interest.[20]

Over the past 50 years, the liability of third parties and agents for their role in enabling or procuring breaches of Trust have also featured in a variety of major commercial and family disputes in common law jurisdictions, including litigation arising from financial transactions and property development.[21]

---

15 Justice R Sackville, 'Mega-litigation: Towards a New Approach' (FCA) [2007] *Federal Judicial Scholarship* 13.

16 *Duke Group Ltd (in liq) v Pilmer* [1998] SASC 6529 (1998) 27 ACSR 1 (Supreme Court of South Australia).

17 *Bell Group Ltd v The v Westpac Banking Corporation & Ors* (2008) WASC 239.

18 For the aftermath, see *Three Rivers District Council v The Governors and Company of the Bank of England* [2006] EWHC 816 ('*BCCI* Case'). This sorry saga, including the extensive interlocutory proceedings, is critically reviewed by A Zuckerman, 'A Colossal Wreck: the BCCI-Three Rivers Litigation' (2006) 25 *Civil Justice Quarterly* 287.

19 For example, in *Fiduciary Ltd & Ors v Morningstar Research Pty Ltd & Ors* [2004] NSWSC 664 (27 July 2004), Austin J considered the question of due allowance claimed by a defendant, against whom allegations of breach of directors' duties had been made. See also, *Warman International Ltd v Dwyer* (1995) 182 CLR 544.

20 *Chan v Zacharia* (1984) 154 CLR 178, 198–199.

21 For example, *Carl Zeiss Stiftung v Herbert Smith & Co (No 2)* [1969] 2 Ch 276; *Karak Rubber Co Ltd v Burden (No 2)* [1972] 1 WLR 602; *Baden Delvaux & Lecuit v Societe General pour Favoriser le Developpement* [1992] 4 All ER 161; [1993] 1 WLR 509; *Westpac Banking Corporation v Savin* [1985] 2 NZLR 41; *Consul Development Ply Ltd v DPC Estates Pty Ltd* (1975) 132 CLR 373; *Cowan de Groot Properties Ltd v Eagle Trust plc* [1992] 4 All ER 700; *Montagu's*

More recently, there has been a creeping emergence of securities litigation relating to the use of crypto-currencies and blockchain technology. According to legal analytics service *LexMachina*, in the 18 months to July 2018, there were 60 cases in the United States alone. According to *LexMachina's 2018 Securities Litigation Report*, the first two quarters of 2018 saw a significant rise in the number of securities cases relating to crypto-currency or bitcoin. Using Legal Analytics' keyword search functionality, *LexMachina* discovered case filings relating to this emerging area surged from seven cases in the fourth quarter of 2017 to 22 cases in the first quarter of 2018 and 23 cases in the second quarter of 2018.[22] For example, in the Tomahawk Exploration dispute, the Securities and Exchange Commission (the SEC) determination that the issuance of digital tokens in exchange for services rather than money constitutes an offering of securities was upheld in a settled enforcement action.[23] In September 2018, the SEC issued an order against TokenLot, LLC, a self-described initial coin offering (ICO) superstore and its founders for operating an unregistered broker-dealership. This was the first time the SEC has made such an allegation in the crypto-currency industry. According to the order, TokenLot served as a platform for both token purchases and secondary trading in more than 200 different digital tokens. The SEC found that 'through these activities, the respondents promoted and sold digital tokens that included securities'.

Tomahawk and TokenLot are typical of the litigation that is emerging from the use of new technologies to represent value. The policy considerations that drive these decisions concern the protection of investors and customers from the uncertainty that surrounds the use of crypto-assets. Crypto-currencies and crypto-assets are notoriously unstable and prone to manipulation. Instability and manipulation erode trust. Trust is essential to the sustainability and tradability of currency and assets. The worth of all currencies from stone coins to bitcoins is based on people trusting the transaction system. As stated by bitcoin

Settlement Trusts [1987] Ch 264; [1987] 2 WLR 1193; *Re Duke of Manchester v National Westminster Bank plc* [1992] 4 All ER 308; *Agip (Africa) Ltd v Jackson* [1992] 4 All ER 385; *Royal Brunei Airlines Sdn Bhd v Tan* [1995] 2 AC 378; *Koorootang Nominees Pty Ltd v Australia & New Zealand Banking Group Ltd* [1998] 3 VR 16; *Twinsectra Limited v Yardley* [1999] EWCA Civ 1290; *Dubai Aluminium Co Ltd v Salaam* [2002] 3 WLR 1913; [2003] 1 All ER 97; *Kalls Enterprises Pty Ltd (In Liq) v Baloglow* [2007] NSWCA 191; *Farah Constructions Pty Ltd v Say-Dee Pty Ltd* (2007) 230 CLR 89; *Byrnes v Kendle* (2011) 243 CLR 253; *Westpac Banking Corporation & Ors v The Bell Group Ltd [No 3]* [2012] WASCA 157; *Grimaldi v Chameleon Mining NL (No 2)* (2012) 200 FCR 296; (2012) 287 ALR 22; (2012) 87 ACSR 260; [2012] FCAFC 6.

22 V Chan, 'Lex Machina's 2018 Securities Litigation Report Reveals Securities Litigation Is At an All-Time High', *Lexmachina.com* (2018) <https://lexmachina.com/media/press/lex-machinas-2018-securities-litigation-report-reveals-securities-litigation-is-at-an-all-time-high/>.

23 *In the Matter of Tomahawk Exploration LLC and David Thompson Laurance*, Securities Act Rel. No. 33–10530, Exchange Act Rel. No. 34–83839, Admin. Proc. File No. 3–18641 (Aug. 14, 2018).

developer Satoshi Nakamoto, the bitcoin system allows for electronic transactions without relying on the trust associated with centralised banking institutions and government issuance of currency.[24]

Actuaries and insurers measure trust by assessing the risk or probability that trust will be breached and then estimating the losses that would be suffered as a result of that breach. With this calculation, it is then possible to charge premiums for insurance to cover the damages that might be suffered should the risk eventuate.

An additional and relatively straightforward method of calculating the cost of trust might be to itemise and aggregate expenditure by private and public sectors on complying with government standards, reporting activities to the market, auditing their accounts and transactions, and making sure that all appropriate licence fees, insurance premiums and taxes are paid in a timely manner.[25] How ever the cost of trust is calculated, it is estimated that the cost of trust accounts for 35% of United States employment in 2010.[26]

In digital economies, adaptability is particularly important for measuring the types and levels of risk that attend upon online businesses and platforms. These include governance risk compliance being automated, financial fraud, misrepresentations and information-privacy. For example, cyber risk relates to the failure of an organisation's information technology systems. However, such events can generate significant financial losses, including a loss of their clients' or customers' trust. This is because the ways that cyber risk can occur changes as rapidly as the development of new technologies. Many cyber breaches are caused by systemic failures and human error. However, there is an increasing threat from nefarious strangers looking to exploit valuable personal and commercial data held by organisations as part of their operations. This rapid development of the risk means that greater reliance must be placed on human judgement, rather than available data, to determine appropriate assumptions as to the cost of that risk. This brings a danger that personal biases may lead to a failure to assess risk levels appropriately.[27]

Often the systems introduced to manage and mitigate these risks are in themselves complex technology systems and computational analytics that measure and predict corporate risk levels and force decisions accordingly. It follows that these systems are also capable of failure. Many organisations outsource these services: amounting to the cost of ensuring trust in these systems. In total, the third-party market for compliance-technology products (known

---

24 S Nakamoto, 'Bitcoin: A Peer-to-Peer Electronic Cash System', *Bitcoin* (31 October 2008) <https://Bitcoin.org/Bitcoin.pdf>. See also, AK Noonan, 'Bitcoin or Bust: Can One Really "Trust" One's Digital Assets?' [2015] 7 *Estate Planning and Community Property Law Journal* 583, 586.

25 S Davidson, M Novak and J Potts, 'The Cost of Trust: A Pilot Study', *SSRN* (24 July 2018), 11 <https://papers.ssrn.com/sol3/papers.cfm?abstractid=3218761>.

26 S Davidson, M Novak and J Potts, 'The Cost of Trust: A Pilot Study', *SSRN*, 1 (24 July 2018) <https://papers.ssrn.com/sol3/papers.cfm?abstractid=3218761>.

27 'Risk Management – An Actuarial Approach' *Institute and Faculty of Actuaries* (June 2017), 8–9 <www.actuaries.org.uk>.

generally as 'governance, risk and compliance' software systems and services) grew to US$52 billion by 2010.[28]

Trust, as manifested in day-to-day purchases over the Internet, requires the purchaser to divulge more personal information for merchants to avoid the issue of fraud.[29] Given the scale and complexity of contemporary business institutions and the massive amount of information involved in corporate operations, the types of risk controls that regulation demands simply cannot function without the use of sophisticated technology systems. These systems manage and process data collection, analysis and monitor the capacities of integrated computer technologies. Using technology to manage risk and hardwire compliance comes with its own risks. Translating natural language rules into code is not straightforward and technology is not neutral. Reduction of regulation to code embodies particular choices as to how the law is interpreted. Those choices may be shaped by a variety of extralegal factors, including the conscious and unconscious professional assumptions of programmers, as well as bottom-line business incentives. Those choices, in turn, may be embedded in a way that is difficult to identify or alter as contexts change.[30]

In light of the increasing sophistication of technology offerings and the geometric increase in computer processing power as compared to cost, a consensus has arisen among regulators, corporate risk managers and risk-management specialists that – for reasons of both efficiency and effectiveness – the trend towards embedding risk management in technology systems is inevitable.[31]

Compliance functions and risk management need to keep pace with the increasing use of digital financial services. Customer demand for online banking, robo-advice and the online purchase of services and products is driving a significant increase in online business volume across all private and government sectors, which is, in turn, putting stress on control frameworks and giving rise to new potential risks, such as those related to cybersecurity and data privacy. These new risks are complex and highly dynamic, and the pace of change continues to accelerate.

Organisations and businesses that suffer legal consequences of a failure to manage different types of social and legal relationships of trust in commerce have the potential to incur significant financial and non-financial costs. With this in mind, it is useful to consider types of social and legal relationships of trust and the particular contexts that expose digital economies to risk.

---

28 KA Bamberger, 'Technologies of Compliance: Risk and Regulation in a Digital Age' (2010) 88(4) *Texas Law Review* 669, 669.

29 S Nakamoto, 'Bitcoin: A Peer-to-Peer Electronic Cash System', *Bitcoin* (31 October 2008) <https://Bitcoin.org/Bitcoin.pdf>. See also, AK Noonan, 'Bitcoin or Bust: Can One Really "Trust" One's Digital Assets?' [2015] 7 *Estate Planning and Community Property Law Journal* 583, 587.

30 KA Bamberger, 'Technologies of Compliance: Risk and Regulation in a Digital Age' (2010) 88(4) *Texas Law Review* 669, 685.

31 See, for example, Ernest & Young LLP, 'Corporate Regulatory Compliance Practices' (2005), 29–30 <https://www.ey.com/Publication/vwLUAssets/EY-corporate-integrity-and-compliance/$FILE/EY-corporate-integrity-compliance.pdf>

3 Distinguishing Between Social Relationships of Trust and Trusts

Until recently, trust has not been a topic of mainstream sociology.[1] Neither classical authors nor modern sociologists use the term in a theoretical context. Empirical research in relation to trust – for example, research about trust and distrust in politics – has relied on rather general and unspecified ideas, confusing problems of trust with positive or negative attitudes toward political leadership or political institutions; with conceptions of alienation, hopes and worries, or with confidence. In order to provide a clear path for analysis it is important to distinguish between trust as an expectation and hope that something will not fail and trust in actors who owe fiduciary duties that they will not fail in their duty by putting their own interests before the interests of others.

Social Relationships of Trust

The notion of a social relationship of trust encompasses in a broad moral sense reliance in social relationships on other people's good will, competence and confidence that general expectations in familiar social circumstances will not be frustrated.[2] The role of social relationships of trust in business and commerce was explored by Stewart Macaulay in empirical research, articles and a series of books published over fifty years, commencing in the early 1960s (including books co-authored with Bill Whitford).[3] Macaulay found that the types of 'exchange relations' that he studied – predominantly before

---

1   N Luhmann, 'Chapter 6 – Familiarity, Confidence, Trust: Problems and Alternatives', in D Gambetta (ed) *Trust: Making and Breaking Cooperative Relations* (Department of Sociology University of Oxford, 2000), 94–107 <http://www. sociology.ox.ac.uk/papers/luhmann94-107.pdf>.

2   R Cotterell, 'Trusting in Law: Legal and Moral Concepts of Trust' (1993) 46(2) *Current Legal Problems* 75, 75.

3   See, S Macaulay, 'Non-Contractual Relations in Business: A Preliminary Study' (1963) 28(1) *American Sociological Review* 55; S Macaulay, 'Elegant Models, Empirical Pictures, and the Complexities of Contract' (1977) 11(3) *Law & Society Review* 507; S Macaulay, J Kidwell and WC Whitford, *Contracts: Law in Action* (LexisNexis, 2nd Edn, 2003); and S Macaulay and WC Whitford, 'The Development of Contracts: The Law in Action' (2015) 87 *Temple Law Review* 793.

the advent of the Internet and e-commerce – could only be understood within a wider social, cultural and political context.[4]

As noted by sociologist and modernist, Emile Durkeim, 'A contract is not sufficient unto itself, but is possible only thanks to a regulation of the contract which is originally social'.[5] Contracts imply a need for individuals to cooperate, at least to the extent of agreeing to the contract. This means entry into a social relationship where each party has a feeling that it is in a state of mutual dependence. The contract must also provide for ways of dealing with future consequences and that are informed by past experiences. Thus the contract is imbued with the history and culture of social experiences of such transactions or relationships.[6]

In this book, social relationships of trust are regarded as fundamental to doing business. Competency and reliability are key to the creation of social relationships of trust. In commercial dealings, social relationships of trust enable and support resource acquisition, personal goodwill, positive reputation and efficiency. In digital economies, these aims are achieved by enhancing the way that participants interact by providing accessibility, visibility, transparency and credibility. Where relationships in digital economies are intermediated by trusted third parties, the risk of failure of trust is managed by charging fees to the entity on one or both sides of the transaction (either directly or via online advertising revenue on the platform's website). These structures are not without their own risks.[7] In distributed and peer-to-peer networks (where there is no trusted third party), trust and risk are managed either via reputation systems or mathematically (for example, using cryptographic proofs).[8]

Trusts

A Trust is an institution developed by Equity[9] and recognised in the court of Equity as imposing obligations enforceable in Equity.[10] The inherent nature of a Trust is a relationship in respect of property, under which one person or one corporate entity, known as a Trustee, is obliged to deal with property vested in

---

4   S Macaulay, 'Elegant Models, Empirical Pictures, and the Complexities of Contract' (1977) 11(3) *Law & Society Review* 507.
5   E Durkheim, *The Division of Labor in Society* (Simon & Schuster, 2014), 350.
6   RA Sydie, 'Social Solidarity' in RA Sydie (ed), *Natural Women, Cultured Men: A Feminist Perspective on Sociological Theory* (Methuen, 1994), 15.
7   These systems and the risks that may arise therein are explored in Part II – Chapters 8 to 12.
8   These systems and their potential risks are explored in Part II – Chapter 13.
9   So as to distinguish it from 'equity' as a notion of fairness or a type of financial interest, the word 'Equity' as a particular jurisdiction or jurisprudence is written throughout this book an uppercase 'E' (unless quoted otherwise).
10 JD Heydon and M Leeming, *Jacobs' Law of Trusts in Australia* (7th edn, Butterworths, 2006), 1.

him for the benefit of another person, known as a beneficiary.[11] A Trustee holds property on Trust for the beneficiaries for a particular purpose.[12]

The Trust concept is an equitable right, title or interest in property, real or personal, distinct from the legal ownership thereof.[13] A Trust is a relationship, recognised by and enforceable in Equity, between a Trustee and property which is held by the Trustee for another person or for a purpose, which gives rise both to personal rights and obligations and to proprietary rights in the Trust property.[14] Lindley LJ described it as: 'An equitable obligation to deal with property in a particular way and as really nothing except a confidence reposed by one person in another, and enforceable in a court of equity.'[15]

Property in the form of 'defined', 'specified' or 'particular' property is an essential ingredient of a Trust.[16] However, it is not a sufficient ingredient. Before a Trust can arise, the property that is to be its subject matter must be linked with the Trustee via a binding trust obligation.[17] In *Westdeutsche Landesbank Girozentrale v Islington LBC*, [18] Lord Browne-Wilkinson identified the relevant principles of Trust law. They can be summarised as follows:

i   Equity operates on the conscience of the owner of the legal interest.

ii The owner of the legal interest cannot be a Trustee of the Trust property until aware of the facts alleged to affect his conscience.

iii In order to establish a Trust there must be identifiable Trust property. The only apparent exception to this rule is a constructive Trust imposed on a person who dishonestly assists in a breach of Trust who may come under fiduciary duties even if he does not receive identifiable Trust property.

iv Once the Trust is established, a Trust beneficiary has an equitable proprietary interest in the Trust property enforceable against subsequent holders other than the bona fide purchaser of the legal interest.[19]

In *Jacobs' Law of Trusts*, [20] the significant features of the Trust are identified as follows:

---

11 AJ Oakley, *Constructive Trusts* (Sweet & Maxwell, 3rd edn, 1997), 2.
12 JD Heydon and M Leeming, *Jacobs' Law of Trusts in Australia* (7th edn, Butterworths, 2006), 10.
13 *Wilson v Lord Bury* (1880) 5 QBD 518, 530.
14 M Leeming, 'What Is a Trust?' (2008) 31 *Australian Bar Review* 211, 211.
15 *Re Williams* (1897) 2 Ch 12, 18.
16 R Wilson, 'Lord Browne-Wilkinson's 'Identifiable Trust Property' Principle' [1998] *Waikato Law Rev* 4, 5.
17 *Re Calgary and Edmonton Land Co Ltd (In liq)* [1975] 1 All ER 1046; [1975] 1 WLR 355 at 1050–1051 (All ER).
18 *Westdeutsche Landesbank Girozentrale v Islington Borough Council* [1996] AC 699; [1996] 2 All ER 961.
19 *Westdeutsche Landesbank Girozentrale v Islington London Borough Council* [1996] AC 699; [1996] 2 All ER 961, 724 (AC).
20 JD Heydon and M Leeming, *Jacobs' Law of Trusts in Australia* (7th edn, Butterworths 2006).

  i The Trustee (or Trustees), individuals or corporate, hold a legal or equitable interest in the Trust property.

  ii The Trustees owe equitable obligations to the beneficiaries to obey the terms of the Trust.

  iii The Trust obligation attaches not only to a nominated Trustee, as in an express Trust, but also to any person in whom the Trust property is vested, unless that person is a purchaser for value without notice.[21]

  iv The Trustee's obligations are *fiduciary* in nature (thus requiring the utmost good faith and prohibiting any conflict of interest). The Trust is a fiduciary relationship. The beneficiaries have equitable proprietary rights in the trust fund.

  v The Trustee may be one of the beneficiaries, but cannot be the sole beneficiary.

  vi The Trustee(s) must be under a personal obligation to deal with the Trust property for the benefit of the beneficiaries.

  vii The Trustee will be personally liable for any loss caused to the Trust by her/their breach of Trust. In this way, the obligation attaches to the Trustee *in personam*. [22]

These features are important as the elements of the Trust and the duties that Trustees owe to beneficiaries must be described with certainty. Without certainty, Trustees and beneficiaries cannot identify and assert their rights and obligations. Identifying and asserting rights and obligations supports trust in the institutional value of using Trusts.[23]

While the Trust emerged in English legal history as a creative response to the disturbance of property rights in Tudor England, their popularity in commerce has caused a proliferation of equitable jurisprudence. Trusts were originally devised to manage property rights between family members so that the deceased's widow or orphans could continue to live in the family home (for example). Debating the value of superimposing equitable principles into modern commercial life, arguments have been made against the regulation of arm's length transactions in commercial life in accordance with standards of behaviour devised for the regulation of relationships of trust and confidence which are distinctly not arm's length relationships.[24] The reasoning here is that Equity never set out to bring to heel what John Maynard Keynes described as 'the uncontrollable and disobedient psychology of the business

---

21 Hence the liability of knowing recipients (for example) in whom trust property has come to be vested, but with the recipient's notice of the trust.

22 JD Heydon and M Leeming, *Jacobs' Law of Trusts in Australia* (7th edn, Butterworths, 2006), 3–5.

23 The risk of failure of trust in the legal institution of the Trust will be discussed in Part III.

24 PA Keane, 'The WA Lee Equity Lecture 2009 – The Conscience of Equity (Speech delivered in the Banco Court, Brisbane, 2 November 2009)' (2009) *Queensland Judicial Scholarship* 62, 87.

world'.[25] However, what has prevailed in commercial and non-commercial arrangements is Equity's role as mitigating the harshness of the common law and its appeal to 'conscience'.[26]

Distrust

Trust is regarded as a fundamental element in successful business relationships.[27] It is the bonding strength that characterises the majority of productive buyer/supplier relationships,[28] the heart of industrial relations[29] and the lubricant of social relationships. There are two broad categories of business trust. The first is based on an expectation of competency and the second on benevolence. Distrust therefore arises where there has been a deception about capacity or ability to deliver a product or service as promised; or where one of the parties to an arrangement or transaction behaves recklessly, opportunistically or fraudulently.

The literature has traditionally been interested in trust in business as a mechanism able to reduce costs and risk,[30] at the same time improving value creation.[31] It therefore follows that distrust will undermine business relationships, erode productivity, harm industrial relations, create friction in social relationships and cause an increase in costs and risk.

Distrust arises when there is a feeling that someone or something is not honest and cannot be trusted. In business, distrust can be difficult to manage. Advances in information technologies have led to major changes in the buyer/supplier relationship. Many theorists prescribe greater trust as a necessary antidote for an increasingly litigious and distrustful society.[32]

Even though trust is functionally necessary for the continuance of harmonious social relationships, its actual continuance in any particular social bond is always problematic. Friends and spouses sometimes come to distrust each other and citizens lose trust in the government, the judicial system, the news

25 JM Keynes, *The General Theory of Employment, Interest and Money* (Palgrave Macmillan 1936).

26 F Burns, 'The Court of Chancery in the 19th Century, A Paradox of Decline and Expansion' (2001) 21(2) *University of Queensland Law Journal* 198, 201.

27 See, MH Charki, 'Does Trust Still Matter in Business Relationships Based on Online Reverse Auctions?', *PhD Thesis, Paris Dauphine University* (2007) <https://pdfs.sema nticscholar.org/d115/897cda27ac2b15d2af4085f6cf8126e9bf14.pdf>

28 JM Hawes, KE Mast and JE Swan, 'Trust Earning Perceptions of Sellers and Buyers' (1989) 9(1) *Journal of Personal Selling & Sales Management* 1.

29 T Miyamoto and N Rexha, 'Determinants of Three Facets of Customer Trust: A Marketing Model of Japanese Buyer–Supplier Relationship' (2004) 57(3) *Journal of Business Research* 312.

30 K Arrow, *The Limits of Organization* (Norton, 1974).

31 See, MH Charki, 'Does Trust Still Matter in Business Relationships Based on Online Reverse Auctions?', *PhD Thesis submitted to Paris Dauphine University* (2007) <http s://pdfs.semanticscholar.org/d115/897cda27ac2b15d2af4085f6cf8126e9bf14.pdf>.

32 JK Lieberman, *The Litigious Society* (Basic Books, 1981).

media or even the monetary currency. There is a direct relationship between the presence of trust and the cohesiveness of society. Where there is distrust, actors become more individualistic in their dealings with each other and their socio-legal and economic institutions.[33]

Social relationships in business depend on minimising distrust. To appreciate the value of managing distrust in e-commerce, it is useful to consider uncertainty, perceived risk and unreliability. The more uncertain the parties are, the more they need to consider whether or not they trust it. When business is conducted online, trust becomes even more important. Distrust is amplified in online dealings because the usual norms associated with personal contact and social interaction are not available. The parties cannot rely on their intuitive judgements about a person's trustworthiness. This is why credit card companies are enlisted for these transactions – the credit card provider has done the due diligence and absorbs the risk by charging fees to cover the cost of any incompetence or fraud (as well as insuring against these outcomes).

Equity as a body of law has sprung from centuries of disputes arising from two main sources. Firstly, it exists to ameliorate the harshness of the Common Law. Secondly, it exists to deal with the real and perceived wrongful administration of Trusts. Equity's appeal to conscience means that complainants can trust the courts to mediate between the letter of the law and justice. If distrust permeates the courts or Trusts the use and relevance of these important legal institutions would naturally wane. A lack of trust in legal systems can lead to inefficiency, discord, erosion of the rule of law and the creation of informal and unregulated alternatives. Whereas informal justice systems and Trust relationships may be sustainable in societies where stable traditions and customs are managed by respected elders, there is a danger that weaker or less-sophisticated participants may be vulnerable to exploitation by dominant controllers of the system, particularly where the mechanics of the institutions are not clearly defined or understood.[34]

In many Common Law and Civil Law jurisdictions, Equity supplements the general law. When compared to the Common Law, Equity adopts a different approach to administering justice – Equity focuses on flexibility and good conscience as opposed to the Common Law's rigid enforcement of strict legal rights. Meanwhile, the evolution of liability for breach of Trust dates back to the early 16th century in the English Court of Chancery.[35] An historical survey

---

33 JD Lewis and A Weigert, 'Trust as Reality' (1985) 63(4) *Social Forces* 967, 969.
34 TJ Roder, 'Informal Justice Systems: Challenges and Perspectives' *World Justice Project* (28 January 2013) <https://worldjusticeproject.org/news/informal-justi ce-systems-challenges-and-perspectives>.
35 For example, *Thoroughgood v Cole* [1582] EngR 40; (1582) 2 Co Rep 5; 76 ER 408; *Humble v Bill* [1703] EngR 55; (1703) 2 Vern 444; 23 ER 884; *Harvey v Harvey* [1729] EngR 125; (1729) T Jones 121; 84 ER 117; *Ex parte Belchier* [1754] EngR 69; (1754) Amb 218; 27 ER 144; *Beckford v Wade* [1805] EngR 116; (1805) 17 Ves 87; 34 ER 34; *Keane v Robarts* [1819] EngR 537; (1819) 4 Madd 332; 56 ER 728; *Attorney-General v Corporation of Leicester* [1844] EngR

of the English Reports reveals that from the late 1500s, the English Court of Chancery adjudicated many complaints where plaintiffs sought to recover misapplied money from errant Trustees and the recipients of their Trust property.

As early as 1468, the English courts heard complaints about Executors and Trustees. In *Ouslowe v Ouslowe; Norris v Lester; Cutting v Huckford*, [36] the court acknowledged that in certain circumstances, proceedings should be brought against the Executor, rather than the heir to the estate. The conduct of the Executor with regard to the estate was considered a determining factor in imposing liability. This is a very early example of Equity expressing its concern that those who manage property on behalf of others must be held to a high standard of conduct.

Equity traditionally approached a Trustee's liability for a breach of Trust through the mechanism of taking an account of the Trust: 'The taking of an account is the means by which a beneficiary requires a trustee to justify his stewardship of Trust property. The Trustee must show what he has done with that property'.[37] In some circumstances this liability is strict. This is a powerful remedy, because it makes the Trustee personally liable for any shortfall in the Trust's account. The liability also extends to errant fiduciaries who have breached their fiduciary duties, as well as any third parties who may be made liable for their knowing participation in a breach by the Trustee or fiduciary.[38]

270; (1844) 7 Beav 176; 49 ER 1031; and [1827] EngR 659 (1827) 3 Car & P 208; 172 ER 389.

36 *Ouslowe v Ouslowe; Norris v Lester; Cutting v Huckford* [1468] EngR 2; (1468–69) Cary 12; 21 ER 7.

37 *Ultraframe (UK) Ltd v Fielding* [2005] EWHC 1638 (Ch) (27 July 2005) [1513] (Lewison J). See also, M Conaglen, 'Equitable Compensation for Breach of Trust: Off Target' (2016) 40(1) *Melbourne University Law Review* 126.

38 *Barnes v Addy* (1874) LR 9 Ch App 244.

4 Distinguishing Digital Economies from Non-digital Economies

In this book, the use of the terms 'non-digital economies' and 'digital economies' is intended to drive a distinction between pre-Internet (traditional) markets and those that operate online (that is, digital markets). With respect to the latter, it is also useful to identify 'crypto-markets' or 'crypto-economies' as a subcategory of digital markets. This classification is important because there are obvious differences between a local grocery store and eBay, and between the Yellow Pages and Google.

It is useful to explore the nature of these differences and their implications for regulators and for the development of the law. The reason why the term 'economies' is preferred here, over the word 'markets', is that this book investigates how the economics of online markets operate against established norms of information and advertising, reputation and anonymity, contract law, employment law and Trusts in governing relationships. The word 'markets' connotes a scope of enquiry that is limited to discussing different types of business in certain sectors, where the word 'economies' indicates that this discussion will include a consideration of the differences in the way that traditional and digital markets are organised and regulated. In addition to the legal institutions that have developed over the past 500 years in traditional markets, the move to digital markets has created new legal and regulatory challenges, including data protection, privacy and the accountability of algorithms. Meanwhile, crypto-markets introduce a further layer of complexity to digital economies, with the advent of crypto-currencies, smart contracts and the automation of trust (as a risk management tool). Particular challenges that arise in digital and crypto-markets include deciding jurisdiction, identifying participants, anti-trust or anti-competition regulation, as well as monitoring taxable events and general financial surveillance.

This chapter provides a brief description of each of the three types of traditional, digital and crypto-marketplaces or economies. Drawing these distinctions will be useful for the discussion that will then follow in relation to the legal consequences of failure to manage trust and risk in digital (and crypto-) economies.

Non-digital Economies

Ledger technology is a fundamental component of economics. Humans have used ledgers to record value and debt for thousands of years. Beginning with clay tablets, followed by more portable media (for example, papyrus and tally sticks), and eventually developing double-entry accounting, modern (pre-digital) economies relied upon bookkeeping conventions developed by the Venetians in the Italian Renaissance period.

In 1494, Luca Pacioli ('the Father of Accounting') recommended the Venetian method of double-entry bookkeeping above all others. He did not invent the system. Instead, he simply described a method used by merchants in Venice. His system prescribed putting debits on one side of a ledger and credits on the other to record capital, separating it from income in order to determine the dividends intended for investors. It also included most of the accounting cycle as we know it today. It involved the use of an inventory book and a receipt and/or payment book.

By the early 1700s, the Court of Chancery was itself acting as an investment conduit, channelling trust estates and fortunes into the informally approved funds of the new Bank of England and other financial entities, such as the by now well-established East India Company. In the decade from its inception in 1711, the South Sea Company also became an investor's favourite. When its investment bubble burst in 1720, many investors lost significant amounts of money. Unscrupulous agents and advisers were exposed.[1]

Digital Economies

With the advent of personal computing, the spreadsheet soon overtook printed books as the method of recording inventory and sales. With the Internet came e-commerce and the automation of many of the processes involved in recording key bookkeeping entries. Digital economies continue to recognise the value and importance of the Venetian method, but emphasis is placed on new ways to value the assets recorded on the inventory. Assets are no longer valued only on the basis of the amount paid for them. Value is updated and manipulated to reflect the price that might be sought on sale or when insuring or re-insuring the item against different types of risk. The most creative valuation processes have been witnessed on secondary markets where assets are fractionalised and prices are set according to speculation of future value (for example, hedging or arbitrage); or possible failure (also known as 'shorting'), enabled by the computerisation of global stock markets in the 1980s.[2]

---

1   A survey of the English Reports reveals that, between 1720 and 1864, more than 350 complaints were brought before the English Courts about South Sea stock and the related conduct of brokers or Trustees.

2   The National Association of Securities Dealers and the Nasdaq Stock Market provide automated execution systems for listed securities and Small Order Execution System (SOES) for Nasdaq securities; automated communications and order

Over the past 30 years, the evolution of digital economies has been enabled and supported at its bedrock by the advent of the Internet and then with the addition of layers of features and apps, as well as the acceptance of electronic signatures and online transactions. The main features of digital economies have been enabled by the development and popularity of information and communication technologies, which have dropped in price and led to the growth of the interconnectedness of users. The adoption of information and communication technologies has reduced operational costs.[3]

Within a few short years of the commercialisation of the Internet, it became clear to businesses that the challenge for the coming years would be to win the trust of the consumers. First, consumers need to trust the Internet in general as a new means of communication. Second, consumers need to trust e-commerce as a new way of transferring ownership or rights to use goods or services by making transactions through computer-mediated networks.[4]

In digital economies, the Internet enables the development of mega-marketplaces. With the combined processing power of personal computers and interconnected devices, traditional third parties and intermediaries are being rendered obsolete by peer-to-peer transactions between strangers. With eBay, Uber and Airbnb leading the way, online applications are running entire networks of consumers, suppliers and distribution networks. Often relying on the accuracy and veracity of ratings and reviews provided by the participants, these networks support new business models for vendors and purchasers whose reputations and trustworthiness are generated by a combination of user feedback and algorithms.

Familiarity is the precondition for trust as well as distrust.[5] In digital economies, familiarity is difficult to establish. Doing business remotely affords

---

negotiation facilities with the SelectNet service; streamlined back-office comparison and reconciliation services with Automated Confirmation Transaction Service (ACT) and Trade Acceptance and Reconciliation Service (TARS); the OTC Bulletin Board service for members entering real-time quotations of issues in the over-the-counter market. More recently, real-time last sale reporting for Nasdaq Small-Cap issues, convertible debt listed on Nasdaq and over-the-counter issues has been implemented. All of these services have increased the speed and volume of trading and similar systems are a key feature in digital economies worldwide. See, RG Ketchum and BE Weimer, 'Market 2000 and the Nasdaq Stock Market' (1994) 19 (3) *Journal of Corporation Law* 559, 576.

3   Significant changes in the provision of information and communication technologies (ICT) services have been taking place in recent years. India has become the leading exporter of ICT services, followed by Ireland, the United States, Germany and the United Kingdom. China has also become one of the major exporters. Together these six countries represent approximately 60% of total ICT services exports. See, OECD: 'OECD Science, Technology and Industry Scoreboard 2013: Innovation for Growth', *OECD Publishing*, UNCTAD (June 2013) <www.oecd. org/sti/scoreboard.htm>.

4   P Balboni, *Trustmarks in E-Commerce: The Value of Web Seals and the Liability of Their Providers* (Information Technnology Law Series, 2009), Introduction.

5   N Luhmann, *Trust and Power* (Wiley, 1979).

little opportunity to get to know the person with whom one is contracting. Indeed, many transactions are conducted internationally and across many time zones. To address these challenges, businesses win new business by collecting positive customer feedback to improve their credibility ratings. Maintaining the integrity of this valuable data requires that this information is not manipulated in any way. In addition to the way that e-businesses deal with their clients and customers, they must also manage regulatory compliance and data protection.

Crypto-economies

The modern world is gradually moving towards full digitalisation of the economy. This means that soon all economic processes will be carried out with the help of digital technologies, and this often means full automation in order to optimise economic processes. Cryptography adds a layer of trust to automation that enables decentralisation. Decentralisation reduces the cost of transactions and makes the whole system more efficient. Cryptography can also automate audit and accounting processes. While cryptography has been around for a while, its role as a solution to some of the fundamental problems preventing the effective digitisation of money has only existed since 2008.

In 2008, the bitcoin blockchain was launched with the publication of Satoshi Nakamoto's white paper, 'Bitcoin: A Peer-to-Peer Electronic Cash System'.[6] That paper introduced the notion that blockchains can create tamper-evident or 'tamper-resistant' records (or blocks) with the implementation of cryptographic protocols. De Filippi and A Wright use the term 'tamper-proof';[7] however, this is not necessarily the case. In most blockchain networks, tampering is possible, but self-correction happens almost automatically. The cumulative effect is that any tampering is reversed and therefore no longer evident. There are two things that make this system theoretically tamper-proof: a cryptographic fingerprint unique to each block, and a 'consensus protocol', the process by which the nodes in the network agree on a shared history.[8]

The records on a blockchain are secured through cryptography. Network participants have their own private keys that are assigned to the transactions they make and act as a personal digital signature. If a record is altered, the signature will become invalid and the peer network will know right away that something has happened. Early notification is crucial to preventing further damage.

It would require massive amounts of computing power to access every instance (or at least a 51% majority) of a certain blockchain and alter them all at the same time. There has been some debate about whether this means

6 S Nakamoto, 'Bitcoin: A Peer-to-Peer Electronic Cash System', *Bitcoin* (31 October 2008) <https://Bitcoin.org/Bitcoin.pdf>.

7 See, P De Filippi and A Wright, *Blockchain and the Law: The Rule of Code* (Harvard University Press, 2018).

8 S Nakamoto, 'Bitcoin: A Peer-to-Peer Electronic Cash System', *Bitcoin* (31 October 2008) <https://Bitcoin.org/Bitcoin.pdf>.

smaller blockchain networks could be vulnerable to attack, but a verdict has not been reached. In any case, the bigger the network is, the more tamper-resistant the blockchain will be.[9]

With the advent of bitcoin and other crypto-currencies, online payments can be made quickly and cheaply to and from anywhere in the world directly from purchaser to vendor, without the need for banks or central clearing houses. These maths-based payments systems have been made possible by the block-chain: distributed ledger technology that enables secure verification, storage and transfer of value or data. This innovative technology gives decentralised marketplaces a platform for conducting business without the need for a third party to authenticate its participants or to guarantee payments. Relationships and transactions in these new digital economies have been variously described as 'riskless' or 'trustless'.

Blockchain is helping to reshape industries in domains as varied as finance, healthcare, government and manufacturing. The technology will continue to evolve and be used in more innovative ways. It is being explored by govern-ments and regulators for its potential to provide transparency and to automate processes, including tax collection, asset registration, supply chain, fraud pre-vention, compliance, delivering welfare benefits, issuing passports, recording land titles, and assuring the quality and supply of goods. Commercial and non-profit organisations are also investigating their ability to manage and track data, assets and value. However, these uses contemplate that the relationship between users and a central authority will exist on and off "chain". This is problematic as these analogue relationships import with them levels of trust and confidence or agency and control, none of which can be managed or negated by cryptography and consensus.

The crypto-economy is an economic system that is not defined by geographic location, legal jurisdiction or political structure. It uses cryptographic techniques to constrain behaviour in place of employing or relying upon trusted third parties.[10] Cryptographic techniques draw on the science of cryptography and allow for the protection of sensitive information (organisational, commercial in confidence, institutional or personal), either in storage, analysis or commu-nication. Initially devised for information security systems, they are now being used in other contexts.[11]

On a blockchain network, trust is established not by powerful intermediaries like banks, governments and technology companies, but through mass colla-boration and sophisticated, complicated code. The rapid development and

---

9   C Miles, 'Blockchain Security: What Keeps Your Transaction Data Safe?', *IBM* (12 December 2017) <https://www.ibm.com/blogs/blockchain/2017/12/blockchain-security-what-keeps-your-transaction-data-safe/>.

10   FX Olleros and M Zhegu (eds), *Research Handbook on Digital Transformations* (Edward Elgar Publishing, 2016), 225–226.

11   N Saper, 'International Cryptography Regulation and the Global Information Economy' (2013) 11 *Northwestern Journal of Technology & Intellectual Property* 673.

implementation of blockchain technology throughout the global economy has created many new opportunities for investing, purchasing goods and services, compensating employees and streamlining business processes. What distinguishes crypto-economics from other business environments is the assumption that all participants in the network are potential adversaries. The challenge in peer-to-peer environments is to manage trust in the absence of a central controller. Unless one assumes that there will be bad actors looking to disrupt the system and unless the designer of the system ensures that there are mechanisms in place to secure the identities and the activities of every node (that is, every participant) on the network, then no one will trust the system.

The advent of bitcoin (and its underlying blockchain technology) brings with it for the first time the possibility of achieving fault-tolerant and attack-resistant consensus among nodes in a peer-to-peer network. The particular consensus that makes blockchain technology trust-worthy is 'proof of work'. A Proof-of-Work ('PoW') system is a process or protocol to deter denial of service attacks and other service abuses, such as spam on a network, by requiring some work from the service requester. This work usually means processing time by a computer. The problem with PoW is that someone or something needs to do the work and it is expensive. Crypto-economics refers to the transactional environment created by the successful incentivisation of (that is, payment of reward for) PoW.[12]

Ultimately, like other business and transactional environments, decentralised peer-to-peer digital networks seek to be safe and to provide value. In the case of crypto-economies, this is achieved by providing trusted execution, open access, irreversible transactions, efficiency and security. Achieving these features without the need for an expensive or controlling third party is radical and revolutionary. Importantly, 'crypto-economics' is not a subfield of economics, but rather an area of applied cryptography that takes economic incentives and economic theory into account.[13]

Crypto-economics imagines marketplaces without money. Bitcoin and other crypto-currencies are not necessarily better than money, but they are a better record-keeping mechanism that works across peer-to-peer networks. Money need not be essential in capitalist economies. But it is essential for valuing the relative price of goods and services in human-to-human exchanges. Money and

---

12 In the case of bitcoin (and other crypto-currencies), the proof-of-work is done by 'miners'. They are rewarded in bitcoin (or other crypto-currency). See also, 'Crypto-economics', *BlockchainHub.net* <https://blockchainhub.net/cryptoeconomics/>.

13 In simple terms, crypto-economics is the use of incentives and cryptography to design new kinds of systems, applications and networks. Crypto-economics is specifically about building things, and has most in common with mechanism design, an area of mathematics and economic theory that takes an engineering approach to designing economic mechanisms. Because it starts at the end of the game, then goes backwards, it is also called reverse game theory. It has broad applications in economics, politics and networked-systems (Internet inter-domain routing, sponsored search auctions). See, J Stark, 'Making Sense of Crypto-economics', *CoinDesk.com* (19 August 2017) <https://www.coindesk.com/making-sense-cryptoeconomics>.

prices deliver efficiencies in human calculation for exchange and this then enables distributed economic activity. A blockchain economy tokenises value so that there is no need for money or money prices. All possible ratios can be represented by tokens. These tokens are unique, traceable and readily used in both online and offline exchanges. With perfect record-keeping of assets and transactions it is possible to envisage economies beyond money.[14]

---

14 C Berg, S Davidson and J Potts, 'Beyond Money: Cryptocurrencies, Machine-Mediated Transactions and High Frequency Bartering', *SSRN* (April 7, 2018), 4, 9–10 <https://ssrn.com/abstract=3158047>.

5 Contract Versus Trust

Distinguishing between contract and trust is useful, particularly when considering their functions in e-commerce. Sometimes we enter into arrangements depending on the express terms of a contract or on terms implied by past custom because we have not yet established a relationship of trust with the other party.

Where there is trust, it seems at the outset that there will be little need for contract. However, trust as a social capital is in fact an essential ingredient in contract, commerce and economic development. Contracts are social tools as well as legal instruments, and so expectations and relationships are as important in contracting as legal obligations. This analysis will be helpful for the discussion of social relationships of trust in Part II of this book. It is helpful because digital economies can only function efficiently if customers and clients trust vendors and service providers to be competent and trustworthy. Because the actors in digital economies do not necessarily have face-to-face interactions, there needs to be other mechanisms in place to support and enable trust and to replace or represent the social capital of trust. The greater the level of trust between contracting parties the more likely they are to resolve any issues or disputes amicably, rather than resorting to fully contested litigation.[1]

For the discussion of legal relationships of Trust in Part III, it will be useful to delineate contract law from Trust law, because the basis upon which the arrangements are made are quite distinct and they give rise to obligations that offer very different remedies for their breach. When there is a breach of contract or a breach of Trust in an online environment, the first question that must be answered is not so much 'Who *do* I sue?', but 'Who *can* I sue?' In

---

1 Stewart Macaulay's seminal 1963 article 'Non-Contractual Relations in Business' explored why merchants and manufacturers often fail to plan their commercial relationships and why they seldom resort to legal sanctions to settle disputes. Macaulay found that, in many business exchanges, detailed planning and legal sanctions play only a small role. See, S Macaulay, 'Non-Contractual Relations in Business: A Preliminary Study' (1963) 28(1) *American Sociological Review* 55. <http://dx.doi.org/10.2307/2090458>. See also, PA Ryan, 'Smart Contract Relations in eCommerce' (2017) 7(10) *Technology Innovation Management Review* 10.

breaches of Trust and breaches of fiduciary duty, the pool of potential defendants is bigger than for breach of contract. Once a defendant has been identified, a complainant must establish a cause of action against the defendant and this will depend upon the relationship (if any) between the complainant and the defendant, and the nature of the defendant's breach. Furthermore, if a Trustee or fiduciary misdirects a client's property, it is important for the purposes of deciding which remedy to impose that the Court determines whether the property was the subject of legal or equitable obligations, or both.[2]

Social Relationships of Trust and Contract

Trust is an expectation in society of honest reliable behaviour according to accepted norms. In this sense, trust is a social capital. Social capital arises where trust exists in small families or large communities. It is distinguished from human capital as it is transmitted through religious, customary or historical traditions. Economists usually argue that the formation of social groups occurs as a result of a voluntary contract between the individuals, on the basis of a rational calculation that forming into cooperative groups is in their long-term interests. On this analysis, trust would not be an essential feature of this social arrangement. Enlightened self-interest and legal mechanisms could regulate behaviour, thereby compensating for the lack of trust. Fukuyama argues that while enlightened self-interest and legal mechanisms are useful, a more fundamental and powerful feature is shared ethical values and that this moral consensus forms the basis of mutual trust.[3]

When a society has a high degree of trust, it can innovate efficiently. The inherent risks usually associated with new ways of manufacturing or communicating are less obstructive when the actors trust each other.

According to Weber, the development of the modern economic world was inextricably bound to the rise of contract. Weber distinguished between two main types of contract: 'status-based' and 'purposive'.[4] Status-based contracts regulate relationships between employers and employees, partners in a partnership, and directors of a company. However, purposive contracts exist to manage the terms upon which a transaction or series of transactions will be effected. This latter type of contract is a characteristic of modernity.

A further question that arises in relation to trust and contract is whether one necessarily precedes the other. Some argue that prior trust may need to be established and tested, to enable open communication and negotiations on the details of the contract, including the thorny sensitive clauses like relationship termination, without evoking a feeling of distrust and conflict, and second, for

---

2   See, P Millett: 'Tracing the Proceeds of Fraud' (1991) 107 *Law Quarterly Review* 71, 82.

3   F Fukuyama, *Trust: The Social Virtues and the Creation of Prosperity* (Free Press Paperbacks, 1995), 26.

4   M Weber, *Economy and Society: An Outline of Interpretive Sociology* (University of California Press, 1922).

partners to be willing to engage in the expensive and specific investment in a detailed contract.[5] In this interpretation, trust serves as a basis for detailed contracting, whereas the contract is seen as deriving from trust. Zaheer and Venkatraman found a positive relationship between trust and formalisation or unified control, but struggled to articulate which of trust and contract came first and how they influenced each other in the relationship.[6] The interaction between trust and contract in relationship development is complex, and thereby trust and contract can go 'hand in hand'.[7]

The rules of contract are very important to modern business and sharing terms and conditions of entering into an arrangement is standard practice in advertising and signing contracts. E-commerce platforms and websites have readily absorbed this practice and accepting legal terms and conditions is easily done by clicking 'OK' or 'I agree' or, in more sophisticated transactions, with a digital signature. The elegant simplicity with which contractors can now accept an offer to enter into a contract is staggering in light of the volumes that have been written by legal theorists on the trials and tribulations of 'offer and acceptance' in contract formation.[8] However, trust as social capital remains vital to all of these contractual arrangements. For example, contracts are not as effective as providing assurance as to competency and reliability as trust. It is for this reason that reputation and feedback ratings feature so predominantly on e-business websites. These devices and their effectiveness in managing the social capital of trust in online relationships will be explored in detail in Part II of this book.

Trusts as a Branch of Law That Is Distinct from Contract

Trust law provides for the creation of an entity known as a Trust that is separate from the settlor, the Trustee and the beneficiary. Title to the property transfers from the settlor to the Trustee for the benefit of a third party. While these three actors can easily rearrange their relationships with any parties with

---

5   RK Woolthuis, B Hillebrand and B Nooteboom, 'Trust, Contract and Relationship Development' (2005) 26(6) *Organization Studies* 813, 831–832 <https://pdfs.semanticscholar.org/772f/92ff106a2e77828b2bba254b6d939068ba82.pdf>.

6   A Zaheer and N Venkatraman, 'Relational Governance as an Interorganizational Strategy: An Empirical Test of the Role of Trust in Economic Exchange' (1995) 16 *Strategic Management Journal* 373 <http://dx.doi.org/10.1002/smj.4250160504>.

7   RK Woolthuis, B Hillebrand and B Nooteboom, 'Trust, Contract and Relationship Development' (2005) 26(6) *Organization Studies* 813, 831–832 <https://pdfs.semanticscholar.org/772f/92ff106a2e77828b2bba254b6d939068ba82.pdf>.

8   For example, the rules as to offer stipulate the number of people who can make the offer, that terms may be included in the offer, that an invitation to treat is not an offer, how it may be communicated to the offeree, when it may be revoked or lapsed, and how and when acceptance can be communicated, so as to be binding on the parties. See, *Gibson v Manchester City Council* [1979] 1 WLR 294; *Harvey v Facey* [1893] UKPC 1, [1893] AC 552; and *Carlill v Carbolic Smoke Ball Company* [1892] EWCA Civ 1.

whom they contract, they could not as easily rearrange their relationship under the Trust. As far as the relationships between the settlor, the Trustee and the beneficiary are concerned, Trust law adds very little to contract law. However, the impact on creditors in a situation of insolvency can be profound.[9] With this analysis in mind, it is difficult to understand why any legal scholars should argue that trust law is part of contract law. However, this is precisely the position pressed by Langbein in his 'Contractarian Basis of the Law of Trusts'.[10]

Langbein claims that,

> In truth, the trust is a deal, a bargain about how the trust assets are to be managed and distributed ... The distinguishing feature of the trust is not the background event, not the transfer of property to the trustee, but the trust deal that defines the powers and responsibilities of the trustee in managing the property.[11]

In Maitland's celebrated lectures on Equity,[12] he observed that in the late 14th century when the English Chancellor first began to enforce the Trust, it had its origin in 'an agreement'.

Writing in 1953 in one of the central works of modern comparative law, FH Lawson suggested that the relationship between settlor, Trustee and beneficiary could easily be explained in the modern law in terms of a contract for the benefit of a third party.[13]

Langbein does acknowledge briefly that the insulation of Trust assets from the Trustee's creditors is a property-like attribute of the Trust.[14] He is at pains, however, to minimise this aspect of Trust law and suggests that it, too, might be replicated by ingenious contracting. Rather, he asserts, 'What is special about the trust is the deal that subjects [the Trust] property to the Trust management regime.'[15] He likens this to the special institution created by marriage, which may also be seen to have terms similar to the foundations of contract.[16]

---

9   H Hansmann and U Mattei, 'The Functions of Trust Law: A Comparative Legal and Economic Analysis' (1998) 73 *New York University Law Review* 434, 470–471.

10 JH Langbein, 'The Contractarian Basis of the Law of Trusts', *Faculty Scholarship Series Paper 502* (1995) <http://digitalcommons.law.yale.edu/fsspapers/502>.

11 JH Langbein, 'The Contractarian Basis of the Law of Trusts', *Faculty Scholarship Series Paper 502* (1995) <http://digitalcommons.law.yale.edu/fsspapers/502>, 627.

12 FW Maitland, 'Equity: A Course of Lectures' (John Brunyate rev. ed., 2d ed. 1936) (AH Chaytor & WJ Whittaker eds., 1st ed. 1909), 28.

13 FH Lawson, *A Common Lawyer Looks at the Civil Law 200* (University of Michigan Law School, 1953), 200.

14 JH Langbein, 'The Contractarian Basis of the Law of Trusts', *Faculty Scholarship Series Paper 502* (1995) <http://digitalcommons.law.yale.edu/fsspapers/502>, 667–69.

15 H Hansmann and U Mattei, 'The Functions of Trust Law: A Comparative Legal and Economic Analysis' (1998) 73 *New York University Law Review* 434, 471.

16 JH Langbein, 'The Contractarian Basis of the Law of Trusts', *Faculty Scholarship Series Paper 502* (1995) <http://digitalcommons.law.yale.edu/fsspapers/502>, 630.

It is useful to separate contract law from Trust law for a number of reasons, one of which relates to the types of relief available for breaches of the obligations that arise from these different areas of private law. A breach of the rights of beneficiaries to a Trust may give rise to particularly powerful remedies against both innocent and dishonest wrong-doers. In the case of a breach of Trust (or breach of fiduciary duty), a wrong-doer might be a third party or a stranger to the Trust, as well as the Trustee. This is important to note as digital economies depend upon computer programmers and telecom service providers to design and deliver the platforms upon which e-commerce is conducted.

In this book, a Trust is treated as an institution quite distinct from a contract and as representing the relationship between the Trustee, Trust property and the beneficiary. An important feature of Trust law is the overlap between the non-custodial duties of Trustees and the duties of loyalty of fiduciaries. Indeed, the Trustee-beneficiary relationship is the paradigm fiduciary-principal relationship. Sometimes fiduciaries owe duties to their principal with respect to the property of their principal. In this case, the term 'deemed Trust property' is used as a convenient label for 'Trust-like' property that was in the hands of a fiduciary and to which fiduciary obligations attach.

Traditionally, arm's-length commercial transactions were not amenable to fiduciary obligations. Commercial arrangements where the parties dealt with each other freely and on an equal footing were historically regarded by courts in Common Law countries as important, if not decisive, in indicating that no fiduciary duty arose. These arrangements were usually founded on contract. However, it is a matter of reasonable expectation that there is scope for fiduciary obligations to arise in a commercial setting, as the consequence of a contract or business arrangement. Under this approach, fiduciary obligations will arise when it is necessary to give effect to the expectations that the parties properly entertain of each other within the particular business setting.[17]

Until the mid-1980s, there was a reluctance to subject commercial transactions to the equitable doctrine of constructive trusts and constructive notice. However, in *Hospital Products Ltd v United States Surgical Corporation*,[18] the High Court recognised that every transaction must be examined on its merits with a view to ascertaining whether it manifests the characteristics of a fiduciary relationship.[19] That contractual and fiduciary relationships may co-exist between the same parties was established before *Hospital Products*.[20] However, in the past decade, the superior courts of the states of Australia and its High Court have consolidated the trend to impose fiduciary obligations in commercial relationships and to recognise that the liability of constructive trusteeship may be imposed on defaulting trustees

---

17 PA Ryan, 'Examining Breaches of Fiduciary Duty by Solicitors in Commercial Arrangements' (2016) 31 *Australian Journal of Corporate Law* 209.
18 *Hospital Products Ltd v United States Surgical Corporation* (1984) 156 CLR 41.
19 *Hospital Products Ltd v United States Surgical Corporation* (1984) 156 CLR 41, 77, per Mason J.
20 *Hospital Products Ltd v United States Surgical Corporation* (1984) 156 CLR 41, 70, per Mason J.

and fiduciaries, in circumstances where the parties had not expressly imposed such obligations on their relationships. As the full Federal Court of Australia noted in *Grimaldi v Chameleon Mining*,[21] unless and until the High Court says otherwise, there is ample authority for the proposition that third party liability for knowing receipt is not confined to persons dealing with Trustees, but extends to dealings with other fiduciaries, in particular company directors.[22]

This imposition of fiduciary obligations on parties to commercial relations means that whereas directors would normally enjoy the protection of the corporate structure, a breach of fiduciary duty may render them personally liable for the plaintiff's loss. In digital economies, this could expose directors to liability in cases where the platform upon which they run their business loses customer assets that were being held on their behalf pending instructions; or where an automated algorithm behaves in conflict of a client's interests. These types of risks are explored in detail in Part III of this book.

---

21 *Grimaldi v Chameleon Mining NL (No 2)* (2012) 200 FCR 296; (2012) 287 ALR 22; (2012) 87 ACSR 260; [2012] FCAFC 6.
22 *Grimaldi v Chameleon Mining NL (No 2)* (2012) 200 FCR 296; (2012) 287 ALR 22; (2012) 87 ACSR 260; [2012] FCAFC 6, [122].

6 Financial Versus Non-financial Goals and Values in Business

The most basic financial goal in business is to make a profit. Profit is the result of revenue less the expense of operating the business. Revenue includes income from sales, interest on investments and income from licensing the use of assets and property. Operating expenses include payroll, rent, materials, vehicle expense, advertising, utilities, interest payments, licenses and taxes.

Non-financial goals may directly or indirectly help to achieve increased profits. For example, non-financial goals that will improve revenue include good customer service, high production quality and employee satisfaction. Improving relationships with agents and contractors may also be beneficial to reducing the propensity for self-interest to compete or conflict with the interests of the organisation.

Non-financial goals are not the same as non-financial values. Non-financial values include aspiration, innovation, confidence, autonomy, creativity, passion, professionalism, diligence and ethical behaviour. What these values have in common is their qualitative nature. They are attributes that an organisation might seek to foster in their people or exude via their brand. While non-financial values might not directly impact on revenue or profits, they serve to enable growth and internationalisation as they underpin the organisational culture.

Organisational culture is like the personality of the organisation and studying it in depth is important to implement processes of change and deal with one's own culture in a more adaptive and effective way. It can be the difference in achieving proposed objectives.[1]

Organisations are both agents of change and the main stability sources of a society, and they affect it in unintended ways through the structuring of social life. By causing an impact on their members, organisations are also active participants in the process of social change.[2] Most analysts conceive social organisations as networks of social relations and shared guidelines, often referred to as social and cultural structure.[3]

---

1   A Dubrin, *Fundamentals of Organisational Culture* (Thomson Learning, 2003).
2   RH Hall, *Organisations: Structure and Processes* (3rd edn, Prentice Hall, 1984).
3   PM Blau, *Introduction to the Study of the Social Structure* (Zahar, 1977).

The influence of cultures (national, professional and corporate) tends to increase as people are socialised into industries, professions and workplaces. Most companies have their own set of norms, values, beliefs and patterns of behaviour that distinguishes them from other organisations. The time a company has been in the market influences the corporate culture.

Poor corporate values and a culture of self-interest will not enable economic success. Business based on unstated moral and family-based obligations soon descend into nepotism, cronyism, secret commissions and kick-backs.[4] Modern prosperity and social well-being are best achieved by embedding transparent and ethical conduct into business practices.[5]

Recent examples of toxic corporate culture in otherwise successful companies have demonstrated the risk of unchecked misconduct and poor organisational values. Uber is one of the most popular start-up tech companies of the past decade. It operates in 65 countries, has 3 million drivers, employs 16,000 people, carries 75 million riders daily and made 4 billion trips worldwide in 2017. However, Uber has recently suffered a reputational crisis.

In 2017, an independent investigation into the sexual harassment complaints at Uber ended with the dismissal for misconduct of twenty employees.[6] Uber's deficiencies in human resource management not only affected the rights and well-being of individual employees, but also undermined Uber's culture and stability. In the first few months of 2017, Uber suffered a wave of high-level departures, and has struggled to fill senior executive positions including the top three key posts of Chief Executive Officer, Chief Operating Officer and Chief Financial Officer.[7]

As well as their harassment woes, Uber has faced a series of allegations of misconduct, including a criminal investigation by the Justice Department for allegedly using software to trick regulators and avoid government scrutiny. Taken together, the probes have tarnished the image of one of Silicon Valley's most aggressive and widely emulated companies and its chief executive, Travis Kalanick.[8] Meanwhile, an analysis of Uber's self-driving car metrics showed that the company's autonomous vehicles needed constant micromanagement, according to a news report. The company's

---

4   F Fukuyama, *Trust: The Social Virtues and the Creation of Prosperity* (Free Press Paperbacks, 1995), 149.

5   F Fukuyama, *Trust: The Social Virtues and the Creation of Prosperity* (Free Press Paperbacks, 1995), 150.

6   C Timburg and E Dwoskin, 'Uber Fires 20 Employees as Part of Harassment Investigation', *Washington Post* (6 June 2017) <https://www.washingtonpost.com/news/the-switch/wp/2017/06/06/uber-fires-more-than-20-employees-as-part-of-sexual-harassment-investigation/?noredirect=on&utmterm=.1c7d79d25a32>.

7   R Jones, 'The Unicorn Governance Trap – Essay' (2017) 166 *University of Pennsylvania Law Review Online* 165, 180.

8   C Timburg and E Dwoskin, 'Uber Fires 20 Employees as Part of Harassment Investigation', *Washington Post* (6 Jun 2017) <https://www.washingtonpost.com/news/the-switch/wp/2017/06/06/uber-fires-more-than-20-employees-as-part-of-sexual-harassment-investigation/?noredirect=on&utmterm=.1c7d79d25a32>.

human testers had to intervene on average once per mile, raising questions about the readiness of the company's autonomous cars despite claims to the contrary during a high-profile launch in Pittsburgh months before.[9] By the end of June 2017, Uber, which a few months earlier was worth US$70 billion, had lost as much as $US20 billion of that value.

Uber has also been investigated for the way that it treats its drivers. The debate continues as to whether the drivers are contractors or employees. According to analysis from The Australia Institute's Centre for Future Work, after Uber takes its 25% cut, an Uber driver's take-home pay is around $14.62 an hour, well below the minimum wage.[10] In 2014, a report emerged that Uber had engaged their own drivers in a deception of falsely generate demand, so as to attract more drivers.[11] In October 2016, Uber concealed a massive cyber-attack that exposed the data of 57 million users and drivers.[12] A system called *Ripley* was reportedly used by Uber in 2015 and 2016 to lock-down staff computers and obstruct tax investigations.[13]

The Uber story has been described as a cautionary tale: 'as parable of the perils of poor governance and how it can spread to a secondary cancer – corporate culture'.[14] In the year that followed, Uber posted more losses amid questions about the behaviour of some senior officials[15] and the death in March 2018 of a pedestrian in Phoenix, Arizona who was struck by one of Uber's autonomous vehicles.[16]

9   B Fung, 'What to Know About Uber's Months of Crises', *Washington Post* (21 June 2017) <https://www.washingtonpost.com/news/the-switch/wp/2017/04/18/from-deleteuber-to-hell-a-short-history-of-ubers-recent-struggles/?utm term=.f1c35c3aa92d>.

10 J Stanford, 'The REAL Diary of an Uber Driver', *The Australia Institute for Research – Centre for FutureWork* (22 January 2019) <https://www.futurework.org.au/the_real_diary_of_an_uber_driver>.

11 P Sims, 'Can We Trust Uber?', *HuffingtonPost.com* (30 September 2014) <http s://www.huffingtonpost.com/peter-sims/can-we-trust-uberb5892668.html>.

12 JC Wong, 'Uber Concealed Massive Hack that Exposed 57m User and Drivers', *TheGuardian.com* (22 November 2017) <https://www.theguardian.com/technol ogy/2017/nov/21/uber-data-hack-cyber-attack>.

13 O Solon, 'Uber Developed Secret System to Lock Down Staff Computers in a Police Raid', *TheGuardian.com* (12 January 2018) <https://www.theguardian.com/technology/2018/jan/11/uber-developed-secret-system-to-lock-down-sta ff-computers-in-a-police-raid>.

14 E Knight, 'Uber Pays a $26 Billion Price for Its Toxic Corporate Culture', *SMH.com.au* (1 July 2017) <https://www.smh.com.au/business/uber-pays-a-26-bil lion-price-for-its-toxic-corporate-culture-20170630-gx1x3w.html>.

15 K Conger, 'Uber Losses Continue in Its March Toward an IPO', *NYTimes.com* (15 August 2018) <https://www.nytimes.com/2018/08/15/technology/uber s-losses-continue-in-march-toward-initial-public-offering.html>.

16 T Griggs and D Wakabayashi, 'How a Self-Driving Uber Killed a Pedestrian in Arizona', *NYTimes.com* (21 March 2018) <https://www.nytimes.com/intera ctive/2018/03/20/us/self-driving-uber-pedestrian-killed.html>.

Analysts, commentators and its own CEO accused Uber's former head of hubris: that is, hubris in relation to the readiness of autonomous vehicles to be tested on public roads, hubris for failing to get the proper permits; and for failing to release accurate data about its testing practices, and hubris in the way that it ran its business.[17]

Hubris is a negative non-financial value. Hubris is the presence of excessive pride or self-confidence of someone in power. Hubris has featured very publicly in Uber's corporate culture, at both organisational and operational levels. Uber's hubris proved to have a corresponding negative impact on its financial position. Uber's troubles are particularly market sensitive because Uber's customers need to be able to trust their drivers and their autonomous vehicles to get them safely to their destination; and its drivers need to trust Uber to treat them fairly and according to the industrial regulations of the jurisdiction in which they operate.

At the heart of everything Uber does there is a need for trust. In fact, Uber now has its own head of trust and safety. Uber's general manager for Australia and New Zealand has been quoted as saying, 'People love our [Uber's] product, they don't necessarily love us'.[18] This raises a critical question of whether brand can beat trust. Once a brand becomes a verb, then its reputation may seem sealed. We Hoover carpets, Google apartments in Rome and, when we need to get to a local restaurant quickly, we Uber it. These brands are powerful, but Uber's brand has been tarnished by the organisation's failure to manage the relationship of trust with its drivers, its employees, the regulators, its customers and the general public.

While trust may seem like a non-financial goal or value, its presence or deficiency can have an immediate financial impact. We need to trust that autonomous vehicles will stop in our path, that the food we eat has been handled according to appropriate standards, that our credit card details are secure during online transactions, that rules and conventions are being followed, that organisations (including tech companies) care about the quality of their goods and services and the treatment of those with whom they interact both internally and externally, in the corporate and operational domains. Importantly, trust is generated by adhering to minimum standards that at the

---

17 R Lanctot, 'Mindboggling Uber Hubris', *StrategyAnalytics* (16 December 2016) <https://www.strategyanalytics.com/strategy-analytics/blogs/infotainment-telema tics/2016/12/16/mindboggling-uber-hubris>; M Kosoff, 'Uber's New CEO Says Travis Kalanick Was "Guilty of Hubris"', *VanityFair.com* (23 January 2018) <http s://www.vanityfair.com/news/2018/01/ubers-new-ceo-says-travis-kalanick-wa s-guilty-of-hubris>; E Newcome, 'Uber's Hubris', *Medium.com-Bloomberg* (19 December 2016) <https://medium.com/bloomberg/ubers-hubris-a67c9aab0b31>.

18 B Head, 'How Uber Trades on Trust', *AICD.CompanyDirectors.com.au* (1 August 2018) <https://aicd.companydirectors.com.au/membership/company-director-ma gazine/2018-back-editions/august/uber-susan-anderson>.

time may seem unnecessarily costly or inconvenient, but if ignored will have consequences that are far more costly, and inconvenient.[19]

Only with reliable systems and processes can we trust strangers and strange new things. This is how and why trust supports innovation and economic growth.

19 N Hooper, 'How Much Does Trust Matter to Your Board of Directors?', *AICD.*
CompanyDirectors.com.au (1 August 2018) <https://aicd.companydirectors.com.
au/membership/company-director-magazine/2018-back-editions/august/its-a
-matter-of-trust>.

Part II
Social Relationships of Trust in Digital Economies

7 Introduction

Since the advent of the Internet, commercial and social processes have been migrating onto platforms. By the end of the second decade of the 21st century, there will be as many types of processes managed online as there are ways for humans to interact. However, these many processes can be broadly categorised into four types: correspondence, transactions, publishing and research. Since becoming commercially available, the Internet has democratised information, enabled global communication and served as a platform for a variety of goods and services.[1]

Information and communications technologies contribute to businesses in many ways. First, the rapid advances in the technology largely reduced the prices of computing hardware within a short timeframe. Second, the hardware market had to reduce the profit margins for traditional manufacturers, which allowed a breakthrough for low-cost, low-margin producers and the growing competition in the software market has compelled software companies to be more innovative and better acknowledge the needs of the consumers. Meanwhile, stored value digital cards and virtual currencies granted a new payment instrument to the digital market. Finally, a prominent trend in the digital economy is the sharing or 'gig' economy, which refers to collaborative consumption that involves the peer-to-peer sharing of goods and services.[2]

Over the past decade, the Internet has become big business. Whereas the list of top ten Fortune 500 companies in 1980 was dominated by petroleum companies and motor car manufacturers,[3] in 2018 the top ten places feature Walmart, Apple, Amazon.com, and AT&T – that is, online retailers

1   P Laudicina, 'This Is the Future of the Internet', *World Economic Forum Agenda* (12 March 2018) <https://www.weforum.org/agenda/2018/03/this-is-the-future-of-the-internet/>.
2   T Budak, 'The Transformation of International Tax Regime: Digital Economy' (2017) 8 *Inonu University Law Review* 297, 300.
3   *Fortune500* – a database of 50 years of Fortune's list of America's largest companies (1980) <http://archive.fortune.com/magazines/fortune/fortune500archive/full/1980/>.

and technology companies.[4] Indeed, of the ten most profitable companies, five are technology companies with Apple topping the chart.[5] One of the reasons that these technology companies have been so successful is the proliferation and increased processing speed of hand-held devices.

According to Domo's *Data Never Sleeps* report, more than half of all web searches are conducted on mobile phones. By mid-2017, the global population of Internet users had reached 3.7 billion; and 90% of all data ever created was generated in the past two years.[6] In 2017, Google users conducted more than 40,000 searches every second and with more than 2 billion active users, Facebook was still the world's largest social media platform.[7] The Internet has become an important platform for conducting business. The two primary drivers of e-commerce in retail and services are convenience to consumers (customers and clients) and lower overheads for suppliers (retailers and providers). However, the entire economic logic of the Internet is based on corporate self-promotion and advertising products and services. The problem with this model is that it exposes the financial ecosystem to human controls and mechanisms that are inherently flawed and easily manipulated. Advertising is an inherently unreliable source of truth about businesses and products; it is the antithesis of due diligence.

While honest advertising practices are required and regulated by law, virtual domains make enforcement very difficult. In most common and civil countries, regulators can impose fines on businesses that mislead consumers. It does not matter whether a false or misleading statement was intentional or not. For example, businesses must not make false or misleading claims about the quality, value, price, age or benefits of goods or services, or any associated guarantee or warranty. Using false testimonials or 'passing off' (impersonating another business) is also illegal.[8] However, navigating the vast expanse that is the Internet so as to detect false or misleading claims is challenging for victims and regulators.

There are other legally problematic or unacceptable behaviours in trade and commerce that are enabled or hidden by online platforms. For example, privacy and data protection, employment relationships, contracts for the delivery of goods or services, and the automation of advice all give rise to particular

---

4   *Fortune500* – Fortune's list of America's largest companies (2018) <http://fortune.com/fortune500/list/>.
5   *Fortune500* – Fortune's list of America's most profitable companies (2018) <http://fortune.com/fortune500/list/filtered?sortBy=profits&first500>.
6   'Data Never Sleeps 5.0', *Domo* (17 July 2017) <https://www.domo.com/learn/data-never-sleeps-5?aid=ogsm0725171&sf100871281=1>.
7   J Constantine, 'Facebook Now Has 2 Billion Monthly Users ... and Responsibility', *TechCrunch* (27 June 2017) <https://techcrunch.com/2017/06/27/facebook-2-billion-users/>.
8   For example, pursuant to section 18(1) of *The Australian Consumer Law*, a person must not, in trade or commerce, engage in conduct that is misleading or deceptive or is likely to mislead or deceive. *The Australian Consumer Law* is found in Schedule 2 to the *Competition and Consumer Act 2010* (Cth).

opportunities to exploit customers, clients, contractors, employees and competitors. In this context, the term 'social relationships of trust' is intended to reflect a particular type of relationship of trust that is to be distinguished from the legal relationship that is created when title over property is settled upon a Trustee for the benefit of beneficiaries (a Trust).

Social relationships of trust in business contracts were explored in the 1960s by Stewart Macaulay. Macaulay found that in the day-to-day workings of developed economies, few disputes arose between consumers and suppliers. Legal scholarship that focuses on the contract lawsuit, as opposed to contractual relationships, creates a distortion of most social norms and economic systems.[9] Since the advent of the Internet, many of the payments and invoices for these transactions are managed online, but the nature of the exchanges remains a social experience. These types of contracts are very different in nature to the purchase of a business or an investment in property, which require due diligence to be conducted on the target and perhaps legal advice to be obtained in relation to the terms and conditions upon which the purchase or investment will be made.

Weber's understanding of different types of contracts is applicable to an analysis of how smart contracts will fit into our future of online exchanges; it favours the characterisation of these relations as conversational and social, rather than strictly legal and purposive.[10] Social trust is strongest when there is a perception that risk is understood and minimised.

When an individual lacks knowledge about a risk, their reliance on the ability of authorities to manage that risk results in the existence of social trust. On the other hand, when an individual has personal knowledge about a risk and therefore does not need to rely on managing authorities, social trust is unrelated to judged risks and benefits. Lacking this knowledge, lay judgements of risks and benefits may be based on assessments of those who are responsible for managing the risk. Social trust is an important dimension in attitudes toward technologies. For example, research has shown that participants who had social trust in the companies and scientists involved in gene technology perceived fewer risks and more benefits associated with this technology than people not having social trust.[11] Where trust requires knowledge of a company and its experts, then it follows that as new companies start-up and their young experts develop novel and complex technologies, it will be more challenging for consumers, businesses and regulators to assess risk and therefore trust what

---

9   See, S Macaulay, 'Non-Contractual Relations in Business: A Preliminary Study' (1963) 28(1) *American Sociological Review* 55; S Macaulay, 'Elegant Models, Empirical Pictures, and the Complexities of Contract' (1977) 11(3) *Law & Society Review* 507.

10 M Siegrist and G Cvetkovich, 'Society for Risk Analysis Perception of Hazards: The Role of Social Trust and Knowledge' (2000) 20(5) *Risk Analysis* 713.

11 M Siegrist, 'A Causal Model Explaining the Perception and Acceptance of Gene Technology' (2006) 1 *Journal of Applied Social Psychology* 29.

is on offer. This is why start-up businesses will often recruit their board members from the boards of other well-established and conservative businesses.

These issues are particularly important when considering digital economies, for three reasons. Firstly, in digital economies, not all businesses are operating with the backing of a known and therefore respected brand or reputation. Dealing with strangers who could be located anywhere in the world presents particular challenges for regulators. Regulators in all economies want to protect consumers without stifling innovation. The types of threats that feature most predominantly for digital economies are identifying and locating potential defendants for breaches of contract and regulation in online business, and data protection generally. These issues will be explored in Chapters 8, 9, 10 and 11 of this Part. Secondly, digital economies are rapidly adopting automated algorithms to manage transactions and to gather and analyse data. Depending on the level of autonomy granted to an algorithm and the nature of its optimal state, business and developers may be at risk of losing control over the behaviour of their robots. The accountability of algorithms is the topic for discussion in Chapter 12. Thirdly, in distributed economies (as contemplated by blockchain technology and demonstrated by the bitcoin network), there will be no trusted third party to manage risk on behalf of the participants. Distributed digital economies have the benefit of efficiency with the removal of central authority. But distributed digital economies depend on sophisticated and complex maths-based trust protocols that need to be secure and scalable. These inherent risks will be discussed in detail in Chapter 13.

8 Social Contracting in e-Business

Digital commerce has transformed the marketplace for all goods and services. The separation by time and distance of point of sale and vendor, and the presence of geographically dispersed sellers who do not engage in repeated transactions with the same customer challenges traditional mechanisms for building the trust required for commercial exchanges. In this changing environment, legal rules and institutions play a diminished role in building trust. Instead, new systems and methods are emerging to foster trust in both one-off commercial transactions and on-going relationships in cyberspace.[1]

Although these conditions seem inimical to the production of trust, commercial Internet transactions have continued to expand and flourish. Technology has enabled innovative forms of exchange to emerge, spanning an ever-broader range of products and services. These new modalities of commerce challenge traditional organisational and market frameworks. They also create peculiar obstacles for recourse via the law, when something goes wrong.

Lawyers regard the law as a means to regulate social relations while sociologists see the law as a part of social systems.[2] The emergence of modern law and its convergence with the formation of capitalism has been driven by economics and both legal and urban forms of social relations. Globalisation, the telecommunications, the Internet and social media have created virtual marketplaces.

There are three significant differences between virtual and non-virtual marketplaces. The first and most obvious difference is the near absence of real-time human-to-human interaction in virtual marketplaces. Businesses that need to provide tailored responses to individual enquiries do so via chat bots that emulate a human customer service or help desk experience. Another clear distinction between non-digital and digital economies is their trading hours. Virtual marketplaces exist entirely online and are not impeded by the time of day, day of the week, seasons or geo-location. Unlike their high street, department

---

1 JY Lee, 'Trust and Social Commerce' (2015) 77 *University of Pittsburg Law Review* 137, 141.
2 DN Schiff, 'Socio-legal Theory: Social Structure and Law' (1976) 39(3) *Modern Law Review* 287.

store, shopping complex or office building equivalents, e-commerce suppliers and service providers are open for business every hour of every day. Shopping online is convenient, fast, often cheaper, and eliminates an unnecessary step when sending purchasers to third parties.

A problem with this physical separation between supplier and consumer is the lack of opportunity to create social relations using the traditional means of handshake, conversation, interaction and – of course – immediate and in person exchange of money for goods. However, a bigger problem arises when entering into agreements and making purchasers with suppliers who are overseas or in another jurisdiction. Consumer rights naturally apply when an online shopping business is inside the consumers' jurisdiction. Those rights may also apply when consumers buy something from an overseas online business, although it may be difficult to get a repair, replacement or refund because the business is outside of the geographical, regulatory and even telecommunications jurisdiction. For example, businesses that sell goods and services to businesses and consumers in Australia must ensure products and services meet Australian safety regulations; not mislead or hide costs and other details; compete fairly to ensure a variety of choices on quality and price; give automatic guarantees with the right to ask for a repair, replacement, refund, cancellation or compensation as appropriate if there is a problem; must not sell items that have been stolen; and the supplier must not be insolvent.[3] Over the past two decades, e-commerce has developed mechanisms for reassuring customers that they can trust online vendors, suppliers, platforms or payments networks.

Devices such as customer reviews, reputation ratings, chat bots and automated dispute resolution stand in place of word-of-mouth recommendations, human interaction, call centres, help desks and courts that featured for so long in physical marketplaces. The relationship between these devices and law is tenuous. The law is guided by precedent and seeks certainty. Modern courts look to documents to admit evidence and characterise relationships. Meanwhile, more and more, dispute resolution is being privatised and democratised so that disgruntled consumers are able to seek recourse via processes that are cheaper, more efficient and ultimately more satisfying than via the courts. Social relationships and the legal institutions that underpin those relationships in business have been completely revolutionised by the Internet and e-commerce. With this in mind, it is useful to identify how this has come about and which particular elements of this new ecosystem are crucial and most reliable. Trust in networks and platforms requires an understanding of not just contract formation, but also contractual relationships, and the features of these systems that make them sustainable.

---

3   'Shopping Online', *ACCC.com.au* (2019) <https://www.accc.gov.au/consumers/online-shopping/shopping-online>.

Non-Contractual Relations in Business

Macaulay's seminal 1963 article 'Non-Contractual Relations in Business' explored why merchants and manufacturers often fail to plan their commercial relationships and why they seldom resort to legal sanctions to settle disputes. Macaulay found that, in many business exchanges, detailed planning and legal sanctions play only a small role. His tentative explanation was that businesses prefer to deal with people or organisations they trust based on their prior dealings or their reputation. According to Macaulay, a manifestation of trust might be a brief conversation followed by a handshake. The rationale is that, if parties cannot rely on promises as being made in good faith, and plan for the future accordingly, the cost of uncertainty would make conducting business impossible. However, this approach to contracting frustrates lawyers, who advise their clients to plan for contingencies and formalise their business arrangements.[4]

It is understood from Macaulay's research and its progeny that mutual trust probably exists and is desired in the future.

All contracts are embedded in a matrix of social relations — contracts are 'relational'.[5] Because these relations are primarily social, there is little knowledge of how these social relationships translate into relationships that are also legal. Macaulay's research shows that parties are often substantially unaware of their legal rights and obligations. However, this does not preclude industry codes from being constructed to embody the values of the relevant industry.[6] It is therefore incumbent up on the market and social system – rather than the courts – to implement any values not reflected in existing contract doctrine (for example, fairness or community).

Where trust exists, formation of contracts often does not occur, in the parties' minds at any single moment, but gradually develops over time as the practices and patterns of contracting are embedded into the relationship.[7]

---

4   See, PA Ryan, 'Smart Contract Relations in eCommerce' (2017) 7(10) *Technology Innovation Management Review* 10. See also, S Macaulay, 'Non-Contractual Relations in Business: A Preliminary Study' (1963) 28(1) *American Sociological Review* 55; S Macaulay, 'Elegant Models, Empirical Pictures, and the Complexities of Contract' (1977) 11(3) *Law & Society Review* 507; S Macaulay, J Kidwell and WC Whitford, *Contracts: Law in Action* (2nd Ed, LexisNexis, 2003); and S Macaulay and WC Whitford, 'The Development of Contracts: The Law in Action' (2015) 87 *Temple Law Review* 793.

5   M Lees, 'Contract, Conscience, Communitarian Conspiracies and Confucius: Normativism through the Looking Glass of Relational Contract Theory' (2001) 25 (1) *Melbourne University Law Review* 82.

6   See further, WD Duncan and S Christensen, 'Section 51AC of the Trade Practices Act: An 'Exocet' in Retail Leasing' (1999) 27 *Australian Business Law Review* 284.

7   WC Whitford, 'J Braucher's Contracts World View' (2016) 58(1) *Arizona Law Review* 13, 16.

Establishing Trust in E-business

It is clear that in the first two decades of the 21st century, consumers have experienced the innumerable benefits of new technology, innovation and data with the commensurate positive impact on their private, social, financial and working lives. However, the speed of these changes has also been bewildering for many in the community. Only in recent years has consumer understanding of the full impact of these changes dawned on them with a growing awareness of the true downside of digital innovation. From worldwide data breaches and increased direct marketing and targeting, to the rise of price discrimination, and even the potential undermining of the political process, consumers are beginning to understand more fully the implications of what they have signed up for.

A modern notion of agreement figures in contemporary contract as a marketing tool (in a conversation between corporations and consumers) as well as an act of compliance with law (in a conversation between corporations and courts).[8] In digital economies, this story is now represented by the visibility of terms, an issue that continues to resonate in the treatment of fine print today. While the tendency of courts to enforce fine print is now a commonplace, it is also regarded as incumbent upon the supplier to draw a bright line around the obligations owed to give consumers notice of terms. In addition, this exposes the aspirational aspect of contract doctrine that there is a duty to read those terms.[9] This latter point raises a practical consideration: can it be reasonable or rational to ask consumers to take up this burden – or any term-reading at all? After all, an individual who depends on Google, Facebook or Twitter is not in a position to negotiate her own separate agreement. Why spend time on a contract you can neither change nor refuse? It may be tantalising to imagine an all-knowing third party or government that can regulate the quality of markets and their products. However, markets are about recognising that information is dispersed in all social systems and that the problem of society is to find, devise and discover institutions that incentivise and enable people to make the right decisions without anyone having to tell them what to do.[10] This is after all the essence of freedom of choice.

The role that trust and reputation play in ordering social cooperation has always been an important, but often overlooked, factor in how the market process actually works.[11] Various forms of reputational mechanisms have developed in order for people to communicate more efficiently their

8   T Kastner, 'How About Them Apples: The Power of Stories of Agreement in Consumer Contracts' (2014) 7(1) *Drexel Law Review* 67, 121

9   T Kastner, 'How About Them Apples: The Power of Stories of Agreement in Consumer Contracts' (2014) 7(1) *Drexel Law Review* 67, 71.

10 RT Simmons, *Beyond Politics: The Roots of Government Failure* (Independent Institute, 2011), 7.

11 See, P Massa, 'Trust It Forward: Tyranny of the Majority or Echo Chambers?', in *The Reputation Society: How Online Opinions Are Reshaping the Offline World* (MIT Press, 2011), 151–152.

judgements and experiences with one another, and to make decisions about whom to trust and what to believe.[12]

Like the Guilds in Medieval London, many trade and professional associations have formed their own clubs with rigorous entry criteria. For example, the New York Diamond Dealers Club was created in the early 20th century and created a rigorous admission process, an arbitration process with industry experts and high standards for maintaining membership. Similar associations use coordinated refusals to deal in order to sustain valuable reputational mechanisms.[13] Merchants refuse to enter into contracts with dishonest firms and demand a risk premium from those who have not lived up to their contracts.[14] Reputation is an essential factor in building trust among others within the market; ultimately it allows for greater specialisation of trade and globalisation of a brand.

Barristers in many common law jurisdictions are required to sit Bar Exams and then complete expensive practical courses and pupillage years. Practising certificates in the legal profession are expensive and misconduct of practitioners is subject to onerous sanctions. Certain types of legal service and advice can only be provided by qualified and licensed practitioners. These restraints are enforced in legislation and in the limits on liability and professional indemnity insurance. These measures ensure that the person providing legal advice and representation both privately and in the courts is qualified, competent and of good character; that is, trustworthy.

These traditional protectionist mechanisms have struggled to sustain the merchants and service-providers they are designed to serve and protect. For decades, London taxis have operated under similar constraints. Acquiring 'the Knowledge' is still regarded as the hardest thing a London cabbie will ever do.[15] Only between a quarter and a third of all applicants are successful. Getting to know London well enough to pass the exam requires up to four years and coverage of 20,000 miles within a six-mile radius of Charing Cross. Applicants head out on their mopeds in any weather or traffic chaos. As well as the exam, 'the Knowledge' demands that novitiates learn thousands of 'points of interest', taking in around 25,000 streets, so that they can recite the perfect route between any two points in the city.[16]

---

12 See, P Massa, 'Trust It Forward: Tyranny of the Majority or Echo Chambers?', in *The Reputation Society: How Online Opinions Are Reshaping the Offline World* (MIT Press, 2011), 159.

13 See, BD Richman, 'The Antitrust of Reputation Mechanisms: Institutional Economics and Concerted Refusals to Deal' (2009) 95 *Virginia Law Review* 325, 332.

14 A Thierer, C Koopman and A Hobson, 'How the Internet, the Sharing Economy, and Reputational Feedback Mechanisms Solve the Lemons Problem' (2016) 70(3) *University of Miami Law Review* 830, 843.

15 I Beetlestone, 'The History of London's Black Cabs', *The Guardian.com* (10 December 2012) <https://www.theguardian.com/world/2012/dec/09/histor y-london-black-cabs>.

16 I Beetlestone, 'The History of London's Black Cabs', *The Guardian.com* (10 December 2012) <https://www.theguardian.com/world/2012/dec/09/histor y-london-black-cabs>.

But this is all changing. In an era of GPS, mini cabs and Uber, it is difficult for London's black cabs to justify their rigorous entry test and the premium they charge their customers. Whatever monopoly once existed and was worth protecting has long been diluted by the chill wind of competition and innovation.

Taxi drivers and lawyers traditionally offer services that are delivered solely offline. However, more and more, the way that they and others in service industries meet the demands of their customers is supported online. For barristers, this means online legal research. For taxi drivers, way-finding does not demand hours of training on a moped in all weathers. A Tomtom, Garmin, Navman or Google Maps will more reliably calculate the driving distance from point A to point B, because these apps can also draw upon third party data to assess real time traffic conditions and the weather.

Whereas diamond merchants, taxi drivers and lawyers tend to deliver products and services in a physical world (albeit with the support of online promotion and big data analytics), many vendors in digital economies are in the business of innovation. Establishing trust in businesses that innovate creates a further layer of complexity for contractual relations.

Innovation implies a rapid rate of change with an appetite for early adoption. These scenarios lack a history of shared understandings, life cycle scenarios and predictive models for causes of disputes and their resolution. In these settings, there is great likelihood of "in good faith" disputes about expectations and what constitutes proper performance. With youthful exuberance and enthusiasm often prevailing over cautious pessimism, this type of business environment creates an atmosphere that can disrupt traditional modalities and frameworks for fundraising, managing resources and communicating with customers. One approach to managing the uncertainty that comes with start-ups and innovation is to resort to the use of formal contracts to support the informality of these new business models and their new relationships.[17] This tendency towards formal contracting to support informal relationships in innovation is entirely consistent with Macaulay's analysis. Start-ups and innovation do not have the benefit of existing reputation, customer reviews or long-term relationships. Without these social relationships and mechanisms, they must resort to formal contracting as a means to establish trust.

Unfortunately, innovation and a climate of disruption will also attract less scrupulous actors who will exploit the novelty and uncertainty that comes with new technologies and new ways of doing business online. It is for this reason, that regulators will step in and try to take the lead with establishing some ground rules for new players, to protect investors and customers.

Corporate regulators in a number of developed economies have favoured the 'sand box' approach to the regulation of innovative start-up businesses.

---

17 GK Hadfield and I Bozovic, 'Scaffolding: Using Formal Contracts to Support Informal Relations in Support of Innovation' (2016) 5 *Wisconsin Law Review* 981.

Australia's regulatory sandbox framework is comprised of three broad options for testing a new product or service without a licence.[18] Those options are: relying on existing statutory exemptions or flexibility in the law – such as by acting on behalf of an existing licensee; relying on the Australian Security and Investments Commission's (ASIC's) 'Fin Tech licensing exemption' for the testing of certain specified products and services; and for other services, relying on individual relief from ASIC.[19]

Singapore's regulatory sandbox was established against the backdrop of a rapidly evolving financial technology landscape, emerging financial products and services that utilise FinTech. Singapore's Monetary Authority (MAS) decided that its FinTech business community was becoming more sophisticated and there may be uncertainty over whether the innovation met regulatory requirements. MAS is encouraging more FinTech experimentation so that promising innovations can be tested in the market and have a chance for wider adoption, in Singapore and abroad. Singapore's regulatory sandbox enables FinTech players to experiment with innovative financial products or services in the production environment, but within a well-defined space and duration. It also includes appropriate safeguards to contain the consequences of failure and maintain the overall safety and soundness of the financial system.[20]

Trust has long been regarded as central to regulatory effectiveness.[21] However, in digital economies, regulation can enable and support trust in a time of disruption and technological innovation. They do this by laying ground rules for the number of clients and the volume of business that start-ups can cater to in their first year or two. They also provide clear guidance in relation to licensing, registration and standards that need to be considered in order to comply with relevant local and international laws and best practice. Businesses that demonstrate active engagement with these rules and recommendations can then advertise their willing compliance on their websites. This transparency helps to build a strong brand and positive reputation with the regulator and establish trust with customers.

---

18 'Regulatory Sandbox', *ASIC.gov.au* <https://asic.gov.au/for-business/your-business/innovation-hub/regulatory-sandbox/>.

19 ASIC has existing relief powers in certain areas that may apply to businesses that qualify for the 'sand box'. Specifically, ASIC has powers to: provide exemptions from the licensing requirements for products or services (or classes of products or services); and modify some of the laws we administer.

20 'Monetary Authority of Singapore' Role in a Smart Financial Centre', *Monetary Authority of Singapore* (1 September 2017) <http://www.mas.gov.sg/Singapore-Financial-Centre/Smart-Financial-Centre/MAS-Role.aspx>.

21 For research on this issue see V Braithwaite, 'Responsive Regulation and Taxation' (2007) 29 *Law and Policy* 3–10; J Job, 'How Is Trust in Government Created? It Begins at Home, But Ends in the Parliament' (2005) 6 *Australian Review of Public Affairs* 1–23; TR Tyler and YJ Huo, *Trust in the Law: Encouraging Public Co-operation with the Police and Courts* (Russell Sage Foundation, 2002).

The Precision Paradox

In any business relationship or agreement, it is not always easy to point to the precise moment when the legal criteria of a contract have been fulfilled. For example, for an agreement and thus a contract to be extracted from circumstances where no acceptance of an offer can be established or inferred, the best a court can do is imply a manifestation of mutual assent from the circumstances.[22] Agreements concerning terms and conditions that might be too uncertain or too illusory to enforce at a particular time in the relationship may by reason of the parties' subsequent conduct become sufficiently specific to give rise to legal rights and duties. In a dynamic commercial relationship new terms will be added or will supersede older terms. It is necessary therefore to look at the whole relationship and not only at what was said and done when the relationship was first formed.[23]

In many cases, what the parties have actually agreed upon represents the totality of their willingness to agree; each may be prepared to take his or her chances in relation to an eventuality for which no provision is made. The more detailed and comprehensive the contract the less ground there is for supposing that the parties have failed to address their minds to the question at issue.[24] However, herein lies the rub: more detail means more precision and more precision means more text in the form of lengthy fine print with terms and conditions. The terms and conditions might cover all eventualities in the proposed agreement between user and service-provider, but studies show that – even where required as a precondition to continuing – most Internet users do not read terms and conditions before clicking, 'OK', 'Join', 'Next', 'Accept' or 'I Agree'.

A Deloitte survey of 2,000 consumers in the United States found that 91% of people consent to legal terms and services conditions without reading them. For younger people, ages 18–34, the rate is even higher with 97% agreeing to conditions before reading.

According to the Deloitte research, the language of the vast majority of terms and conditions is understandably too complex for many. Given the absence of a choice, consumers do not consider these as a barrier to purchasing and accepting many forms of new technology.[25]

Researchers at the University of Connecticut conducted a study to gather empirical data about how extremely consumers could be deceived into signing

---

22   *Vroon BV v Foster's Brewing Group Ltd* [1994] VicRp 53; [1994] 2 VR 32, 81 per Ormiston J.

23   *Integrated Computer Services Pty Ltd v Digital Equipment Corp (Aust) Pty Ltd* (1988) 5 BPR §11,110, §11,118 (per McHugh JA).

24   *Codelfa Construction Pty Ltd v State Rail Authority of New South Wales* (1982) 149 CLR 347.

25   '2017 Global Mobile Consumer Survey: US Edition The Dawn of the Next Era in Mobile', *Deloitte* (2017) <https://www2.deloitte.com/content/dam/Deloitte/us/Documents/technology-media-telecommunications/us-tmt-2017-global-mobile-consumer-survey-executive-summary.pdf>.

up to something. Jonathan Obar and Anne Oeldorf-Hirsch created a fake social networking site called 'Name Drop', and wrote up a terms and services agreement for users to agree to before signing up. In the agreement they included the disclosure that users give up their first-born child as payment, and that anything users shared would be passed along to the United States National Security Agency. A staggering 98% of participants agreed.[26]

A number of organisations and regulators have suggested ways to improve user experience with terms and conditions. In Australia, financial rights activists and consumer data rights representatives were invited to make a submission on behalf of their constituency in relation to the proposed Open Banking regime. In their joint submission to Treasury, the Financial Rights Legal Centre and Consumer Action Legal Centre observed that there are many opportunities for improved outcomes for consumers. For example, a Consumer Data Right would provide a once in a generation opportunity to fix issues with consent and the unbundling of reams of unread terms and conditions.

To understand how consumers can get better informed about the content of terms and conditions and how their trust in them can be enhanced, the European Commission has carried out a study that provides fresh insights and recommendations on how consumer readership, comprehension and trust in terms and conditions can be improved. The study investigated two different ways to help consumers assess the substantive quality of the terms and conditions. Their findings are based on data collected through a literature review, online surveys and online behavioural experiments with consumers in 12 European Union Member States. The first study focused on increasing consumer readership and understanding of terms and conditions. The second study focused on increasing consumer trust in the sellers and the quality of the terms and conditions without necessarily expecting consumers to read the terms and conditions. The European Commission's study found that when consumers had to scroll through terms and conditions, 77.9% indicated that they read them at least in part, while terms and conditions that could only be accessed via a separate link were read by only 9.4% of consumers.[27]

The researchers in the University of Connecticut's Name Drop experiment suggested as a possible solution that it may make sense to hand off the work to specialists who could provide users with very brief bullet summaries of the relevant terms and conditions with an overall rating of their quality from the user's standpoint. This would establish a measure of trustworthiness of the site and could be a handy guide to the rights and obligations created and imposed by the terms and conditions.[28]

26 D Berreby, 'Click to Agree with What? No One Reads Terms of Service, Studies Confirm', *TheGuardian.com* (3 March 2017) <https://www.theguardian.com/technology/2017/mar/03/terms-of-service-online-contracts-fine-print>.

27 European Commission, 'Consumers' Attitudes to Terms and Conditions' (21 March 2016) <https://ec.europa.eu/info/publications/consumers-attitudes-terms-and-conditions-tcsen>.

28 D Berreby, 'Click to Agree with What? No One Reads Terms of Service, Studies Confirm', *TheGuardian.com* (3 March 2017) <https://www.theguardian.com/technology/2017/mar/03/terms-of-service-online-contracts-fine-print>.

The European Union's study also found that a promise by the seller to be fair accompanied by an expert endorsement were not effective in garnering the trust of the user. Indeed, some consumers reported a decrease in trust and purchase intentions. Conversely, a positive customer feedback cue, an endorsement by a national consumer organisation and an endorsement by a European consumer organisation generally increase consumers' trust and purchase intentions.[29]

These studies suggest that a better alternative to lengthy terms and conditions that will not be read at all is briefly summarised terms and conditions. The most read and trusted option seems to be endorsements of trustworthiness. The problem with over-brevity and endorsements is that they do not define or describe the terms upon which the user is dealing or contracting with the business behind the website. From a legal perspective, this leads to imprecision, thus increasing the probability of disputes. The more detailed the terms and conditions, the more defensible they will be in court for suppliers, but the less likely they are to be read or relied upon by consumers. Hence, the 'precision paradox'.

---

29 'Consumers' Attitudes to Terms and Conditions', *European Commission* (21 March 2016) <https://ec.europa.eu/info/publications/consumers-attitudes-terms-and-conditions-tcsen>.

9 Trust in Online Advertising

The Internet's early architecture was built on a foundation of trust,[1] but as it has matured, its uses and relationship with users has become increasingly complex. Due to concerns over Internet security, reliability and complexity, the National Science Foundation in the United States began funding research in 2008 into the building of a 'next-generation' or 'clean-slate' Internet. Improving the Internet might solve some problems like viruses, spam, phishing and worms. But it would cost billions of dollars and there is a debate among experts about how long it might take.[2] One difficulty is that the path of technological change is clouded in mystery.[3] Any attempt to predict this path would be expensive and necessarily uncertain. It is difficult to make laws future-proof without predicting the future.[4] At the time that the Pew team was formulating their solution for a broken Internet, concern was expressed that if a next-generation Internet were to be built, it might be characterised by intrinsic features that will allow governments and corporations to exercise more control over what happens online. Ten years after the Pew Research Centre launched its project to reinvent the Internet, the focus of power and control over the mega platforms and virtual global marketplaces is more concentrated than ever.

Together Facebook, Amazon, Apple, Netflix and Google dominate all marketing on the Internet of the West. In China, the likes of Baidu, Alibaba and Tencent dominate the big four marketing categories (shopping, social, streaming and searching) in the world's most populous country.[5]

1   J Hurwitz, 'Trust and Online Interaction' (2013) 161 *University of Pennsylvania Law Review* 1580.
2   J Quitney Anderson and L Rainie, 'The Future of the Internet III – Scenario 7: The Evolution of the Architecture of the Internet', *Pew Research Centre* (14 December 2008) <http://www.pewinternet.org/2008/12/14/scenario-7-the-evolution-of-the-architecture-of-the-internet/>.
3   See, CS Diver, 'The Optimal Precision of Administrative Rules' (1983) 93 *Yale Law Journal* 67.
4   L Bennett Moses, 'Recurring Dilemmas: The Law's Race to Keep Up With Technological Change' [2007] *UNSWLRS* 21.
5   A Fry, 'BAT vs FAANG: The Battle for Digital Dominance', *IBC.org* (21 August 2018) <https://www.ibc.org/content-management/bat-vs-faang-the-battle-for-digital-dominance/3103.article>

Across the globe, these tech giants have accumulated power in ways that existing regulatory and intellectual frameworks struggle to comprehend. A consensus is emerging that the power of these new digital monopolies is unprecedented, and that it has important implications for journalism, politics and society. It is increasingly clear that democratic societies require new legal and conceptual tools if they are to adequately understand, and if necessary check, the economic might of these companies. Equally, it is apparent that we need a better comprehension of the ability of such organisations to control personal data and to shape the flow of news, information and public opinion.[6] Their combined access to global markets is unprecedented.

The failure of trust is in part a product of the secrecy with which the tech giants manage their automated 'back-office operations'; that is, their algorithms. For example, Google has always refused to disclose how its search engine prioritises advertising content on the web.[7] In December 2018, Google CEO Sundar Pichai testified before the United States Congress in a wide-ranging hearing about data breaches, misinformation campaigns, potential political bias on the company's platforms and concerns about working with China. The hearing ended a tough year for big tech companies, as lawmakers and the public have become increasingly sceptical about the role big tech companies play in manipulating democracy, misinformation and privacy.[8] Among other concerns, lawmakers are expected to ask about the controversial algorithms powering Google's search engine. Google declares on its website that 'Google's mission is to organise the world's information and make it universally accessible and useful'. Google generates billions of dollars from advertising globally. This is achieved in part via its very successful Google Ads (previously known as *AdWords*). Google Ads is an online advertising platform developed by Google, where advertisers pay to display brief advertisements, service offerings, product listings, video content and generate mobile application installs within the Google advertising network to web users. This form of advertising represents more than 86% of Google's revenue.[9] As revealed in Google's Quarterly Earnings Summary for the quarter ending 30 September 2018, those earnings exceeded US$33.7 billion.[10]

In addition to Google's search engine and advertising model, online social networks are now a major part of everyday life and the method by which many

6   D Tambini and M Moore, eds, *Digital Dominance: The Power of Google, Amazon, Facebook, and Apple* (Oxford University Press, 2018).
7   E Rosenberg, 'How Google Makes Money', *Investopedia* (5 December 2018) <http s://www.investopedia.com/articles/investing/020515/business-google.asp>.
8   J D'Onfro, 'Google's Sundar Pichai Was Grilled on Privacy, Data Collection, and China During Congressional Hearing', *CNBC Tech* (11 December 2018) <http s://www.cnbc.com/2018/12/11/google-ceo-sundar-pichai-testifies-before-con gress-on-bias-privacy.html>.
9   E Rosenberg, 'How Google Makes Money', *Investopedia* (5 December 2018) <http s://www.investopedia.com/articles/investing/020515/business-google.asp>.
10   Alphabet Investor Relations, 'Alphabet Announces Third Quarter 2018 Results' (2018) <https://abc.xyz/investor/static/pdf/2018Q3alphabetearningsrelease.pdf>.

of us stay connected with friends, consume news and conduct business. They are a prominent method by which people foster social connections and are mostly funded by online advertising. The significance and depth of these connections between consumers of the Internet, as well as their relationship with fostering trust, have been extensively studied. Social networks and online advertising have positive and negative aspects, with corresponding effects on social trust.[11]

Social networking on the Internet takes place in a context of trust, but trust is complex and can be fragile.[12] Studies suggest that the lay (non-expert) public relies on social trust when making judgements of risks and benefits, particularly when their own personal knowledge about a subject is lacking.[13] In this way, Internet users place trust in other Internet users who are perceived or believed to have expertise or personal experience.[14] This can often cause distress or harm as a result, with a corresponding drop in social trust.

Gone are the days when there was a clear delineation between entertainment, information and advertising. For example, in the early days of radio and television, the breaks for advertisements were preceded by an announcement indicating that what followed was an advertisement from a sponsor. In newspapers and other print journalism, advertisements had their own look and feel and were accompanied by text indicating price and availability of the product. These devices ensured that the audience knew they were being marketed to. However, these days, online advertising is delivered in countless ways and the marketers have sufficient data to know to whom they should target their products and how. Sometimes online advertising is designed to mimic news content, or manipulates our voting intentions, or is simply misleading and deceptive conduct. The challenge for regulators is that even if these breaches of advertising standards are detected, it is not always possible to identify those responsible. In this chapter, different methods of establishing trust in online advertising are explored, followed by a discussion of challenges for regulators.

Customer Reviews and Reputation Ratings

Customer reviews are online comments provided by users of different services to provide feedback about the quality of their experience. This is popular with

11 J Hurwitz, 'Trust and Online Interaction' (2013) 161 *University of Pennsylvania Law Review* 1580. See also, P McBride, 'Digital Technologies and the Erosion of Social Trust', in *Essays* (8 November 2017) <https://paulmcbride.me/2017/11/08/essay-digital-technology-and-the-erosion-of-social-trust/>.

12 S Grabner-Krauter and S Bitter, 'Trust in Online Social Networks: A Multifaceted Perspective' (2013) 44 *Forum for Social Economics* 48.

13 M Siegrist and G Cvetkovich, 'Perceptions of Hazards: The Role of Social Trust and Knowledge' (2000) 20(5) *Risk Analysis* 713, 713.

14 LS Lai and E Turban, 'Groups Formation and Operations in the Web 2.0 Environment and Social Networks' in *Group Decision and Negotiation* (Springer, 2008), 387–402.

sites that were established for the purpose of hosting customer reviews about travel and restaurant experiences (like TripAdvisor and UrbanSpoon) as well as customer reviews that form part of the business model (like eBay and Uber). Customer ratings are often represented on a scale of 1 to 5 starts (where 5 is the best rating). These can be gathered manually from customers who took the time to provide the feedback or it can be generated automatically on the basis of number of transactions without complaint. These systems are very popular because people tend to rely on the reviews of other consumers, rather than believing the word of the service provider or even an expert third party.[15]

The desirability of using customer reviews and reputation ratings is equally balanced on both sides of the transaction. On the supply side, users receive better prices for their goods and services when they have higher reputation scores. On the demand side, participants rely on reviews to make informed selection decisions.[16] In the case of some businesses, the entire advertising model depends on all participants reviewing each other. A successful example is Airbnb, which has 60 million users.[17] Indeed, one study revealed that before making a purchase, 77% of online consumers consider ratings and reviews.

However, reputation systems suffer from a fundamental intrinsic flaw: reputational information is sourced from many different data points, but information about quality, safety and other regulatory compliance are not in the possession of participant reviewers and so not included in the rating.[18] With millions of users of different apps relying on the lay opinions of users based solely on their particular experience, there is asymmetric or unjustified level of trust in those reviews and in the business which receives the most positive feedback and favourable ratings.

One example of the trials and tribulations of ratings platforms is TripAdvisor. Created in 2000, TripAdvisor built its brand on the trademark 'World's most trusted travel site'.[19] But after countless lawsuits in multiple countries, by

---

15 'Consumers' Attitudes to Terms and Conditions', *European Commission* (21 March 2016) <https://ec.europa.eu/info/publications/consumers-attitudes-terms-and-conditions-tcsen>.

16 A Stemler, 'Feedback Loop Failure: Implications for the Self-Regulation of the Sharing Economy' (2017) 18(2) *Minnesota Journal of Law, Science and Technology* 673.

17 'Study Finds Consumers Rely on Ratings, Reviews and Recommendations During Recession,' *Targetmarking* (26 February 2009) <http://www.targetmarketingmag.com/article/study-finds-consumers-relyratings-reviews-and-recommendations-during-recession/>.

18 See generally, P Resnick et al., 'Reputation Systems: Facilitating Trust in Internet Interactions', *Communications of the Association of Computing Machinery* (2000), 45, 45. See also, A Stemler, 'Feedback Loop Failure: Implications for the Self-Regulation of the Sharing Economy' (2017) 18(2) *Minnesota Journal of Law, Science and Technology* 673.

19 From October 2002: 'TripAdvisor is the world's most popular, largest, and most trusted travel community. We provide a comprehensive travel planning experience. Not only do we have 30+ million real traveler reviews, we power a robust flights search engine, hotel compare and check rates search, vacation rental search, in addition to restaurant ratings and reviews, worldwide' <http://www.travelclix.info/tags/ski.htm>.

2013 TripAdvisor quietly removed the words 'trusted' and then 'honest' from all of its website marketing. It now describes itself more objectively as 'the world's largest travel site'.

The suits were against reviewers, with hoteliers and restaurateurs threatening to sue in response to critical reviews. After a stay in an Ohio hotel in 2010, a disgruntled guest wrote a review on TripAdvisor to complain about the housekeeping. Less than 24 hours later, the critique was taken down by its author — after the hotel said it would sue. In another instance, a hotel in Quebec sued a traveller who took to the website to complain about an alleged infestation of bedbugs.[20] The type of lawsuit that would be filed against a reviewer is likely to seek damages for defamation (also known as libel or slander in some jurisdictions). The object of the law of defamation is to protect reputation. The person whose reputation is lowered by a defamatory imputation has a cause of action in respect of that imputation.[21] Usually, a corporation does not have a cause of action in defamation.[22] This means that only the particular housekeeping staff identified and impugned by the review can pursue such a claim, as opposed to the hotel or restaurant.

In defence of a defamation suit, a reviewer might argue that the offending part of the review was factually correct or a comment based on matters on fact.[23] This defence is often seen to protect the right to free speech.[24]

Since early 2006, largely uniform defamation legislation has operated in Australia, collectively referred to as the 'uniform Defamation Acts'.[25] Under the uniform Defamation Acts, there is a statutory defence of honest opinion.[26] It is also common defence to the publication of defamatory matter if the defendant proves that the matter carried, in addition to the defamatory imputations of which the plaintiff complains are substantially true, and the defamatory imputations do not further harm the reputation of the plaintiff because of

20 K Conti, 'TripAdvisor Wants Tougher Law Protecting Online Reviewers from Suit', *BostonGlobe.com* (28 September 2017) <https://www.bostonglobe.com/business/2017/09/28/tripadvisor-wants-tougher-state-law-protecting-online-r eviewers-from-lawsuits/ojcWjYVjprYiR5OPwXafRM/story.html>.

21 New South Wales Law Reform Commission – *Defamation* (1995) NSWLRC 75.

22 There are exemptions for small corporations. For example, under section 9 of the *Defamation 2005* (NSW), a corporation that has 10 or fewer employees is exempt and can sue for defamation.

23 See, RE Brown, *The Law of Defamation in Canada* (Carswell, 2nd ed, 1994), 964. See also, for example, *Meckiff v Simpson* [1968] VR 62, 66 (Winneke CJ, Adam and Gowans JJ); *Sims v Wran* [1984] 1 *New South Wales Law Report* 317, 323.

24 AT Kenyon, 'Six Years of Australian Uniform Defamation Law' (2012) 35(1) *University of New South Wales Law Journal* 31, 49–50

25 See, *Defamation Act 2005* (NSW); *Defamation Act 2005* (Qld); *Defamation Act 2005* (SA); *Defamation Act 2005* (Tas); *Defamation Act 2005* (Vic); *Defamation Act 2005* (WA); *Civil Law (Wrongs) Amendment Act 2006* (ACT) (amending the *Civil Law (Wrongs) Act 2002* (ACT)); *Defamation Act 2006* (NT). The state Acts commenced on 1 January 2006; the territory Acts early in 2006 (ACT: 23 February; NT: 26 April).

26 See, for example, *Defamation Act 2005* (NSW), section 30.

the substantial truth of the contextual imputations. For example, in September 2003, the *Sydney Morning Herald* published a review by Matthew Evans of a Sydney restaurant called 'Coco Roco', which had been established by the plaintiffs only shortly before. In his review, Mr Evans wrote of his meal:

> Why anyone would put apricots in a sherry-scented white sauce with a prime rib steak is beyond me. ... A generous chock of meat comes perfectly rested, medium as ordered. But the halves of apricot are rubbery and tasteless (which is probably a good thing). I scrape the whole wretched garnish to one side ... In a city where harbourside dining has improved out of sight in recent years, Coco Roco is a bleak spot on the culinary landscape.[27]

Coco Roco subsequently closed – within six months of the review – and the owners sued the publisher, John Fairfax Publications, as well as the author of the review, for defamation.

A jury subsequently found that the publication conveyed three imputations that were defamatory of the three plaintiffs. They were first, that the plaintiffs sold unpalatable food at the restaurant. Secondly, that they provided bad service. Thirdly, that they were incompetent as restaurant owners because they employed a chef at the restaurant who made poor quality food. The defendants contended that the second and third imputations were true and that the plaintiffs suffered no loss as a result of the first imputation because it was contextually true. The defendants relied upon the defence of comment in respect of all three imputations. The newspaper and Evans were unable to prove the statements were true or fair comment. The trial judge found for the plaintiffs, and awarded damages.[28] But to make matters worse, the defendants failed to apologise and Fairfax did not remove the review from its website. Six years later, the first instance decision was set aside and an even higher award was made by the Court of Appeal.[29] That one review cost the defendants over $600,000.[30]

The problem with the threat of or actual claim against a reviewer is that it means many reviewers will back down from being candid for fear of being sued. This erodes the integrity and trustworthiness of the platform as a repository for honest reviews.

---

27 M Evans, 'Coco Roco', *Sydney Morning Herald* (30 September 2003) <https://www.smh.com.au/national/coco-roco-20020615-gdfdbo.html>.

28 *Gacic v John Fairfax Publications Pty Ltd* [2009] NSWSC 1403 (18 December 2009).

29 *Gacic v John Fairfax Publications Pty Ltd* [2015] NSWCA 99 (16 April 2015).

30 A Meade, '$600,000 Restaurant Review: Fairfax Loses 11-year Defamation Battle', *The Guardian, Australia Edition* (10 June 2014) <https://www.theguardian.com/law/2014/jun/10/600000-restaurant-review-fairfax-loses-11-year-defamation-battle>.

More insidious than the reticent reviewer is the 'fake news' reviewer. An entire industry of 'reputation management' businesses can be hired to create highly believable fake reviews, or to 'fix' bad reviews, or sabotage their competitors. To prove how easy this is, an Italian magazine managed to elevate a fake restaurant to number one on in the restaurant ratings. Italian magazine *Italia a Tavola* decided to 'reveal alleged flaws in the asking system, which they say leave TripAdvisor vulnerable to fraudulent reviews'. To do this, the magazine created an imaginary restaurant on the site called Ristorante Scaletta and added 10 fake, perfectly scored reviews to the listing. Within a month, the non-existent restaurant was rated the best restaurant in Moniga del Gara.[31]

Writing fake reviews to bolster reputation is not new. In 1855, American poet, essayist and journalist Walt Whitman anonymously published a 3,000 word review of his own work in *The United States Review*.[32] It opens with the declaration, 'An American bard at last!' Whitman goes on to extravagantly applaud his dress sense ('manly and free'), his posture ('strong and erect'), his voice ('bringing hope and prophecy to the generous races of young and old'), and his compassion ('the largest lover and sympathizer that has appeared in literature').[33]

Outside the publishing industry, the practice known as 'review brushing' exists on a vast and industrial scale. It is popular because consumers typically see positive customer reviews as a more reliable indicator of quality than advertising.

For online retailers, the war on the fake-review industry is now a major part of the business. Today, when a review is submitted to TripAdvisor, it goes through a tracking system that examines hundreds of different attributes, from basic data points, such as the unique user IP address of the reviewer or even the screen resolution of the device that was used to submit the review. TripAdvisor defends this levels of scrutiny on the basis that quickly identifying unusual patterns of review behaviour helps to generate a data map of where reviews are coming from. If there is a flood of reviews in relation to one establishment from a single source, then they can identify and block content from 'review farms'.[34] Whether the fake review is in relation to a product or service, TripAdvisor's success underscores the illegality of such behaviour.[35]

31 K Shah, 'Magazine Creates Fake Restaurant to Show How Easy It Is to Post False Reviews on TripAdvisor', *Eater.com* (2 Jul 2015) <https://www.eater.com/2015/7/2/8884687/magazine-fake-restaurant-tripadvisor-scam>

32 E Folsom and K Price, *The United States Review* 5 (September 1855).

33 E Folsom and K Price, *The United States Review* 5 (September 1855), 205–212.

34 In 2015, TripAdvisor took legal action against sixty offshore review farms. See, S Parkin, 'The Never-ending War on Fake Reviews', *The New Yorker* (31 May 2018) <https://www.newyorker.com/tech/annals-of-technology/the-never-ending-war-on-fake-reviews>.

35 S Osborne, 'Amazon Suing More Than 1,000 for Fake Product Reviews', *The Independent UK* (18 October 2015) <https://www.independent.co.uk/news/world/americas/amazon-suing-more-than-1000-for-fake-product-reviews-a6698556.html>.

Social Media Marketing, Bloggers and Influencers

Disgraced wellness blogger Belle Gibson built an online community and sold a recipe book off the back of claims she cured terminal brain cancer through diet and lifestyle alone. Gibson's wellness empire included a mobile phone app called *The Whole Pantry* and a website and recipe book of the same name. However, Gibson's story was eventually revealed to be a sham. The young Instagram star had raised substantial funds for charity with the help of her hundreds of thousands of followers. However, by early 2015, it became apparent that she had failed to donate thousands of dollars that she had promised to charity: money raised through the success of her ruse. Then in March 2015, she admitted that she did not have cancer at all.[36]

The phenomenon that emerged in Gibson's story is complex and a product of a combination of individual and institutional faults, and of social trends both centuries old and very, very new. Gibson's cancer scamming is a variation on a type of confidence trickster often characterised as 'snake-oil salespeople'. There have always been people like Gibson. But her explosion to success, and her incredible reach was made possible by a number of intensely modern forces, including the emergence of social media and online 'influencers'; and the seismic shift in the media industry that has radically changed how the public consumes news. Gibson had 200,000 followers without ever having gone through the checks and balances that are provided by traditional media.[37]

At the time of the very public collapse of Gibson's fake empire, the term 'fake news' was not yet the concept it became in the wake of the 2016 United States election, but Gibson's story does seem to reflect some essential quirk in online media that facilitates, if not encourages, the spread of misinformation and untruth.

The story of Gibson's elaborate scam and her success in raising significant funds from her unsuspecting followers is not unique. In November 2017, a *GoFundMe* page was established after Johnny Bobbitt, a homeless veteran with a history of drug addiction, apparently gave Katelyn McClure his last $20 to get home safely after her car ran out of petrol.[38] Within weeks of the launch of the fundraiser, the story was a pre-Christmas good news sensation: a homeless man whose act of kindness had gone viral was to receive $500,000 raised for him online by more than 15,000 strangers.[39]

36 M Davey, "'None of It's True': Wellness Blogger Belle Gibson Admits She Never Had Cancer', *The Guardian* (22 April 2015) <https://www.theguardian.com/a ustralia-news/2015/apr/22/none-of-its-true-wellness-blogger-belle-gibson-adm its-she-never-had-cancer>.

37 JR Douglas, 'Behind Belle Gibson's Cancer Con: "Everything About This Story Is Extreme"', *The Guardian (Australia edition)* (13 November 2017) <https:// www.theguardian.com/books/2017/nov/13/behind-belle-gibsons-cancer-con-e verything-about-this-story-is-extreme>.

38 'Fundraiser by Kate McClure: Paying It Forward', *GoFundMe.com* (10 November 2017) <https://ca.gofundme.com/hvv4r-paying-it-forward>.

39 'Johnny Bobbitt: Homeless Man Who Helped Stranded Woman Buys Home after Nearly $400K Raised', *McKoy's News* (7 December 2017) <https://mckoysnews. com/johnny-bobbitt-homeless-man/>.

However, in April 2018, a journalist decided to contact Bobbitt and see how he was coping. Bobbitt – whose addiction to heroin and opioids led to his homelessness in the first place – had used some of the campaign money to buy drugs. This saw him return to a rehabilitation centre and another attempt at sobriety. By November 2018, the entire lie was exposed. Almost no part of the tale was true. McClure did not run out of petrol. Bobbitt did not spot her in trouble and give her money. Instead, the pair met near a Philadelphia casino in October 2017, shortly before they concocted and then shared their story.

These scams are just two examples of online confidence trickery. They are shocking and brazen, because from the outset the perpetrators made their real identities known to their online audience. This meant that they would have to maintain their lie despite the knowledge of their friends and family. In both cases, this is where they failed and their lie was exposed. A more insidious type of Facebook user is the nefarious identity operating and hiding behind a fake account. In the first half of 2018, Facebook disabled almost 1.3 billion fake accounts.[40] Fake accounts are a problem for Facebook because they artificially inflate the user statistics, which in turn impacts the data Facebook provides advertisers. All of this uncertainty further increases scepticism over Facebook's ultimate value as a third party data source.[41] Facebook has undertaken to start publishing data about its fake accounts. The organisation argues that publishing this data is a way for the company to hold itself accountable and to improve user trust in the platform.[42]

Not all objectionable online marketing is based on a scam. Some forms of digit advertising are subtle; for example, 'native advertising'. Native advertising is the latest incarnation of the long-running practice of blurring the lines between paid advertisement and independently created publisher content.[43] Native advertising is the use of paid ads that match the look, feel and function of the media format in which they appear. Native advertisements are often found in social media feeds, or as recommended content on a web page. Unlike display advertisements or banner advertisements, native ads do not look like advertisements. They look more like news or

40 K Wagner and R Molla, 'Facebook Has Disabled Almost 1.3 Billion Fake Accounts Over the Past Six Months', *Recode* (15 May 2018) <https://www.recode.net/2018/5/15/17349790/facebook-mark-zuckerberg-fake-accounts-content-policy-update>.

41 A Wolk, 'Facebook's Got Billions Of Fake Users, Though That May Be The Least Of Their Problems', *Forbes.com* (29 June 2018) <https://www.forbes.com/sites/alanwolk/2018/06/29/facebooks-got-billions-of-fake-users-though-that-may-be-the-least-of-their-problems/#37ca022f5853>.

42 K Wagner and R Molla, 'Facebook Has Disabled Almost 1.3 Billion Fake Accounts Over the Past Six Months', *Recode* (15 May 2018) <https://www.recode.net/2018/5/15/17349790/facebook-mark-zuckerberg-fake-accounts-content-policy-update>.

43 AC Bakshi, 'Why and How to Regulative Native Advertising in Online News Publications' (2015) 4 *University of Baltimore Journal of Media Law and Ethics* 4, 4.

other forms of traditionally reliable and reputable journalism.[44] The problem with 'native advertising' is that – like Gibson and McClure's scams – it is designed to deceive the reader into thinking that the content is something it is not. However, unlike Gibson and McClure, the perpetrators of 'native advertising' scams are not readily identifiable to consumers or regulators. And the sheer volume of content on the Internet makes it very difficult to detect all instances that breach advertising standards or regulations.

With the use of technology to exploit and deceive consumers and the regulators too overwhelmed to identify and prosecute all perpetrators, it is useful to imagine ways that technology might help combat this problem. For example, attempts have been made to design natural language processing software that can analyse text and detect 'fake news'. However, published results indicate that this has so far not been successful. The very nature of fraud, deception and fake information makes it difficult to distinguish it from truth. This is because fake news is intended to seem real. However, given the massive amount of Web content, automatic fake news detection is a practical problem that needs to be addressed by all users of the Internet.[45]

While customer reviews and reputation ratings are designed to defeat the 'puff' generated by advertising agencies to promote products and services, trust in the reviewing and rating systems themselves is on the wane. Indeed, there is a dearth of trust in most online content and it seems more difficult than ever to differentiate truth from lies, whether the content is in relation to product promotion by businesses or self-promotion by bloggers. A possible solution that has been explored for more than a decade is the use of 'trustmarks'.

Use and Abuse of Trustmarks

In e-commerce, a trustmark is an electronic commerce badge, image or logo displayed on a website to indicate that the website business has been shown to be trustworthy by the issuing organisation. A trustmark is intended to give confidence to customers and to indicate to them that it is safe to do business with the website displaying it. With consumers' growing concerns about fake ratings and reviews, fraud and identity theft when dealing with business online, e-commerce trustmarks aim to reduce consumer privacy and address security fears. If this is achieved, the business operating the website will be trusted by its customers. Hence the name 'trustmark'.

---

44 E Goodman, et al, 'Native Advertising – AELJ Spring Symposium: New Impressions on Advertising Law: Panel 2' (2016) 34(3) *Cardozo Arts & Entertainment Law Journal* 580.

45 A recent study found that detection of fake news using natural language processing is difficult. The problems mainly arise from the limits of these data sets and problem formulations. See, R Oshikawa, J Qian and WY Wang, 'A Survey on Natural Language Processing for Fake News Detection', *Cornell University* (2 November 2018) <https://arxiv.org/abs/1811.00770>.

The trustmark shows that the website being visited offers consumer protection of data and privacy of interaction so that their purchases may be made safely and their personal information only ever shared with authorised recipients. Some trustmarks simply confirm that a business has been accredited by another organisation. Accreditations from well-known organisations are usually of more value from a customer confidence viewpoint.

For these reasons, trustmarks are particularly useful and popular where the website provides access to a service that can only be provided with accreditation or licensing. This protects the expertise or professional qualifications of service-providers from being undermined by cheaper unqualified alternatives.[46] An unaccredited trustmark system is not enough for a businessperson whose lifeline depends on the integrity and operations of their business partners. To address the concern of whether there is a real business operating behind a website, or whether it is just a front for a sham, Alibaba suggests that customers call the telephone number advertised on the website to confirm that the office exists and is staffed by a responsible adult. If a trustmark requires that users conduct this level of due diligence into the quality and credibility of the mark itself, then it would lose its value as a mark of trust.

The European Union has actively encouraged the use of trustmarks (including with accreditation) since the 1999 eEurope initiative.[47] A number of trustmarks and international codes have emerged from this programme. For example, online dispute resolution (ODR) is regulated by standards and must complement the court system into which it operates. It is therefore useful for ODR service providers to display the European trustmark on their websites, assuring parties to civil disputes of their compliance with procedural standards. In addition, the participation in accredited ODR may be mandatory and their decisions may be enforced by the courts.[48] However, these and other trustmarks have proved to be an imperfect solution. The disparity in national laws regarding the treatment of certification marks will also affect the treatment of trustmarks.[49] The numerous trustmarks were generated but a lack of information or marketing campaigns have led to some confusion among consumers. Trustmarks need to be addressed at a national or regional level by public authorities in order to avoid the existing confusion among Internet users. At

46 L Webb, 'International BBB Ratings a la EBay: A Proposal for an Improved Online Better Business Bureau to Facilitated International Business Transactions' (2004) 35(1) *California Western International Law Journal* 127, 141.

47 In order to create an 'information society for all', in 1999 the European Commission launched the eEurope initiative, an ambitious programme aimed at making information technologies as widespread as possible. See, EurLex – access to European Law <https://eur-lex.europa.eu/legal-content/EN/TXT/?uri=LEGISSUM%3Al24221>.

48 P Cortest, 'Accredited Online Dispute Resolution Services: Creating European Legal Standards for Ensuring Fair and Effective Processes' (2008) 17(3) *Information & Communications Technology Law* 221, 222.

49 A Endeshaw, 'Legal Significance of Trustmarks' (2001) 10(2) *Information & Communications Technology Law* 203.

present, there are too many trustmarks and too little knowledge of their existence and credibility.[50]

Registrants of trustmarks openly disclaim any liability for the acts or omissions of the members or subscribers (licensees) of such trustmarks. The more detailed the disclaimers, the less trust the user will have in the mark. Because trustmarks are not subject to an independent quality assessment or audit, the *carte blanche* for anyone to be able register a trustmark of their choice will eventually erode the value of all trustmarks.[51]

Despite all the efforts of regulators and the ingenuity of trustmarks, there remains the age-old vice of counterfeit. Since 2013, the European Commission and Japan's equivalent certification authority have warned consumers about fake trustmarks and the use of trustmarks without permission.[52] For marks to be truly trustworthy, they need to have the same qualities as watermarks on minted notes, artwork on postage stamps, micro-tagging used in supply chains and sophisticated 'fingerprinting' technology of the sort used to identify diamonds. Benjamin Franklin once said 'to counterfeit is death', in recognition of the importance to a nation of the reliability of its currency.[53] Franklin would almost certainly have appreciated the value of trustmarks to digital economies.

Regulating Misleading, Deceptive and Illegal Conduct in Virtual Marketplaces

Misleading and deceptive conduct describes certain types of misrepresentations in trade and commerce. It may seem that there is nothing particularly unique about misleading and deceptive conduct in digital markets, that sets it apart from non-digital economies. However, there are two particularly prevalent features of online or virtual marketplaces that make it particularly difficult to detect and regulate misleading and deceptive conduct. The first is the pricing complexity that e-business enables. The second feature is complicated refund and replacement conditions that can be hidden behind the curtain of a website. With respect to both of these, regulators are particularly mindful to ensure that websites do not bind their customers to terms and conditions that offend or dilute their statutory rights.

It is not unusual to be offered up to four different prices for hotel rooms, air fares and holidays to reflect payment options and level of luxury. For example, many hotels charge less if the customer is prepared to make an immediate non-refundable payment. Some third party meta-search platforms (like Trivago,

---

50 T Schultz, 'An Essay on the Role of Government for ODR: Theoretical Considerations about the Future of ODR', 7(8) *ADR Online Monthly UMASS* (2003) <http://www.ombuds.org/center/adr2003_8.html>.

51 A Endeshaw, 'Legal Significance of Trustmarks' (2001) 10(2) *Information & Communications Technology Law* 203.

52 'Please Be Careful of Online Shops With Fake Trustmarks', *TradeSafe Trustmark* (13 September 2013) <https://www.tradesafe.co.jp/english/fakemark/>.

53 K Scott, *Counterfeiting in Colonial America* (University of Pennsylvania Press, 2000).

Booking.com, LastMinute and Wotif) can source cheaper last-minute prices for hotel rooms. Airfares also offer different types of deals for the same economy seat depending on the purchaser's willingness to commit to the flight, without the level of flexibility to cancel or change flights that may be on offer at a higher price. These hotels and airlines are putting a price on the value of cancellation risk. The less the customer pays for their room in a hotel or seat on a plane, the more they will pay if they need to change their arrangements. Many hotels only give free upgrades to guests who booked directly through the hotel's website. These hotels are rewarding these customers for paying the higher rate offered directly via the hotel's own booking engine. Most organisations that offer different prices for otherwise identical services and experiences usually comply with the regulations of their jurisdiction in relation to consumer rights. But recent revelations by Australia's consumer watchdog in relation to the published policies of four major airlines have shone a bright light on how easy it is for consumers to be misled by relatively trusted brands. The Australian Competition and Consumer Commission (ACCC) – Australia's competition watchdog – found that Qantas, Jetstar, Tigerair and Virgin Australia had to varying degrees misrepresented their refund policies in a way that violated their customers' statutory rights.[54] In this case, the ACCC investigated the airlines based on concerns over published refund policies that included statements that certain flights are non-refundable, or that consumers would need to pay a fee to process a refund. Such policies contravene Australian Consumer Law (ACL) provisions about the handling of refunds. The head of the ACCC warned: 'Airlines cannot make blanket statements that flights are non-refundable or charge consumers a fee to get a refund when they are entitled to one free of charge under the ACL.'[55]

Importantly, businesses must have the right to sell the product or service and must not mislead consumers or hide costs and other details. Whether it is for a movie, a rock concert, a cruise or a flight, the ticket must match the description provided on the website.

This case was not the first time the ACCC has tussled with the airlines over the wording of their booking engines. In March 2017, the Federal Court of Australia penalised Jetstar $545,000 for misrepresenting its prices through its mobile site. In 2015, the ACCC action against Jetstar and Virgin Australia led the Federal Court to rule that the airlines had contravened the Australian Consumer Law over the way their mobile websites were structured to conceal credit-card booking fees.

54   D Braue, 'Airlines Slammed Over Dodgy Online Refund Claims – Published Policies Contravened Australian Consumer Law', *Australian Computer Society* (14 January 2019) <https://ia.acs.org.au/article/2019/airlines-slammed-over-dodgy-online-refund-claims.html>.

55   D Chau, 'Jetstar named "Worst Offender" as Qantas, Virgin and Tigerair Also Investigated For Misleading Refund Policies', *ABCNews.net.au* (17 December 2018) <https://www.abc.net.au/news/2018-12-17/qantas-virgin-tigerair-jetstar-refund-probe-by-accc/10627160>.

The Unites States Federal Trade Commission (FTC) is responsible for truth in advertising and for protecting America's consumers. It seeks to ensure that when consumers see or hear an advertisement on the Internet, radio or television (or anywhere else), that the content and representations in the advertisement are truthful. Truthful advertising must not be misleading, and, when appropriate, it should be backed by scientific evidence.[56]

The FTC enforces these truth-in-advertising laws, and it applies the same standards no matter where an advertisement appears. This principle also applies to social media, so long as the statement is being made in the course of trade or commerce (in other words, as an inducement to pay for something). The FTC looks especially closely at advertising claims that can affect consumers' health or their pocketbooks – claims about food, over-the-counter drugs, dietary supplements, alcohol and tobacco – as well as conduct related to high-tech products and the Internet.[57]

The aim of the European regulators, the ACCC and the FCT (as well as their counterparts in other jurisdictions) is to bring perpetrators before courts for immediate and permanent orders to stop scams; to prevent fraudsters from perpetrating future scams; to freeze the assets of fraudsters; and to get compensation for victims. Of course, these measures depend upon identifying and locating the would-be respondents to these proceedings. If perpetrators are out of the relevant jurisdiction, enforcement may be difficult. In many foreign countries, the recognition and enforcement of foreign judgments are governed by local domestic law and the principles of comity, reciprocity and res judicata (that is, that the issues in question have been decided already).

The general principle of international law applicable in such cases is that a foreign state exercises the right to examine foreign judgments for four causes: (1) to determine if the court that issued the judgment had jurisdiction; (2) to determine whether the defendant was properly notified of the action; (3) to determine if the proceedings were vitiated by fraud; and (4) to establish that the judgment is not contrary to the public policy of the foreign country. While procedures and documentary requirements vary widely from country to country, judgments that do not involve multiple damages or punitive damages generally may be enforced, in whole or in part, upon recognition as authoritative and final, subject to the particulars cited above, unless internal law mandates a treaty obligation.[58]

---

56 *Truth in Advertising*, Federal Trade Commission (2019) <https://www.ftc.gov/news-events/media-resources/truth-advertising>.

57 *Truth in Advertising*, Federal Trade Commission (2019) <https://www.ftc.gov/news-events/media-resources/truth-advertising>.

58 Examples of relevant United States authority in relation to the personal jurisdiction of the courts against non-residents include, *Kulko v Superior Court*, 436 US 84 (1978); *Pennoyer v Neff*, 95 US 714 (1878); *International Shoe Co v Washington*, 326 US 310 (1945); *Hanson v Denckla*, 357 US 235 (1958); *Shaffer v Heitner*, 433 US 186 (1977); and *World-Wide Volks-Wagen Corp v Woodson*, 444 US 286 (1980). Of course, different countries have different interpretations of how to enforce judgments abroad.

In cases where a responsible person or an accused is out of the jurisdiction, it is possible to stop the offending conduct by disabling the platform. In such cases, Internet service providers and operators may be joined to the proceedings to give effect to the court's orders. In 2013, the United States Department of State shut down *Silk Road*, a website that traded in guns, fake identity documents, credit card numbers and drugs. An informant directed investigators to the site, accessible only through the Tor anonymising network, and explained how transactions for the sale of heroin, cocaine and LSD were managed using the digital currency bitcoin.

While investigators in New York focused on gathering evidence around the drug sales, law enforcement in Maryland began mapping the operation. They focused on identifying and nabbing two groups connected to Silk Road: the top 1% of sellers, as well as the moderators and system administrators, whose computers and credentials, once seized, could open the door to the site's private communications and account details. Once identified, law enforcement connected with sellers and, under the same cover of anonymity as its other users, they posed as drug dealers and gathered the crucial evidence they needed to identify the bank accounts of the platform's users. Once the Federal officers had these details, they were able to disable the servers upon which the network was operating.[59]

Federal agents say the use of Tor and bitcoin were major obstacles for them and that investigating the site was 'uncharted territory' that involved a reversal of their usual investigative methods.[60] Within the Tor network are computer servers that are not accessible directly through the Internet – servers such as Silk Road.[61] Indeed, the investigation was run counter-intuitively and in the reverse-order of usual policing. Instead of starting with probable cause against a specific suspect who is already identified and then obtaining a search warrant to collect more evidence, the investigation of Silk Road involved collecting evidence from the site first and then trying to identify individuals. Ironically, one of the key masterminds arrested during the operation complained in his defence that the way that the FBI had conducted their investigations breached his Fourth Amendment right to privacy. The FBI refuted the allegation by demonstrating how the key information leaked from the accused's server due to a configuration error, and not because they had infringed his rights.[62]

59 R Fordyce, 'End of the Silk Road: How Did Dread Pirate Roberts Get Busted?', *The Conversation* (4 October 2013) <https://theconversation.com/end-of-the-silk-road-how-did-dread-pirate-roberts-get-busted-18886>.
60 A Greenberg, 'The FBI Finally Says How It Legally Pinpointed Silk Road's Server', *Wired* (9 May 2014) <https://www.wired.com/2014/09/the-fbi-finally-says-how-it-legally-pinpointed-silk-roads-server/>.
61 R Fordyce, 'End of the Silk Road: How Did Dread Pirate Roberts Get Busted?', *The Conversation* (4 October 2013) <https://theconversation.com/end-of-the-silk-road-how-did-dread-pirate-roberts-get-busted-18886>.
62 A Greenberg, 'The FBI Finally Says How It Legally Pinpointed Silk Road's Server', *Wired* (9 May 2014) <https://www.wired.com/2014/09/the-fbi-finally-says-how-it-legally-pinpointed-silk-roads-server/>.

In *Google Inc v Equustek Solutions Inc*, the Supreme Court of Canada upheld an order which enjoined Google to de-index the websites of the defendants to an intellectual property dispute. Google offers a global service and, as this was a global injunction, this in turn impacted web searches conducted anywhere in the world. As Abella J explained for the majority:

> The problem in this case is occurring online and globally. The Internet has no borders — its natural habitat is global. The only way to ensure that the interlocutory injunction attained its objective was to have it apply where Google operates – globally.[63]

In 2018, Facebook was sued by a television personality for repeatedly allowing fake advertising that featured his name and image. One of the complaints brought against Facebook was its failure to check the veracity of its paid advertising content. For this purpose, many courts have either statutory or inherent powers to prevent abuse of their own processes.[64]

'Post truth' was the Oxford English Dictionary *Word of the Year* for 2016. Truth-telling is not part of Facebook's business model. Instead, hyperbolic, outrageous and attention-grabbing posts are its meal ticket. This conflict of interest with the demands of regulators for truth in advertising has yet to be resolved. Facebook may not care about the truth in an abstract sense, but when untruths are being deployed in trade and commerce and Facebook is a beneficiary of that activity, it is possible to convince to its board of directors that the courts have power to control its content.

---

63 *Google Inc v Equustek Solutions Inc* (2017) SCC 34. See also, M Douglas, 'A Global Injunction Against Google' (2018) 134(Apr) *The Law Quarterly Review* 181.

64 *Jago v The District Court of NSW and others* [1989] HCA 46. See also, W Lacey, 'Inherent Jurisdiction, Judicial Power and Implied Guarantees Under Chapter III of the Constitution' (2003) 31(1) *Federal Law Review* 57.

10 Industrial Relations in the Gig Economy

The 'gig-economy' is the name given to virtual marketplaces created by online platform companies to allow consumers to search for service providers. Examples include Uber, Lyft, TaskRabbit and Airbnb. Advances in technology and the proliferation of smartphones have made it much easier for consumers to connect with providers of goods and services via the Internet or mobile applications. Most of the service providers in these arrangements are sole proprietors or individuals. They are not operating through an incorporated entity or other separate entity.[1] This creates particular complexities for regulators of tax obligations, licensing, workplace safety and employment law.

Though the size of the gig economy is inherently difficult to measure, from 2003–2013, the number of 'non-employer businesses' associated with the gig-economy grew by over 1 million.[2] In 2018, the United States Bureau of Labor Statistics provided its first initial reading in relation to the level of participation of Americans who rely on temporary work, freelancing and on-demand apps to make ends meet. The report found that 16.5 million people are working in 'contingent' or 'alternative work arrangements'.[3]

On-demand, Informal and Cheap

On-demand employment, also known as the 'gig economy', is growing at a rapid rate along with the supply of gig-workers who provide their labour on a short-term basis via digital platform technologies. In the United States, Uber alone has nearly half a million drivers in its fleet.[4]

---

1   KD Thomas, 'Taxing the Gig Economy' (2017–2018) 166(6) *University of Pennsylvania Law Review* 1415, 1419.
2   E Torpey and A Hogan, 'Working in a Gig Economy', *United States Department of Labor* (May 2016) <http://www.bls.gov/careeroutlook/2016/article/what-is-the-gig-economy.htm>.
3   C Gayle, 'US Gig Economy: Data Shows 16m People in "Contingent or Alternative" Work', *The Guardian* (8 June 2018) <https://www.theguardian.com/business/2018/jun/07/america-gig-economy-work-bureau-labor-statistics>.
4   L Orly, 'The Gig Economy and the Future of Employment and Labor Law' (2017) 51 *University of San Francisco Law Review* 51.

Uber's business model is the envy of start-ups worldwide. It has made it possible for people to simply tap their smartphone and have a cab arrive at their location in the minimum possible time, leaving a lot of budding start-ups yearning for an app like Uber. Uber's success further inspires gig-based business models. Venture capitalists report hearing dozens of pitches every week formulated as 'Uber but for X'.[5] It is no surprise that Uber has been so successful in the 'taxi business'. Any short-term arrangement that is a one-off relationship lends itself to delivery via an app.

Gig workers are drivers, delivery-people, personal assistants, handymen, cleaners, cooks, dog-sitters and babysitters, but increasingly are also more specialised professionals, including nurses, doctors, teachers, programmers, journalists, marketers and lawyers. For example, the rising start-up InCloudCounsel offers an army of lawyers providing on-demand, routine legal services.[6]

The genius behind the gig economy is that at any given time, human capital that might otherwise be working is under-utilised or dormant. An app is introduced to find business to fill in this 'down time'. Instead of a limousine or taxi driver waiting in a queue or not having an advanced booking for the next hour or day, an app matches the driver in real time with a nearby passenger looking for a ride.

There is an elegant simplicity to the gig economy business model. However, the problem with this premise is that it is feeds upon down-time or availability that would otherwise be valueless. Its reward structure feeds on this notion of valueless, useless time now made useful by happenstance, accident or serendipity. This notion of paying someone for their time – time that would have otherwise been spent unrewarded – devalues that time. Freelance relationships in the gig economy are on the whole uninsured and unregulated. Customers do not pay to use the app. The entire cost of arrangement is borne by the contractor who first pays a fee to get the gig and then charges customers below the traditional market rate. All of these forces drive down prices and places pressure on competing and more traditional business models. For many, the 'gig economy', in which short-term jobs are assigned via online platforms, is a potent symbol of how modern capitalism has failed.[7]

McKinsey's report on the gig economy, *Independent Work: Choice, Necessity, and the Gig Economy*, finds that up to 162 million people in Europe and the United States – or 20 to 30% of the working-age population – engage in some form of independent work. The report observed that on average, these low-skilled freelancers are on the whole are paid 20 to 30% less than their employed

5   M Kaufman, '4 Ways the On-demand Economy Will Evolve in 2016', *VentureBeat* (2 January 2016) <http://venturebeat.com/2016/01/02/4-ways-the-on-demandeconomy-will-evolve-in-2016/>.

6   See, 'Company', *InCloudCounsil* (25 September 2016) <https://www.incloud counsel.com/company>.

7   'How Governments Should Deal With the Rise of the Gig Economy', *The Economist* (6 October 2018) <https://www.economist.com/leaders/2018/10/06/how-governments-should-deal-with-the-rise-of-the-gig-economy>.

counterparts. While demographically diverse, independent workers largely fit into four segments: *free agents*, who actively choose independent work and derive their primary income from it; *casual earners*, who use independent work for supplemental income and do so by choice; *reluctants*, who make their primary living from independent work, but would prefer traditional jobs; and the *financially strapped*, who do supplemental independent work out of necessity.[8]

Critics rail that it allows firms to rid themselves of well-paid employees, replacing them with cheap freelancers. As the gig economy grows, more workers are finding ways to participate. Common side jobs range from driving for Lyft or Uber to picking up freelance work that uses writing, technical or design skills. For some workers, participating in the gig economy can provide a safeguard against unemployment. For the unemployed, the gig economy represents both opportunity and challenge. Because lots of small, casual jobs are available, any workers who are employed only part-time can find gigs to help make ends meet. However, because gigs and contracts are more affordable for employers, it becomes harder for workers to find the full-time jobs they need for financial security and the kind of regular income that banks require (to approve loan applications, for example).[9]

In a number of countries, the underpayment and terms of employment of workers offering their services via apps has come under scrutiny.[10] The informality of gig economy arrangements can attract freelancers who would not otherwise be able to secure insurance, registration or on-going employment. Without the protection of licensing and regulation, all parties to the gig arrangements are more vulnerable than they would be in a traditional model. This attitude applies to suppliers and the culture that pervades in a growing economy that operates across mega-platforms enabling the provision of millions of rides, deliveries and repairs all over the world every day. The operators of platforms and apps that support the gig economy charge the freelancers a percentage of their fare to use the app.

---

8   J Manyika, S Lund, J Bughin et al., 'Independent Work: Choice, Necessity, and the Gig Economy', *McKinsey Global Institute* (October 2016) <https://www.mckin sey.com/~/media/McKinsey/Featured%20Insights/Employment%20and% 20Growth/Independent%20work%20Choice%20necessity%20and%20the%20gig% 20economy/Independent-Work-Choice-necessity-and-the-gig-economy-Full-rep ort.ashx>.
9   L Alton, 'Why The Gig Economy Is The Best And Worst Development For Workers Under 30', *Forbes.com* (24 January 2018) <https://www.forbes.com/ sites/larryalton/2018/01/24/why-the-gig-economy-is-the-best-and-worst-deve lopment-for-workers-under-30/#98816fa6d765>.
10 'How Governments Should Deal with the Rise of the Gig Economy', *The Economist* (6 October 2018) <https://www.economist.com/leaders/2018/10/06/ how-governments-should-deal-with-the-rise-of-the-gig-economy>.

Contractors or Employees?

In the 'gig economy', with workers no longer employed in traditional 9–5 jobs, self-employed freelancers have replaced employees.[11] In each instance, a digital platform serves as the readily accessible meeting ground or marketplace that connects those who are offering the performance of services with workers seeking payment to perform them. An advantage to workers in the gig economy is their autonomy. Independent workers have a high degree of control and flexibility in determining their workload and work portfolio. They can decide which assignments to accept based on criteria such as the fee, the desirability of the client or the timing, and they can change those choices over time. However, these are freelancers without entitlements and who are still paid only by the hour in conditions where the work is precarious.[12]

Despite the relative newness of this work arrangement, gig-economy non-employer businesses have already been hit with numerous lawsuits related to or affected by how they classify their workers. They have been sued over workers' tortious conduct, worker classification and worker pay.[13]

In 2018, the question of whether food delivery bicycle riders were employees or contractors was tested in Australia. The national workplace watchdog, the Fair Work Ombudsman, questioned whether online platform workers are in fact employees not contractors, as claimed by food delivery company Foodora. The Ombudsman launched legal action in the Federal Court that related to two bicycle delivery riders who delivered food and drinks to customers in Melbourne and a delivery driver who delivered food and drinks by car to customers in Sydney.

Foodora faced allegations that it engaged in sham contracting that resulted in the underpayment of workers who were classified as contractors instead of employees. However, those proceedings did not continue as the company was later placed in voluntary administration.[14] This case was still significant because it put other 'gig economy' employers on notice in relation to the types of personal services arrangements they enter into with their purported contractors.

---

11 M Taylor, 'Good Work, the Taylor Review of Modern Working Practices', *Department of Business, Energy and Industrial Strategy (UK)* (2017) <https://www.gov.uk/government/publications/good-work-thetaylor-review-of-modern-working-practices >.

12 'How Governments Should Deal with the Rise of the Gig Economy', *The Economist* (6 October 2018) <https://www.economist.com/leaders/2018/10/06/how-governments-should-deal-with-the-rise-of-the-gig-economy>.

13 See, for example, D Levine, 'Uber Settles Wrongful Death Lawsuit in San Francisco', *Reuters* (15 July 2015) <http://www.reuters.com/article/us-uber-tech-crash-settlement-idUSKCNOPO2OW20150715>; D Alba, 'Some Drivers Really Aren't Happy About the $100M Uber Settlement', *Wired* (16 May 2016) <https://www.wired.com/2016/05/drivers-really-arent-happy-100m-uber-settlement/>. See also, P Gibbins, 'Extending Employee Protections to Gig-Economy Workers through the Entrepreneurial Opportunity Test of Fedex Home Delivery' (2018) 57 *Washington University Journal of Law and Policy* 183.

14 *In the matter of Foodora Australia Pty Ltd (Administrators Appointed)* [2018] NSWSC 1426 (11 September 2018), [12].

Short-term Relationship Between the Worker and the Customer

Independent earners perform short-term assignments, such as giving someone a ride, designing a website, treating a patient or working on a legal case. Both the worker and the customer acknowledge the limited duration of the relationship. Some contracts may extend for months or even years, at which point the individuals become indistinguishable from traditional employees; we therefore define independent work as assignments lasting less than 12 months.

The independent contractor relationship significantly limits the rights and protections afforded workers, and, by extension, it significantly reins in costs for businesses. However, some companies are concerned about the sustainability of gig-work for those who rely on gigs for a significant portion of their income and as a result are unable to access many of the benefits available to traditional employees.[15] Meanwhile, the gig economy and the autonomy and flexibility it affords to all users means the popularity of this service model is unlikely to wane. This raises the question of how to improve and secure the circumstances of freelancers in the gig economy.

Etsy, an online marketplace utilised by small-scale producers of a variety of goods, released a white paper discussing the need for those not traditionally employed to have a single place to manage benefits, a simple, common way to fund those benefits and 'a way to manage income fluctuations'.[16] The Etsy white paper suggests that non-traditional workers would be better served if rules could be amended to allow them to form formal associations, platforms and worker groups to offer group plans to their membership.[17]

By allowing association, freelancers in similar classes of gig economy work would have the power to negotiate for more favourable working conditions and other benefits through collective bargaining. The two proposed models follow either unions or guilds.

The Case for Unions and Guilds

The problem of sustainability of gigs for workers has even prompted academics, labour leaders and industry leaders to sign an open letter calling for, among other things, basic universal protections for workers regardless of how they earn their income. Workers cannot form a union unless they are employees. The traditional option for freelancers and independent workers to achieve collective bargaining and thereby improve working conditions is to form guilds. The benefit of forming a union is that a union can advocate for a

---

15 P Gibbins, 'Extending Employee Protections to Gig-Economy Workers through the Entrepreneurial Opportunity Test of Fedex Home Delivery' (2018) 57 *Washington University Journal of Law and Policy* 183, 183–184.

16 'Economy Security for the Gig Economy: A Social Safety Net That Works for Everyone That Works', *Etsy* (Fall 2016) <https://extfiles.etsy.com>.

17 'Economy Security for the Gig Economy: A Social Safety Net That Works for Everyone That Works', *Etsy*, 7 (Fall 2016) <https://extfiles.etsy.com>.

minimum wage for its members. However, in guilds, it is not possible to set or agree a minimum wage for members. This is because members of a guild are freelancers in competition with each other. Freelancers and independent workers, like other businesses, are statute-barred from price-fixing. It is illegal for competitors to work together to fix prices rather than compete against each other. Price-fixing and the forming of cartels amounts to anti-competitive behaviour and is illegal in most developed countries.[18]

Most workers in developed economies are guaranteed a legal right to join or form a union without interference, restraint or coercion from their employer. In the United Kingdom, the rights of freelancers have recently been lobbied by the Independent Workers Union (IWU). In 2017, the UK Central Arbitration Committee heard a case in which the Independent Workers Union of Great Britain sought recognition of rights to collective bargaining with Deliveroo on behalf of Deliveroo riders.[19] They sought to have the drivers treated as workers who could join the IWU. An integral part of the hearing concerned the employment status of riders, who claimed they were workers. Deliveroo claimed that riders it engaged were instead 'suppliers' and as such were entitled to rights as independent contractors. During the inquiry, the key considerations included that while logged into the app, Deliveroo riders were free to accept and reject 'offers' at any time; there were no consequences for not accepting work; riders were expected to login to the app and work just once every three months; and while Deliveroo riders were expected to provide their own clothing and equipment necessary to complete the work, they were explicitly permitted to wear 'whatever kit you want to'.

In deciding on the nature of the relationship and its finding that the Deliveroo drivers are not 'workers' as defined under statute and so not entitled to a minimum wage, the UK Central Arbitration Committee was convinced by one key finding of fact, which it saw as outweighing all others. This was the contractual right to substitute work to another rider, once accepted by the rider through his or her account on the app. In effect, Deliveroo drivers have the right to subcontract driving services to almost any other person (with limited restrictions).[20]

In May 2016, the United States Independent Drivers Guild (IDG) was formed. This guild or association is operated in partnership with the

---

18 See, C Beaton-Wells and B Fisse, 'Criminalising Serious Cartel Conduct: Issues of Law and Policy' [2008] *University of Melbourne Law Review* 3; A Duke, 'Broadening the Extraterritorial Reach of Australia's Cartel Prohibition: Adopting the "Effects" Doctrine without the Negative Effects' (2010) 38(1) *Federal Law Review* 97; P Wirz, 'Imprisonment for Hard Core Cartel Participation: A Sanction with Considerable Potential' (2016) 28(2) *Bond Law Review*, Article 1.

19 *Independent Workers' Union of Great Britain (IGWB) and RooFoods Limited TA/ Deliveroo*, Central Arbitration Committee, 14 November 2017 (TUR1/985 (2016)).

20 *Independent Workers' Union of Great Britain (IGWB) and RooFoods Limited TA/ Deliveroo*, Central Arbitration Committee, 14 November 2017 (TUR1/985 (2016)).

International Association of Machinists and Aerospace Workers. It is partially funded by Uber and has already agreed never to strike or to engage in more concerted union organising. The motto of the IDG is 'We are Uber, Lyft, Juno, Via workers united for a fair industry'.[21] All for-hire vehicle workers that work with these companies are entitled to basic membership of the IDG. Currently, that includes all of New York City's nearly 65,000 drivers who use the Uber app. The IDG provides a number of benefits to its members and advocates on their behalf. For example, a recent success for the IDG was the introduction of a facility for customers to tip Uber's driver in New York.

Guilds in the gig economy can act as a bargaining agent, although this is not actual union representation.[22] Though the guild arrangement for New York falls short of traditional union rights, Uber is making concessions in allowing some form of organising to occur among its contractors. Some criticise Uber's move to allow drivers' associations as simply a self-serving attempt to prevent them organising traditional – more powerful – unions.[23]

Guilds composed of workmen from specific trades and crafts were established in the middle ages. Their purpose was to defend the interests of the trade, regulate the quality of workmanship and the training of new members, and provide support and welfare for their members. The history of guilds begins in England with the oldest laws of pre-Norman Anglo Saxons. From the late 17th century, the powers of the London guilds to regulate entry into their trades and enforce standards of workmanship declined. With industrialisation and the growth of urbanisation, skilled and unskilled workers turned to employment in factories, banks and large companies. Industrial disputes in the 18th century took place with little reference to the guilds. The formation of unions of workers was a next logical step.

Despite the decline of guilds in England and across Europe, their popularity resurfaced across the Atlantic in the 20th century with screen actors and writers in America. Guilds have served Hollywood workers who are independent and compete with each other, but need to bargain for certain rights collectively. For example, collective bargaining by writers who exercise supervisory and production executive roles has contributed to the successes of the Writers Guild. It has been suggested that lessons should be drawn from the experience of the writers' union in Hollywood and that the gig economy should embrace bargaining by independent workers in order to realise the potential of the disruptive economy of the future.[24]

---

21 Independent Drivers Guild <https://drivingguild.org/>.

22 D Wiessner and D Levine, 'Uber Deal Shows Divide in Labor's Role in Gig Economy', *Reuters* (23 May 2016) <https://www.reuters.com/article/us-uber-tech-drivers-labor/uber-deal-shows-divide-in-labors-drive-forrole-in-gig-economy-idUSKCNOYEODF>.

23 J Eidelson, 'Uber Found an Unlikely Friend in Organized Labor', *Bloomberg Businessweek* (27 October 2016) <https://www.bloomberg.com/news/articles/2016-10-27/uber-found-an-unlikely-friend-in-organized-labor>.

24 CL Fisk, 'Hollywood Writers and the Gig Economy' (2017) 2017 *University of Chicago Legal Forum* 177, 203.

Some critics have expressed concern that the gig economy creates opportunities for small companies to create an app that charges thousands of workers for the opportunity to deliver their services at their own expense and liability to customers, casting it in a romantic light as a democratised peer-to-peer relationship, when in fact the app owner wields significant control over the arrangement between the app users.[25]

It is important to note that in some developed economies, social welfare and medical cover is tied to employment. In these economies, independent workers and freelancers are more vulnerable when they experience workplace injury or fall ill or when their equipment is not working. In these circumstances, the need to organise representation (for example, via guilds) will be more pressing than in countries that do provide comprehensive medical and unemployment benefits. There is no social or fiscal benefit to be derived (in digital or non-digital economies) from creating classes of underpaid workers. It costs most people money to earn money. This is why being underpaid is worse than not being paid at all.

In *Trust and the Poverty Trap*, Farah and Hook describe the problems that flow from underpayment.[26] The working poor do not have savings to weather time between jobs or an emergency expense. Workers who are struggling financially are less likely to agree to deferred payments or to trust that they will get paid by strangers. This is because in workers in lower socio-economic circumstances are more likely to accept a discounted rate for their efforts in order to receive payment immediately. This makes them vulnerable to the suggestion that payment will be 'in full and delayed' or 'immediate for a discount'. Of course, most working poor are aware that this strategy is used against them and will therefore (quite understandably) not trust those who ask permission to delay payment. The reluctance to wait to be paid also means that the type of work that is done will be low-paid, one-off tasks for strangers. There is no establishment of an ongoing social relationship of trust that normally develops between suppliers and consumers.

A major attraction for the working poor in a gig economy is the prospect of immediate reward. The payment systems through apps mean that the customer pays by credit card to the business running the app. The business keeps an agreed share of the payment and then remits the balance to the worker. This all happens in minutes. However, because work is unreliable and inconsistent, it is difficult to predict future income or make financial plans. Wealth and security is usually generated over long periods of time and in conjunction with buying a home. The relation between present-mindedness and poverty is complex and multi-faceted. It is one of many reasons that working poverty persists over lifetimes and across generations.

25 O Lobel, 'The Gig Economy and the Future of Employment' (2017) 51(1) *University of San Francisco Law Review* 51, 73.

26 MJ Farah and CJ Hook, 'Trust and the Poverty Trap' (2017) 114(21) *Proceedings of the National Academy of Sciences of the USA* 5327.

11 Protecting Privacy in a World of Big Data

Information privacy has given rise to rules governing the collection and handling of personal data, such as credit information, and medical and government records.[1] These rules are known as 'data protection'. In this context, the word 'data' connotes information that is stored in digital from. Personal data is private when the person who possesses it does not intend that it shall be imparted to the general public.

Data protection is a problem that arises where data is collected by government or business and there is a need to protect the individual records in that data from falling into the hands of third parties, either inadvertently or by force. It is important to note here that many data breaches occur at the hands of employees and officers of organisations, both the well-meaning and the nefarious. Accidentally sending a confidential email to the wrong recipient is a data breach. Leaving a laptop on a bus is a data breach. However, these data breaches are not the type that affect millions or even billions of the organisations customers. Over the past decade, the big data breaches were – on the whole – perpetrated by malicious hackers. These big data breaches play havoc with the relationship of trust between consumers and organisations and their systems.

This problem is amplified by an increasing interest in the problem of building massive virtual warehouses of data to mine and analyse, while protecting. The need to protect the privacy of those who give their personal information to organisations (usually in exchange for a service) has become big business. Cyber security is about protecting technology and information from accidental loss or illicit access, as well as corruption, theft or damage.

Data protection is a key factor in building trust between business and customers. The rapid increase in consumer digital data held by businesses makes

---

1 'Information privacy' is to be distinguished from: 'Bodily privacy' (which concerns the protection of people's physical selves against invasive procedures such as genetic tests, drug testing and cavity searches); 'Communications privacy' (which covers the security and privacy of mail, telephones, e-mail and other forms of communication); and 'Territorial privacy' (which concerns the setting of limits on intrusion into the domestic and other environments such as the workplace or public space. This includes searches, video surveillance and ID checks).

data security a topic of scrutiny among the public and policymakers. The public demand for data security is reflected in improving data regulations, including the requirement to notify customers and regulators of certain types of data breaches within strict timeframes. New data compliance rules demand that all organisations re-evaluate their processes to improve data management. Updating company data regulations is also an opportunity for businesses to achieve competitive differentiation and a way to drive greater customer confidence and trust in their online interactions and their brands.

The Nature of Privacy

Privacy (as a moral right) inheres in the basic dignity of the individual. This right is of intrinsic importance to the fulfilment of each person, both individually and as a member of society. Without privacy it is difficult for an individual to possess and retain a sense of self-worth or to maintain an independence of spirit and thought.[2]

The genesis of modern legal academic discussion of the topic of privacy is generally acknowledged to be Samuel Warren and Louis Brandeis's article, 'The Right to Privacy', published in the *Harvard Law Review* in 1890.[3] During the 1960s 'information revolution', the storage of personal information in computer data banks fuelled widespread debate about what this might mean for the protection of privacy.[4]

2   See for example, *Vickery v Nova Scotia Supreme Court (Prothonotary)* [1991] 1 SCR 671, 687. As a general definition, privacy is to be distinguished from confidence and secrecy. Confidential information does not have to be inherently 'private' in nature. Indeed, the information may quite properly be made public at a later time – for example, with inventions, market sensitive intelligence or similar commercial-in-confidence information. At the heart of an action for breach of confidence is the relationship of confidence or the defendant's knowledge that the information was confidential – *Duchess of Argyle v Duke of Argyle* [1967] Ch 302. Liability arises where a reasonable person standing in the shoes of the recipient of the information would have realised that it was provided in confidence – *Coco v AN Clark (Engineers) Ltd* [1969] RPC 41. A third party who receives confidential information may be subject to an obligation of confidence, if the party is aware of or has reasons to suspect the confidential nature of the information. Secrecy, however, is a general right to privacy warranting legal protection and as such is a relatively modern phenomenon – R Gavison, 'Privacy and the Limits of Law' (1980) 89 *Yale Law Journal* 421, 465.

3   S Warren and L Brandeis, 'The Right to Privacy' (1890) 4 *Harvard Law Review* 193.

4   See, for example, R Prosser, 'Privacy' (1960) 48 *California Law Review* 383; E Bloustein, 'Privacy as an Aspect of Human Dignity: An Answer to Dean Prosser' (1964) 39 *New York University Law Review* 962; C Fried, 'Privacy' (1967) 77 *Yale Law Journal* 475. This is not to suggest an absence of legal discourse between the late 19th century and the 1960s. For example, see the articles cited in E Bloustein, 'Privacy as an Aspect of Human Dignity: An Answer to Dean Prosser' (1964) 39 *New York University Law Review* 962, n 4. See also, J Stephen, *Liberty, Equality, Fraternity* (1967 ed, 1873), 160.

Advances in technology in the 1980s led to a modern concern for the protection of privacy that can be attributed primarily to a change in the nature and magnitude of threats to privacy, due at least in part to advances in the technology of surveillance and the recording, storage and retrieval of information have made it either impossible or extremely costly for individuals to protect the same level of privacy that was once enjoyed.[5]

Privacy Protection as a Fundamental Value

Privacy protection has become a fundamental value. That value lies in both private and public interests.[6] Privacy has been defended for centuries and is evidenced in the laws of England and as received or adopted in America and Common Law countries.[7] William Pitt the Elder– later the first Earl of Chatham – wrote in the early 1800s:

> The poorest man may in his cottage bid defiance to all the force of the Crown. It may be frail; its roof may shake; the wind may blow though it; the storms may enter; the rain may enter – but the King of England cannot enter; all his forces dare not cross the threshold of the ruined tenement.[8]

Pitt made these remarks on 27 March 1763 in the course of a debate in relation to the *Excise Bill*, which was before the House of Commons. The Excise Bill of 1763 was also known as *the Cider Act* because it levied a tax on cider. To enforce the Act, agents of the Crown would be able to search any suspected business premises for untaxed cider. This was an apparent violation of Common Law restrictions on the power of the King's agents to enter a man's property without the owner's permission. However, there was already ample precedent for such illegal searches in England. For example, numerous and various excise statutes on sugar and molasses gave customs officials the right to search vessels and warehouses on mere suspicion that there were untaxed goods on the

---

5   R Gavison, 'Privacy and the Limits of Law' (1980) 89 *Yale Law Journal* 421, 465. See also, D Lindsay, 'An Exploration of the Conceptual Basis of Privacy and the Implications for the Future of Australian Privacy Law' (2005) 29 *Melbourne University Law Review* 131, 135–136; M Jackson, *Hughes on Data Protection in Australia* (2nd ed, Law Book Company, 2001), 10.
6   The public interest in protecting privacy and private freedoms is recognised as key to maintaining peace, order, comfort and well-being in the community. Protecting these rights supports the personal safety and feeling of security of all citizens. The general view is that no one should be subjected to arbitrary interference with his or her privacy, family, home or correspondence, nor to attacks on his or her honour or reputation. Of course, protecting privacy requires balancing privacy with other important interests.
7   The *Justices of the Peace Act 1361* in England provided for the arrest of peeping toms and eavesdroppers.
8   W Pitt, 'Speech on the Excise Bill, House of Commons (March 1763)', quoted in *Lord Brougham, Historical Sketches of Statesmen Who Flourished in the Time of George III* (1855), I, 42.

premises. The proposed Cider Act went a step further and permitted inspection even of private homes in which a farmer or cider merchant might well store some of his product.[9]

Article 8 of the 1950 Convention for the Protection of Human Rights and Fundamental Freedoms states that everyone has the right to respect for his private and family life, his home and his correspondence; there shall be no interference by a public authority with the exercise of this right except as in accordance with the law and is necessary in a democratic society in the interests of national security, public safety or the economic well-being of the country, for the prevention of disorder or crime, for the protection of health of morals, or for the protection of the rights and freedoms of others.[10]

Interest in the right of privacy increased in the 1960s and 1970s with the advent of information technology. The surveillance potential of powerful computer systems prompted demands for specific rules governing the collection and handling of personal information.

In December 2013, the United Nations General Assembly adopted resolution 68/167, which expressed deep concern at the negative impact that surveillance and interception of communications may have on human rights and called upon member states to respect and protect the right to privacy in digital communication; to review their procedures, practices and legislation related to communications surveillance, interception and collection of personal data; and to ensure the full and effective implementation of their obligations under international human rights law. This resolution is particularly framed around the growing use of technology by governments to monitor the online activities of their citizens and to collect data about them.

The Hard and Fast Facts About Big Data

Big data is a term that describes the large volume of data – both structured and unstructured – that inundates a business on a day-to-day basis. But it is not the amount of data that is important. Big data can be analysed for insights that lead to better decisions and strategic business moves. Berkeley researchers estimated that the world had produced about 1.5 billion gigabytes of information in 1999 and in a 2003 replication of the study found out that amount to have doubled in three years.[11]

9   T Fleming, 'Defending the Family Castle – Part I', *Chronicles – Magazine of American Culture* (24 March 2014) <https://www.chroniclesmagazine.org/blogs/thomas-fleming/defending-the-family-castle-part-i/>.

10 Article 8 of the United Nations *Convention for the Protection of Human Rights and Fundamental Freedoms* (Rome, 4 November 1950) <https://treaties.un.org/pages/showDetails.aspx?objid=080000028014a40b>.

11 P Lyman, 'How Much Information?', *Berkeley School of Information* (1999) <https://datascience.berkeley.edu/>; P Lyman et al., 'How Much Information?', *School of Information Management and Systems, UC Berkeley* (2003) <http://www2.sims.berkeley.edu/research/projects/how-much-info-2003/>.

Whereas in the 1970s and 1980s the top ten spots in the list of Fortune 500 companies were dominated by companies exploiting oil and gas and car manufacturers, the major players are now the FAANG corporations. FAANG is an acronym that represents the combined for the world's five big tech companies: Facebook, Amazon, Apple, Netflix and Google (the brand name for holding company Alphabet Inc). The top 10 companies in the United States account for 53% of the total gains of the S&P 500 index in 2018.[12] Netflix (NFL), Facebook (FB) and Google (GOOGL) are the biggest stocks on the market, in terms of market capitalisation. In 2018, FAANG stocks also dominated the NASDAQ.[13] While these so-called FAANG companies offer search engine, retail, entertainment and social media services via their digital platforms, they also enhance the delivery of those services by analysing the data they gather from their customers. Indeed, this further layer of strategic engagement with information gleaned from the market they provide is so lucrative that many other big players in the market have positioned themselves with the sole commercial aim of gathering, managing and analysing data as a complete business model. The world's big data companies also include the incumbents – IBM, Microsoft, HP Enterprise, and Oracle – who traditionally offered information technology and hardware computer products. These have branched into the business of big data. In 2012, IBM was the world's biggest vendor of big data products, with US$1.2 billion in revenue in this sector alone.[14]

The newer players in the big data market, like Cloudera, provide sophisticated Cloud-based or on premises services to deliver enhanced services including data warehousing and engineering, predictive analytics and machine learning. Alpine Data Labs is an advanced analytics interface working with Apache Hadoop and big data to provide a collaborative, visual environment to create and deploy analytics workflow and predictive models.[15]

It is clear that data is a resource in its own right. Referencing its power to fuel economies has been called the world's most valuable resource: the 'new oil'.[16] It provides companies with information from which to draw insights. Big data is a growing field in both technology and business. Whether the data

---

12 R Vlastelica, 'Why Investors Shouldn't Fear the Dominance of the FAANG Stocks', *MarketWatch.com* (2018) <https://www.marketwatch.com/story/why-investors-shouldnt-fear-the-dominance-of-faang-stocks-2018-10-04>.

13 'Fang Stocks Dominate the Market', *Gulf News* (5 May 2018) <https://gulfnews.com/business/markets/faang-stocks-dominate-nasdaq-1.2216707>.

14 C Versace, 'Talking Big Data and Analytics with IBM', *Forbes.com* (1 April 2014) <https://www.forbes.com/sites/chrisversace/2014/04/01/talking-big-data-and-analytics-with-ibm/#3bc5dc53a66e>.

15 B Gourley, 'The Analyst One Top Technologies List: The Breakthrough Technologies Every Analyst Should Know About', *Analyst One* (17 October 2013) <https://web.archive.org/web/20140308233907/http://www.analystone.com/the-analyst-one-top-technologies-list/>.

16 'The World's Most Valuable Resource Is No Longer Oil, But Data', *The Economist* (6 May 2017) <https://www.economist.com/leaders/2017/05/06/the-worlds-most-valuable-resource-is-no-longer-oil-but-data>.

is sourced from third parties or gathered in-house, any organisation that engages with its clients or customer online will seek to gain a competitive edge with the use of data. Meanwhile, billions of social media users all over the world are generating significant volumes of data through messaging, posting, blogging and sharing. According to Domo's sixth annual *Data Never Sleeps* report,[17] in every minute of every day in 2018, Instagram users posted 49,380 photos, Google conducted 3.8 million searches, Twitter users sent 473,400 tweets and Tumblr users published 79,740 posts. Every minute. Every day. In the six years since the first of the *Data Never Sleeps* reports, the number of Internet users has grown from 2.5 to 3.8 million.[18]

The proliferation of social applications and websites and the use of the Internet has opened the door to a new realm of data. By liking a brand on Facebook, shopping online or posting a restaurant review, consumers are adding to the massive amount of data categorised as unstructured behavioural data. From user preferences, sentiment, trends and location, each person is leaving a digital footprint behind for analysis and targeted marketing. In December 2018, Facebook reached more than 2.27 billion active monthly users constantly updating their profiles about what they are up to. The platform is the most popular in the world.[19]

In addition to all of this 'declared' data, companies are scraping, aggregating, inferring, imputing and adding value to social data as well as their customers' and clients' inputs, so as to gain insights into the values and trends that make their sector or market tick. This information is pivotal to strategic decision-making for recruitment, investment and marketing.

The volume of data captured and stored is also increasing rapidly. Companies such as Facebook, Google and Yahoo! have jointly and independently developed new technologies for the unlimited storage and use of data that each individual is knowingly or unknowingly creating. Current estimates suggested that 90% of the world's information has been generated in just the past two years.[20] As we all know, vastly improved data capture, processing speed and developments in machine learning are reshaping the way our economy functions before our eyes. And each movement leaves a trace element of our past, present and future movements and attitudes.

---

17 'Data Never Sleeps 6.0', *Domo* (18 November 2018) <https://www.domo.com/learn/data-never-sleeps-6>.
18 See 'Data Never Sleeps Infographic', *Domo* (2012) <https://www.domo.com/learn/infographic-data-never-sleeps>.
19 'Number of Monthly Active Facebook Users Worldwide as of 3rd Quarter 2018 (in Millions)', *Statistica* (2019) <https://www.statista.com/statistics/264810/number-of-monthly-active-facebook-users-worldwide/>.
20 B Marr, 'How Much Data Do We Create Every Day? The Mind-Blowing Stats Everyone Should Read', *Forbes.com* (21 May 2018) <https://www.forbes.com/sites/bernardmarr/2018/05/21/how-much-data-do-we-create-every-day-the-mind-blowing-stats-everyone-should-read/#66d9d21860ba>; Australian Productivity Commission, 'Data Availability and Use' (8 May 2017) <https://www.pc.gov.au/inquiries/completed/data-access#report>.

However, for all the benefits that may derive from big data, there is a darker side to the creation of valuable lakes or 'honey pots' of data. Internal data breaches and external cyber-attacks cause losses, commercial risk and breaches of privacy that annually cost organisations and individuals billions of dollars. Cyber events include data breaches, security incidents, privacy violations and phishing crimes.

There is research suggesting that when compared with the cost of bad debts and fraud, public concerns regarding the increasing rates of data breaches and legal actions may be excessive compared to the relatively modest financial impact to firms that suffer these events.[21] However, the regulatory approaches to data breaches that have developed in many of the more developed countries place the obligation to protect data and to report any breaches squarely on the data gatherers. The penalties that can be imposed when a breach does take place and the reputational damage to the organisation suffering the breach adds significantly to the real cost of a failure to secure data.

The global average cost of a data breach is $3.86 million, up 6.4% from 2017. The average cost, globally, for each lost or stolen record containing sensitive and confidential information is also up from 2017, landing at $148 per record. The costs associated with 'mega breaches' ranging from 1 million to 50 million records lost, projecting that these breaches cost companies between $40 million and $350 million respectively.[22] Internet users cannot afford to embrace active intermediaries without assurances that their data will be handled in accordance with their expectation'.[23]

Privacy Breaches in a World of Big Data

Big data experts predict that 'The organisation of tomorrow will be built around data' – its collection, distribution, analysis and automation, using artificial intelligence.[24] Tech giants, service providers and businesses track our data via transactions, mobile telephone use and posts on social media. They use this information to advertise more intelligently and intuitively. Capturing and analysing consumer data is big business in its own right. With this information, companies are able to tailor advertising to target particular demographics or individuals with advertising for specific products or services. The problem with this practice is that when the advertising or suggestions that appear in our

---

21 S Romanosky, 'Examining the Costs and Causes of Cyber Incidents' (2016) 2(2) *Journal of Cybersecurity* 121.

22 'IBM Study: Hidden Costs of Data Breaches Increase Expenses for Businesses', *IBM.com* (11 July 2018) <https://newsroom.ibm.com/2018-07-11-IBM-Study-Hidden-Costs-of-Data-Breaches-Increase-Expenses-for-Businesses>.

23 J Hurwitz, 'Trust and Online Interaction' (2013) 161 *University of Pennsylvania Law Review* 1580, 1582.

24 M Van Rijmenam, 'How to Build the Organisation of Tomorrow?', *Blog Technology* (17 October 2018) <https://vanrijmenam.nl/how-build-organisation-of-tomorrow/>.

Google ads or social media feeds are too accurate, it can create a feeling of being surveilled. If the particular product or service that is fed back to us relates to something personal, then it may feel like a breach of privacy.

A data breach occurs when personal information held by an agency or organisation is lost or subjected to unauthorised access, modification, disclosure or other misuse or interference. The types of harm to individuals that could result from a data breach include identity theft, financial loss, threat to physical safety, threat to emotional wellbeing, loss of business or employment opportunities, humiliation and damage to reputation. The impact on the target organisation might be the loss of public trust in the organisation, reputational damage, loss of assets (for example, stolen computers or storage devices), financial exposure (for example, if bank account details are compromised), regulatory penalties (for example, for breaches of relevant data protection and privacy legislation), extortion, legal liability and breach of secrecy provisions in legislation.

There are various legal and trust consequences to big data breaches. The following four examples demonstrate the precarious position that can be created by a data breach – for the target organisation, its customers and third parties.

Target (2012)

In 2012, the privacy of a pregnant teen was invaded by the results of predictive analytics conducted at a local store. Andrew Pole, a statistician and 'Director of Guest Data Management' at Target in the United States, created a data analysis program that captured information via its customers' Target loyalty cards. When customers paid for their purchasers, their loyalty card was scanned so as to record the value of the purchases and to reward the customer with loyalty points. This step was also storing a record of the purchases for analysis in conjunction with the personal information about the shopper that was provided on the shopper's application for a loyalty card. Pole noticed a shopping pattern for women who were expecting a baby that included the purchase of pregnancy tests kits, unscented lotions and vitamin supplements. Using the pregnant teen's home address that was required on her loyalty card application, the store sent her a catalogue of new baby supplies. The teenager lived at home with her parents, but had yet to tell them of her pregnancy.[25]

The fact that the girl was pregnant is not a dark secret in the sense that it is something that would pose a threat to the government, society or the state. It is, however, something deeply personal and something that she might want to keep to herself. She is not required to keep this secret, but it is her secret to tell, or not to tell, which ever she prefers. Because of Target's interference, the

---

25 K Hill, 'How Target Figured Out A Teen Girl Was Pregnant Before Her Father Did', *Forbes.com* (16 February 2012) <http://www.forbes.com/sites/kashmirhill/2012/02/16/how-target-figured-out-a-teen-girl-was-pregnant-before-her-father-did/#2b973a734c62>.

girl lost some of her autonomy. She lost the freedom to choose how and when she would tell her parents and others. Target's use of the pregnant teen's data in that way and its clumsy inadvertent disclosure to her parents made headlines. *Forbes* warned that 'Target isn't just predicting pregnancies'.[26] The *New York Times* wrote it up as companies learning our secrets.[27]

Yahoo (2013–2014)

In September 2016, the once dominant Internet giant, while in negotiations to sell itself to Verizon, announced it had been the victim of the biggest data breach in history. Yahoo described the perpetrator as 'very likely a state-sponsored actor'. The attack compromised the real names, email addresses, dates of birth and telephone numbers of 500 million users. The company said the 'vast majority' of the passwords involved had been compromised. Then just three months later (in December 2016), Yahoo disclosed a more alarming breach that occurred before the 2014 attack. In 2013, a different group of hackers had accessed the details relating to 1 billion accounts (including names, dates of birth, email addresses and passwords, as well as security questions and answers).

In October 2017, Yahoo revised the December 2016 estimate, admitting that in fact all 3 billion user accounts had been compromised. Following its acquisition by Verizon in June 2017, Yahoo said it obtained new intelligence while investigating the breach with help from outside forensic experts. The breaches knocked an estimated $350 million off Yahoo's sale price. Verizon eventually paid $4.48 billion for Yahoo's core Internet business.[28] Verizon argued that despite Yahoo's seeming inability to safeguard customer data, the acquisition made strategic sense. The strategy in this case is to improve its position in relation to access to consumer data. The more information Verizon can amass about people's online behaviour and activities, the more it can compete with the likes of Google and Facebook in leveraging that info with marketers.[29]

---

26 K Hill, 'Target Isn't Just Predicting Pregnancies: "Expect More" Savvy Data-Mining Tricks', *Forbes.com* (24 February 2012) <https://www.forbes.com/sites/kashmirhill/2012/02/24/target-isnt-just-predicting-pregnancies-expect-more-savvy-data-mining-tricks/#516bb17f598a>.

27 C Duhigg, 'How Companies Learn Your Secrets', *New York Times* (16 February 2012) <https://www.nytimes.com/2012/02/19/magazine/shopping-habits.html>.

28 'Yahoo Hack: 2013 Breach Affected All 3 Billion of Its Accounts, Tripling Originally Reported Number', *ABC News* (4 October 2017) <https://www.abc.net.au/news/2017-10-04/yahoo-says-that-a-2013-breach-affected-all-3-billion/9013502>.

29 D Lazarus, 'Your Privacy: Verizon's Takeover of Yahoo Is All About User Data', *LA Times* (24 February 2017) <https://www.latimes.com/business/lazarus/la-fi-lazarus-verizon-yahoo-privacy-20170224-story.html>.

Remijas v Neiman Marcus Group (2015)

In January 2015, news broke of a card hack at Neiman Marcus where hackers accessed the debit and credit card information of customers who shopped at its chain between mid-July and the end of October 2013. Only in-store customers were affected, not online transactions. Originally, the company estimated that as many as 1.1 million cardholders could have been affected. But further investigation found that it affected a maximum of 350,000 customers. The breach occurred when malicious software was installed onto the Neiman Marcus system that collected payment card data from customers who made purchases during those dates.[30]

These events led to a class action against Nieman Marcus brought by its customers who sought compensation for leaving customers' personal information vulnerable to computer hackers. However, a legal problem arose during the proceedings because it was discovered that not all customers had been affected by the hack. Not every store was infected by hackers' malware, and even at stores that were affected, the malware operated intermittently. The personal data of some Neiman Marcus cardholders, in other words, was not compromised at all. The presiding judge's concern was that members of the class action might have opted into the settlement deal with Neiman Marcus not knowing how they were situated compared to other members. The judge observed that this creates an appearance of manipulation or dishonesty, undermining the integrity of the class action mechanism.[31] A lack of certainty about the extent and impact of a data breach has the potential to undermine the rights of victims who may want to seek compensation through the courts.

Vidal-Hall v Google Inc (2014)

In February 2012, the *Wall Street Journal* published allegations that Google was circumventing the Safari browser's privacy settings. In 2012, Safari was a popular Internet service, accounting for 6% of all desktop browsing and 50% on mobile devices. During this time, Google intentionally changed the default privacy settings of Apple's Safari browser to secretly re-enable disabled cookies.

Companies have long used cookies to remember users' past visits. This can be helpful for saving sign-in details and preferences. But they are also used to profile users so as to fine-tune advertising to users' tastes and interests. Cookie use goes beyond visiting a particular website. As other sites embed Facebook 'like' and 'share' buttons, for instance, Facebook's servers are being pinged and can access users' stored cookies. This is the means by which Facebook mines user data to ascertain sentiment, political views and social values. With this information, Facebook's advertisers can more effectively tailor marketing

---

30 B Hardekopf, 'The Big Data Breaches of 2014', *Forbes.com* (13 January 2015) <https://www.forbes.com/sites/moneybuilder/2015/01/13/the-big-data-brea ches-of-2014/#5c974f7fefe6>.

31 *Remijas v Neiman Marcus Group, LLC*, 794 F.3d 688 (2015).

content. Safari users would deliberately disable cookies in order to protect their privacy. However, Google was re-enabling cookies without the users' knowledge. Stanford University's Jonathan Mayer caught Google, along with a number of ad servers, avoiding this block by using a loophole in Safari that lets third parties set cookies if the browser thinks a user is filling out an online form.[32]

Google tried to justify this practice by arguing that they made this change to the behaviour of Safari's cookies so that users could more easily share advertisements with other users. However, the problem for Google was the secrecy with which they had made the change. Usually, when a technology giant introduces a new feature to its platform that is a benefit to users, it is announced in an upgrade or media release. It is usually made public so as to leverage the goodwill that is generated by user-friendly improvements. Google had made no such announcement and it was alleged that its sneakiness was telling of the real purpose behind the move: to improve the reach of advertisements, so as to attract more advertising revenue.

Six months later, Google had agreed to pay a record $22.5 million penalty to the United States Federal Trade Commission for misrepresenting to its users what it was doing. However, it was not required to make any admission of wrong-doing. The following year, three claimants from the United Kingdom sought to bring a claim against Google for the tort of misuse of their private information and for a breach of its statutory duties as a data controller.[33] These claims were filed under the *Data Protection Act 1998* (UK).[34] The claims arose because Google tracked and collated information relating to their Internet usage on the Safari browser between mid-2011 and early 2012. As Google is a registered corporation in Delaware with its principal place of business in California, the claimants were required to obtain permission from the Master under the United Kingdom's Civil Procedure Rules to serve proceedings abroad (that is, to serve them in the United States, which they were successful in doing). Google appealed that decision to the High Court and then the Court of Appeal.

In March 2015, the English Court of Appeal found against Google on three key issues arising out of its so-called Safari cookie workaround: the claimants could serve proceedings on Google in the United States for the misuse of their private information and for breach of the Data Protection Act 1998; there is an arguable case that browser-generated information, such as cookies, constitutes

---

32 Mayer's suspicions were confirmed by Ashkan Soltani, a cyber-security consultant. See, V Valentine-deVries, 'The Google Cookie That Seems to Come Out of Nowhere', *WSJ* (28 February 2012) <https://blogs.wsj.com/digits/2012/02/28/the-google-cookie-that-seems-to-come-out-of-nowhere/>.

33 *Vidal-Hall v Google Inc* [2014] EWHC 13 (QB) (16 January 2014).

34 The *Data Protection Act 1998* is a United Kingdom Act of Parliament designed to protect personal data stored on computers or in an organised paper filing system. It enacted the European Union's Data Protection Directive 1995's provisions on the protection, processing and movement of data.

'personal data', bringing a whole swathe of Google's online activities into the scope of European data protection laws; and the Court found that the claimants could claim for distress without having to prove pecuniary loss (greatly increasing the scope for compensation claims in the future given an invasion of privacy will rarely be accompanied by actual monetary loss).

In November 2013, Google agreed to pay $17 million to 37 states and the District of Columbia in a wide-reaching settlement over tracking users online without their knowledge. Responding to this outcome, the Attorney General of New York commented, 'Consumers should be able to know whether there are other eyes surfing the web with them ... by tracking millions of people without their knowledge, Google violated not only their privacy, but also their trust'.[35]

Google's case is another example of public admonition and financial penalty making very little difference to its customer-base or popularity. While users may trust Google less, they will still use its browsers. This was noticed in 2017, when Facebook announced that it had handed more than 80 million user profiles to Cambridge Analytica – an election strategy firm. While Facebook was excoriated for their behaviour and suffered a major stock loss, there was not a corresponding drop in the number of user accounts.[36] It seems that losing the trust of your users does not immediately make them flee your business.

A Trust Trade-off Analysis

Security requirements often reflect implicit assumptions about trust relationships among actors. The more actors trust each other, the less stringent the security requirements are likely to be. Trust always involves the risk of mistrust; hence, trust implies a trade-off: gaining some benefits from depending on a second party in trade for getting exposed to security and privacy risks.[37] For consumers the trade-off is gaining some benefit from convenience while accepting that our data is being tracked and used. This acceptance extends to knowing that our private date is being gathered and sometimes misused. When trust assumptions are implicit, these trust trade-offs are made implicitly and in an ad-hoc way. This agent- and goal-oriented analysis allows for a better appreciation of where the limits of trust and convenience sit on a trade-off continuum. The aim for technology providers and users is to make these trade-offs in a way that reaches a balance between costs and benefits. Trust in

35 CC Miller, 'Google to Pay $17 Million to Settle Privacy Case', *NYTimes.com* (18 November 2013) <https://www.nytimes.com/2013/11/19/technology/google-to-pay-17-million-to-settle-privacy-case.html>.

36 M Green, 'Why I'm Worried About Google', *Slate* (3 October 2018) <https://slate.com/technology/2018/10/google-is-losing-users-trust.html>.

37 G Elahi and E Yu, 'Trust Trade-off Analysis for Security Requirements Engineering', *IEEE* (2009) *IEEE International Requirements Engineering Conference, Atlanta GA*<https://ieeexplore.ieee.org/document/5328522>.

technology is a balance between accessibility and security. Information must be accessible so that it can be used and it needs to be secure. Managing these competing requirements is a delicate balance.[38]

However, this analysis is from an engineering perspective and the particular aspect of security it refers to is technical. It is the security of the system from external cyber-attack. It does not (and cannot) speak to how secure a user's personal data will be at the hands of their service provider.[39] This is because the technical security provided by the engineers does not (and cannot not) block the service provider from accessing the data and providing it to third parties in exchange for reward. In other words, the engineers are not programming against an 'inside job'.

What differentiates the Target, Google and Facebook privacy breaches from the Yahoo hack is that the former were all 'inside jobs'. While Yahoo was charged with failing to secure its customers' data from external attack, Target, Google and Facebook were entirely responsible for the intentional misuse of their users' personal information. The way to prevent service providers from breaching the trust of their customers and consumers is to create transparent governance models that reflect and uphold the values and culture of the organisation. Building governance models into technical systems is not easy, but it can be done by requiring – for example – multiple digital signatures, including from a board member, for certain features to be added to or removed from client- and regulator-facing systems. As well as securing high-level authority, governance models can require transparency in relation to these decisions and their consequences for users and regulators. Louis Brandeis's line that 'sunlight is the best disinfectant' summarises the philosophy of the transparency. Transparency means that decision-makers in organisations and the platforms they provide can be more effectively held to account, which will lead to a re-building of trust in technology giants.

Regulatory Approaches to Data Protection and Privacy

The particular type of data that needs to be protected under most privacy and data protection legislation is the personal information of customers that has been gathered by organisations. That is, personal data. According to the European Commission, personal data is any information relating to an individual, whether it relates to his or her private, professional or public life. Examples of personal data include the individual's name, their photo, an email address, bank details, their posts on social networking sites, medical information or a computer's IP address.

---

38 See, H Glass, 'Trust by Design: Balancing Accessibility and Security in Blockchain', *King & Wood Mallesons* (26 October 2017) <https://www.kwm.com/en/au/knowl edge/insights/trust-design-blockchain-accessibility-security-information-20171026>.
39 G Elahi and E Yu, 'Trust Trade-off Analysis for Security Requirements Engineering', *IEEE* (2009) *IEEE International Requirements Engineering Conference, Atlanta GA*<https://ieeexplore.ieee.org/document/5328522>.

The genesis of modern legislation in this area can be traced to the first data protection law in the world enacted in Germany in 1970. This was followed by national laws in Sweden (1973), the United States (1974), Germany (1977) and France (1978).

The European Union's General Data Protection Regulation (EU) 2016/ 679 came into force on 25 May 2016. It is regulation by which the European Commission intends to strengthen and unify data protection for individuals within the European Union (EU). The EU's regulation imposes more rigorous requirements for obtaining consent for collecting personal data; raises the age of consent for collecting an individual's data from 13 to 16 years; requires a company to delete data if it is no longer used for the purpose it was collected; requires a company to delete data if the individual revokes consent for the company to hold the data. It also requires that companies notify the EU government of data breaches in 72 hours of learning about the breach; firms handling significant amounts of sensitive data or monitoring the behaviour of many consumers will be required to appoint a data protection officer; and imposes fines up to €20m or 4% of a company's global revenue for non-compliance. These statutory obligations impose an expensive compliance burden on all organisations regulated by the legislation.

Furthermore, under the General Data Protection Regulation (the GDPR), it is not just member nations that are bound to comply; the regulation also binds any organisation doing business with Europeans. For example, Australian businesses of any size may need to comply if they have an establishment in the EU, if they offer goods and services in the EU, or if they monitor the behaviour of individuals in the EU.[40]

The European Commission's definition of 'personal data' is much wider than Australia's. A general right to privacy does not exist in Australia. However, under the common law, an individual's privacy can be defended by reference to other laws, such as those relating to defamation, nuisance and trespass.[41] Since 1988, Australia has had a statutory regime to protect information about people that is gathered by government and businesses.[42] Australia's *Privacy Act* regulates the handling of personal information.[43] In 2000, amendments to the *Privacy Act*

---

40 To manage this obligation, many countries outside of the European Union have been forced to incorporate accommodate any GDPR provisions that are inconsistent with local data protection rules. For example, the Office of the Australian Information Commissioner has published new guidance for Australian businesses on the European Union's General Data Protection Regulation (GDPR) requirements.

41 *Victoria Park Racing and Recreation Grounds Co Ltd v Taylor* (1937) 58 CLR 479.

42 *Privacy Act 1988* (Cth)

43 Initially, the Australian Privacy Act applied exclusively to the Commonwealth public sector. Public sector agencies are required to comply with the Information Privacy Principles. The Act was amended shortly after its enactment 'to deal with government data-matching activities and the activities of credit providers' and was also extended to cover 'the Australian Capital Territory public sector'.

established a separate set of privacy principles, known as the National Privacy Principles (NPPs), which apply to the private sector in all States.

Australia also has a notifiable data breaches regime.[44] Pursuant to these regulations, any entity bound by Australia's Privacy Principles (an APP entity) is required to notify the Privacy Commissioner and affected individuals if there are reasonable grounds to believe that an 'eligible data breach' has occurred. This notification must happen as soon as reasonably practicable. Where an APP entity merely suspects that there has been an eligible data breach, it must undertake an assessment within 30 days of detecting the breach. Subject to some exceptions, an 'eligible data breach' happens when there is unauthorised access to, unauthorised disclosure of, or loss of, personal information held by an entity; and a reasonable person would conclude that the access, disclosure or loss is likely to result in serious harm to any of the individuals to whom the information relates. The penalties for breach under this regime are much lower than those imposed by the European Union under their GDPR and its mandatory notification requirements.[45]

In the United States legislation has been enacted by all 50 states, the District of Columbia, Puerto Rico and the Virgin Islands that requires private entities or government agencies to notify individuals who have been impacted by security breaches that may compromise their personally identifiable information. These laws typically define what is classified as personally identifiable information in each state, entities required to comply, what specifically constitutes a breach, the timing and method of notice required to individuals and regulatory agencies, and consumer credit reporting agencies, and any exemptions that apply, such as exemptions for encrypted data. Entities that conduct business in any state must be familiar with not only federal regulations, but also individual state laws that apply to any agency or entity that collects, stores or processes data pertaining to residents in that state. While the laws in many states share some core similarities, state legislators have worked to pass laws that best protect the interests of consumers in their respective states. As a result, some states have much more stringent laws or more severe penalties for violations.

It is to be expected that the cost of compliance with data breach and other privacy laws all over the world will be passed on to customers. The cost of cyber security measures, the cost of data protection compliance and the cost of a hack are therefore to be borne by the targeted companies and their

---

44 *Privacy Amendment (Notifiable Data Breaches) Act 2017* (Cth). On 13 February 2017, the Australian Senate passed the *Privacy Amendment (Notifiable Data Breaches) Bill 2016* (Cth) (the Bill). The Governor-General gave formal assent to the Bill on 22 February 2017, which saw the Bill enacted into law from 22 February 2018.

45 The Privacy Commissioner can issue civil penalties for 'serious or repeated interferences of privacy'. The penalties are AU$420,000 for individuals and AU$2.1 million for corporations. See, *Privacy Amendment (Notifiable Data Breaches) Act 2017* (Cth).

customers. It seems law makers everywhere have taken the view that it is of little utility to expect that perpetrators will be identifiable, within any jurisdiction, or that they will be in a position to compensate their victims. Mandatory reporting rules and the sanctions for failure to report an attack shift liability for the consequences of the attack from the gate crasher to the host. Although the hackers are the bad guys, it is the good guys who are made to pay.

The pressure is on all organisations to secure data using technology that is more sophisticated than being deployed by the hackers. However, all indicators point to this being a complex and expensive problem, mainly because the hackers are only in the business of committing cyber-attacks, while their targets regard defending themselves as only secondary to their primary concern, which is the business they are running. There is an asymmetry in the focus of the relative application of resources and energy between the two sides of the attack. The uncertainty created by the very real danger of cyber-attack is just one more catalyst in the ever-decreasing trust being felt by consumers towards organisations and their systems.

12 The Accountability of Algorithms

An algorithm is a step-by-step logical method of solving a problem. It is commonly used for data processing, calculation and other related computer and mathematical operations.

Automated algorithms make decisions that can breathe a new level of power into businesses and governments. Autonomous algorithms rely on data analysis and artificial intelligence to replace human controls and decision-making. Not all automation is algorithmic, but all algorithms automate, and the extension of algorithmic automation from purely mathematical and computational terrains to extended sociotechnical infrastructures has produced profound, ongoing and open-ended transformations in the organisation and function of contemporary social worlds.[1] Automation can include the automatic control of the manufacture of a product through a number of successive stages; the application of automatic control to any branch of industry or science; or, by extension, the use of electronic or mechanical devices to replace human labour.[2] In this context, automation refers to a device or system that accomplishes (partially or fully) a function that was previously, or conceivably could be, carried out (partially or fully) by a human operator.[3]

Algorithms and other 'smart' devices carry out or perform calculations, data processing and automated reasoning tasks. Increasingly, algorithms implement institutional decision-making based on analytics, which involves the discovery, interpretation and communication of meaningful patterns in data. Especially valuable in areas rich with recorded information, analytics relies on the simultaneous application of statistics, computer programming and operations research to quantify performance. That said, there is growing evidence that some algorithms and analytics can be opaque, making it impossible to determine when their outputs may be biased or erroneous.[4]

---

1   I Lowrie, 'Algorithms and Automation: An Introduction' (2018) 33(3) *Cultural Anthropology* 349 <https://doi.org/10.14506/ca33.3.01>.
2   *Oxford English Dictionary* (1989).
3   R Parasuraman and VA Riley, 'Humans and Automation: Use, Misuse, Disuse, Abuse' (1997) 39 *Human Factors* 230.
4   'Statement on Algorithmic Transparency and Accountability', *Association for Computing Machinery US Public Policy Council (USACM)* (12 January 2017) <https://

Algorithms influence almost every aspect of society. The explosive growth of data collection, coupled with increasingly sophisticated algorithms, has resulted in a significant increase in automated decision-making, as well as a greater reliance on algorithms in human decision-making.[5]

Every day automated algorithms make decisions that can amplify the power of businesses and governments. When Facebook delivers us clickbait and conspiracy theories, it uses an algorithm that determines our interests. With notifications and geolocation services switched on, our mobile apps know where we are. This data can be fed back to an algorithm, which in turn suggests (because, for example, it is Friday night and we are still on the way home from work) that we may want to place an advance order for take-away food from our local Thai restaurant. These predictive analytics are driving business marketing strategies all over the world.

This chapter explores the legal issues arising from the development of algorithms to automate and replace professional advice (robo advice) and decision-making in government and commercial contexts (robo decision-making). The particular legal issues to be explored here are pre-programmed bias, anti-competitive behaviour and lack of transparency. The overarching aim of policy-makers and regulators is to ensure that algorithms can comply with the same ethical and regulatory frameworks in which their human counterparts operate. For victims of algorithmic misconduct or wrong-doing, the challenge is to bring to account the actors responsible for the algorithm's behaviour.

The Automation of Algorithms

Algorithms can be programmed to operate independently or in concert with raw or analysed data. This level of automation can relieve individuals of repetitive and low-grade processing tasks and improve the quality of decision-making.

A number of models for levels of automation of algorithms have been suggested to assist in the analysis of action selection and the need for some human control.[6] The model to be used here is the author's model (see Table 12.1),

---

www.acm.org/binaries/content/assets/public-policy/2017usacmstatementalgo
rithms.pdf>.

5   R Dopplick (ACM Director of Public Policy), 'New Statement on Algorithmic Transparency and Accountability by ACM U.S. Public Policy Council', *United States Association for Computing Machinery* (14 January 2017) <https://techp olicy.acm.org/2017/01/new-statement-on-algorithmic-transparency-and-a ccountability-by-acm-u-s-public-policy-council/>.

6   For example, R Parasuraman et al.'s model has 10 levels of automation of decision and action selection, where 10 is the most automated and 1 is the least. At level 10, the computer decides everything, acts autonomously, ignoring the human. At level 1, the computer offers no assistance: the human must take all decisions and actions. See, R Parasuraman, TB Sheridan and CD Wickens, 'A Model for Types and Levels of Human Interaction with Automation' (May 2000) 30(3) *Transactions On Systems, Man, And Cybernetics – Part A: Systems and Humans*, 287.

Table 12.1 A taxonomy for automated algorithms adopting by analogy a taxonomy for autonomous vehicles

Level of autonomy	Description for self-driving vehicles	Description for automated algorithms
0	No driving automation. The driver (human) controls it all: steering, brakes, throttle, power. Warning systems on, but no self-control.	Traditional use of computer program, where every step is known and the sequence of instructions is written to perform a specific task with a computer. No conditional logic.
1	'Hands on' (e.g. cruise control). Driver still responsible for monitoring the conditions of the road and traffic. This driver-assistance level means that most functions are still controlled by the driver, but a specific function (like steering or accelerating) can be done automatically by the car.	Algorithms that execute exactly as they are set up to by their creators. The algorithm will only proceed if certain conditions are met. In this case, the algorithms would depend upon human control to input data so that it could execute the desired command.
2	'Hands off' (e.g. assisted parking). At least one driver assistance system is automated (e.g. cruise control and lane-centring). Driver's hands off steering wheel, foot off pedal.	Algorithm is triggered by a human. The algorithm can perform functions when a required set of conditions are met (including for example, that a set of data satisfies a test). Human can override.
3	'Eyes off' (e.g. car knows when to slow down). Driver still necessary, but are able to completely shift 'safety-critical functions' to the vehicle, under certain traffic or environmental conditions.	Algorithm is triggered by a data set or another algorithm. Human intervention is still possible. Human intervention is required under certain conditions.
4	'Mind off' (car may need to stop in new scenarios). Vehicles are designed to perform all safety-critical driving functions and monitor roadway conditions for an entire trip. Limited to operational domain of vehicle - not all driving scenarios.	Algorithm is capable of functioning without the participation of external systems. However, as with vehicles, this autonomy is limited to the operational domain of the algorithm. It does not cover every scenario. New or unusual conditions may call for human intervention.
5	Full driving automation - no human intervention required, no steering wheel required	Full algorithm automation - no human intervention required.

based upon the Society of Automotive Engineers' taxonomy used for levels of driving automation.[7]

According to this model, algorithms at automation levels 0, 1 or 2 would be relatively benign programs and would not raise concern about their behaviour. Any level of automation above level 3 would deliver efficiencies and cost savings, but the application of these high levels of automation may need to be limited to use cases where there is a low level of risk for the network or ecosystem in which they operate. This security-efficiency trade-off must be applied consciously within a transparent governance regime in order to maintain trust in the system.

How particular functions are automated and the characteristics of the associated sensors, controls and software are major priorities in the development of automated systems. This is perhaps not surprising given the sophistication and ingenuity of the design of many such systems (for example, the automatic landing of a jumbo jet, or the docking of two spacecraft). The economic benefits that automation can provide, or are perceived to offer, also tend to focus public attention on the technical capabilities of automation.[8]

Deterministic and Probabilistic Behaviour of Algorithms

Big data and data science have transformed organisational decision-making. It is important to identify the different frameworks for the use of big data. Data analysis can support or replace human decision-making; and the output can be either probabilistic or deterministic. The behaviour of deterministic algorithms can be predicted because all data upon which the algorithm relies is known at the outset. With probabilistic behaviour there is an element of chance involved in the outcome, because not all data is known. Knowing which of these behaviours an algorithm will adopt and why is important for any assessment of risk.

Everything else being equal, it may seem that deterministic algorithms would be less risky and the outputs more trustworthy than their probablistic counterparts. This impression arises from the certainty surrounding the content of the data set that is used. Although it is tempting to arrive at this conclusion, it is not necessarily the case. Some algorithms need to analyse data based on characteristics that are hard to predict.

A good example of the difference between deterministic and probabilistic outputs is seen in data matching. In deterministic matching, either unique identifiers for each record are compared, or an exact comparison is used between fields, to determine a match. Deterministic matching is generally not

7   'SAE J3016 Levels of Driving Automation', *SAE International* (2014) <https://blogs. forbes.com/samabuelsamid/files/2018/07/SAE-Driving-Levels-5July18-1.jpg>.

8   R Parasuraman, TB Sheridan and CD Wickens, 'A Model for Types and Levels of Human Interaction with Automation' (May 2000) 30(3) *Transactions On Systems, Man, And Cybernetics – Part A: Systems and Humans*, 286.

completely reliable since in some cases no single field can provide a reliable match between two records. This is where probabilistic, or 'fuzzy', matching comes in. In probabilistic matching, several field values are compared between two records and each field is assigned a weight that indicates how closely the two field values match. The sum of the individual fields weights indicates the likelihood of a match between two records.[9]

One way to manage risk in all algorithms is to increase the complexity of the conditional logic to account for known problems with the data. However, with this higher level of complexity comes a risk that unknown problems have been overlooked, and that the operation of the algorithm is harder to explain and manage from a governance perspective.

One way of managing the use of probabilistic data is for the algorithm to disclose its level of certainty in its results. For example, IBM's super computer 'Watson' employs more than 50 scoring components that produce scores ranging from formal probabilities to counts of categorical features based on evidence from different types of sources. Such sources include unstructured text, semi-structured text and triple stores (that is, the generation of multiple search queries for a single question, and backfilling hit lists to satisfy key constraints identified in the question). These scorers consider a range of factors including the degree of match between a passage's predicate-argument structure, (for example, *Alice ran for office*, or *Bob ate his dinner*), and the question, passage source reliability, geospatial location, temporal relationships,[10] taxonomic classification, the lexical and semantic relations the subject is known to participate in, the subject's correlation with question terms, its popularity (or obscurity) and its aliases.

Because of the varying levels of certainty with which these outputs are delivered, different algorithms are suited to difference use-cases. Although not absolute, the clearest division is in giving advice versus reaching a decision. The former lends itself to providing a probabilistic output, whereas the automation of decision-making requires a clear determination. Where an output is probabilistic, a next step must be considered before automating its output. That step is whether a system's percentage of probability of accuracy will suffice to continue the automated process or whether human intervention is required. In the case of Watson, its goal is not to replace a human, but to augment their decision-making. Watson is well-suited to those grey areas where there is no perfect right or wrong answer. It considers millions of hypotheses, tests them against what it knows to be true and gives its best answer, with a percentage of

9   'Deterministic and Probabilistic Data Matching', *Oracle – Master Index Match Engine Reference* (2010) <https://docs.oracle.com/cd/E19182-01/821-0919/refsme-deter-problc/index.html>.

10 Temporal reasoning is used in Watson to detect inconsistencies between dates in the clue and those associated with a candidate answer. See, 'The AI Behind Watson – The Technical Article', *AI Magazine* (2010) <https://www.aaai.org/Magazine/Watson/watson.php>.

certainty. It is then up to a human - say a doctor or an investment banker - to make the relevant decision.[11]

Understanding this distinction between deterministic and probabilistic outcomes or outputs is important when deciding how to programme an algorithm and what data it will use in order to reach its decision. The automation of decision-making is fundamentally distinguishable from the automation of advice-giving. Decision-making is determinative, whereas advice is probabilistic.

Robo Advice

One of the most significant recent technological developments concerns the application of robotics and AI to skill-intensive, and knowledge-based jobs. The financial adviser is a role that has been identified as being under threat from automated 'robo-advice' services. Financial advice is big business. In 2010, registered investment advisers in the United States, (who are regulated by the Securities Exchange Commission) managed more than US$38 trillion for more than 14 million clients.[12]

For the purposes of this discussion, it is important to note the difference between the automation of giving 'personal advice' and merely providing 'product information'.[13] Both of these types of output may be provided via an algorithm based on the way that particular declared data is inputted by a client or customer. However, receiving general financial product or legal information from a website is very different to receiving tailored personal advice that has been pre-programmed and then generated automatically.

In Australia, factual information is considered to be 'objectively ascertainable information, the truth or accuracy of which cannot reasonably be questioned'.[14] Businesses providing factual information are not required to hold an Australian Financial Services Licence (AFSL). However, professional financial advisers who provide general advice or personal advice are required to hold an AFSL or be an authorised representative of a license holder.[15]

11 J Niccolai, 'IBM Watson Will Know What You Did Last Summer', *ComputerWorld* (24 September 2015) <https://www.computerworld.com.au/article/585275/ibm-watson-will-know-what-did-last-summer/>.

12 'Study on Investment Advisers and Broker-Dealers (As Required by Section 913 of the Dodd-Frank Wall Street Reform and Consumer Protection Act)', *US Securities Exchange Commission* (January 2011) <https://www.sec.gov/news/studies/2011/913studyfinal.pdf>.

13 'Personal advice' is defined in section 766B(3) of Australia's *Corporations Act 2001* (Cth) as: 'financial product advice given or directed to a person (including by electronic means) in circumstances where the provider of the advice has considered one or more of the client's objectives, financial situation and needs; or a reasonable person might expect the provider to have considered one or more of these matters'.

14 'Giving Financial Product Advice', *Australian Securities and Investments Commission* (20 December 2018) <https://asic.gov.au/regulatory-resources/financial-services/giving-financial-product-advice/>

15 'Regulatory Guide 175 – Licensing: Financial Product Advisers – Conduct and Disclosure', *Australian Securities and Investments Commission* (March 2017)

In March 2016, Australia's corporate watchdog, ASIC, issued guidance in the form of a consultation paper in relation to the provision of 'robo-advice'. The consultation paper sets out ASIC's proposed approach to the regulation of digital financial advice in Australia.[16] According to ASIC, digital advice (also known as 'robo-advice' or 'automated advice') is the provision of automated financial product advice using algorithms and technology and without the direct involvement of a human adviser. It can comprise general or personal advice, and range from advice that is narrow in scope (for example, advice about portfolio construction) to comprehensive financial product advice. 'General advice' will generally be treated as 'financial product advice' and is therefore not 'personal advice'.[17]

It is also useful to distinguish robo-advice from hypothetical clients. With developments in data analytics, digital advisers can create a hypothetical client who is (for example) of a certain age, gender, profession, marital status and residential area. Using this information, a digital adviser could ascertain the typical financial situation, needs, objectives and risk appetite of a client, based on data from previous clients who share similar characteristics. Advice given in this context may not be personal advice, as it has been given based on a theoretical client's needs and objectives. This raises interesting policy questions. For example, is the advice prepared for the hypothetical client just general information or has it become tailored financial advice?

Replacing human financial advisers with robo-advisers seems to make sense from an economic perspective – as they cost less than their human counterparts and make fewer mistakes.[18] Degeling and Hudson argue that the 'robot' in this scenario is not the financial adviser, 'Rather, the financial robot is the digital means by which the advice is manifested and/or communicated'.[19] However, the Australian regulator describes robo-advice as, 'Advice that's delivered by a computer instead of a human financial adviser'.[20] These definitional inconsistencies can create challenges for lawyers and courts that seek to

<http://download.asic.gov.au/media/4191992/rg175-published-22-march-2017.pdf>.

16 'CP 254 – Regulating Digital Financial Product Advice', *Australian Securities and Investments Commission* (21 March 2016) <https://asic.gov.au/regulatory-resources/find-a-document/consultation-papers/cp-254-regulating-digital-financial-product-advice/>.

17 General advice is financial advice that does not take into account an individual's objectives, financial situation or needs, while personal advice is financial advice tailored to an individual's unique situation. In Australia, the authority for this proposition is *Corporations Act 2001* (Cth), section 766B 'Meaning of financial product advice'.

18 C Coombs and A Redman, 'The Impact of Robo-Advice on Financial Advisers: A Qualitative Case Study', *UK Academy for Information Systems* (2018) <https://dspace.lboro.ac.uk/2134/32441>.

19 S Degeling and J Hudson, 'Financial Robots as Instruments of Fiduciary Loyalty' (2018) 40(1) *Sydney Law Review* 63, 63.

20 'Robo-advice', *ASIC MoneySmart* (12 November 2018) <https://www.moneysmart.gov.au/investing/financial-advice/robo-advice>.

interpret and apply the law. However, it is likely that simply 'looking under the hood' of what is being automated may resolve any confusion that arises from these conflicting views. For example, if the algorithm that is driving the process of delivering advice is programmatic and not self-learning, then the Degeling-Hudson definition should apply. However, if the algorithm is self-learning and has been optimised to use data to improve its own processes, then the computer has taken over.

Robo Decision-making

Automation of decision-making through application of machine learning algorithms is one way to pursue efficiency and accuracy.[21] The popularity of robo decision-making is evidenced in the number of amendments to UK and Australian legislation to allow ministers to use computer programs to make decisions at their discretion. In Australia, for example, these include in relation to migration,[22] social security,[23] taxation,[24] citizenship,[25] superannuation,[26] consumer credit,[27] paid parental leave,[28] carbon credits[29] and business names registration.[30]

However, in public administration and administrative review, the automation of decision-making requires particularly close scrutiny before implementation. An example of the negative consequences that can flow from outsourcing administrative decision-making to an algorithm played out in Australia in 2016–2018 in what came to be known as the 'robo-debt debacle'.[31]

Australian law explicitly allows computers to make important decisions previously made by the ministers or staff of at least 11 federal government departments. This has been going on since at least 2001 and, despite a recent push for more openness, there remains little clarity about exactly what decisions are being entrusted to the computers. One example was the amendment to the *Social Security (Administration) Act 1999* (Cth) granting power to the

---

21　T Carney, 'The New Digital Future for Welfare', *University of New South Wales Law Journal Forum* 1, 1 (2018) <http://www.unswlawjournal.unsw.edu.au/wp-content/uploads/2018/03/006-Carney.pdf>.

22　*Migration Act 1958* (Cth), s 495A.

23　*Social Security (Administration) Act 1999* (Cth), s 6.

24　*A New Tax System (Family Assistance) (Administration) Act 1999* (Cth), s 223.

25　*Australian Citizenship Act 2007* (Cth), s 48.

26　*Superannuation (Government Co-contribution for Low Income Earners) Act 2003* (Cth), s 48.

27　*National Consumer Credit Protection Act 2009* (Cth), s 242.

28　*Paid Parental Leave Act 2010* (Cth), s 305.

29　*Carbon Credits (Carbon Farming Initiative) Act 2011*(Cth), s 287.

30　*Business Names Registration Act 2011* (Cth), s 66.

31　J Revanche, 'After the "Robo-Debt" Debacle, Traumatised Users Find Support in Online Communities', *The Guardian* (4 January 2018) <https://www.theguardian.com/commentisfree/2018/jan/04/after-the-robo-debt-debacle-traumatised-users-find-support-in-online-communities>.

Commonwealth Government to automate notices to welfare recipients demanding repayment of overpayments. In 2016, the Australian Government introduced an automated 'online compliance intervention' that compared information gathered from the Australian Taxation Office and the Department of Human Services to assess whether recipients of welfare and other Centrelink payments had been overpaid. If the system detected overpayment, then (employing a statutory power to convert overpayment into a debt) a letter was sent to the debtor demanding repayment. Before automating this process, the Australian Government sent 20,000 'intervention' letters each year. After automation, the number of letter swelled to 20,000 per week.[32]

The Australian Government's implementation of its debt recovery programme resulted in a backlash from welfare recipients, the Commonwealth Ombudsman, community legal centres and the press. The main problems were threefold: a significant number of the letters contained estimates of debt that were plainly wrong; the debt letter did not include a review mechanism so that the debt would be stayed pending further correspondence; and the debt letters for many of recipients (whether correct or not) caused significant distress to members of the community who are already vulnerable or dependent upon welfare and therefore ill-equipped to repay the asserted debts within the period given. The Ombudsman was later accused of not having properly assessed the legality of the 'robo-debt' initiative.[33]

What the Australian example revealed was a need for due diligence before algorithms are used to replace decision-making on behalf government agencies. Allowing an algorithm to make decisions raises more than just ethical questions.

In order to trust the automation of complex decision-making, minimum technical standards must be assured in relation to the way that algorithms are programmed. These minimum standards must include ensuring that accuracy of any data that the algorithm will calculate or analyse; considering whether the system will be purely programmatic (and therefore predictable) or self-learning (in which case it may be hard for humans to understand or monitor how the system decides to optimise); and ensuring that all processes will be transparent. However, the most important factor is the instructions provided by the human director of the automated programme. As one critic of the Australian 'pay up letter' debacle commented, 'This isn't a bug in an IT system: it's an executive giving systems developers instructions to implement a malicious system'.[34]

32 H Pett and C Cosier, 'We're All Talking About the Centrelink Debt Controversy, But What Is "Robodebt" Anyway?', *ABC News* (3 March 2017) <https://www.abc.net.au/news/2017-03-03/centrelink-debt-controversy-what-is-robodebt/8317764>.

33 P Karp, 'Ombudsman Failed to Check Legality of Robo-Debt, Former Tribunal Member Says', *The Guardian* (7 April 2018) <https://www.theguardian.com/a ustralia-news/2018/apr/07/ombudsman-failed-to-check-legality-of-robo-debt-former-tribunal-member-says>. See also, T Carney, 'The New Digital Future for Welfare', *University of New South Wales Law Journal Forum* (2018) <http://www.unswlawjournal.unsw.edu.au/wp-content/uploads/2018/03/006-Carney.pdf>.

34 R Chirgwin, 'Australia: Stop Blaming Centrelink Debts on Its IT Systems', *The Register Co UK* (6 January 2017) <https://www.theregister.co.uk/2017/01/06/australiastopblamingcentrelinkdebtsonitsitsystems/>.

Trust in decision-making by government agencies is central to citizen satisfaction and a functioning economy. Radical information technologies may work to alter the production or maintenance of trust.[35] When government adopts technologies that automate their processes, it is just as important to ensure that these systems can be and are trusted. This is because when a government decides to adopt technology to interact with citizens, the website, chat bots and automated reporting systems begin to look and feel like they are government. It is possible that citizens will only interact with their government via online systems. This is particularly the case where agencies have long waiting periods for telephone customer service.

There are examples of algorithms that are designed to help reduce human bias in decision-making. For example, predictive judicial analytics technologies have been developed with a view to increasing efficiency and fairness in the law. Judicial analytics can assess extra-legal factors that influence decisions.[36]

The most effective strategies that Western governments and courts can adopt to improve trust in official decision-making are transparency and interactivity. If citizens feel that government websites are interacting with them in a way that is fair, understandable and open, they will feel satisfaction with and trust in e-government. As it currently stands, trust in government can improve. Trust in the way that government delivers services and enforces rules (whether this is through human or digital agents) directly influences compliance and therefore corruption. If business owners and individuals do not trust government and its systems, they will work around them. They will flout the law. This in turn erodes social cohesion and economic health. Decision-making by government, trust in government and the health of the economy are inextricably interwoven.

Robo Sellers

In the United States, anti-competitive use of 'robo sellers' or automated pricing systems has already been the target of enforcement actions by the Department of Justice as well as the subject of intense debate among anti-trust practitioners and academics.[37]

---

35 EW Welch, CC Hinnant and MJ Moon, 'Linking Citizen Satisfaction with E-Government and Trust in Government' (2005) 15(3) *Journal of Public Administration Research and Theory* 371, 371.

36 D Chen, 'Judicial Analytics and the Great Transformation of American Law', *Journal of Artificial Intelligence and the Law* (2019) 27.1 *Artificial Intelligence and Law* 15. <http://users.nber.org/~dlchen/papers/JudicialAnalyticsandtheGreatTransformationofAmericanLaw.pdf>.

37 SK Mehra, 'Antitrust and the Robo-Seller: Competition in the Time of Algorithms' (2015–2016) 100 *Minnesota Law Review* 1323.

Pricing algorithms are designed to collect and analyse a large quantity of market data in order to price products and services - taking into account a range of factors. With the help of a pricing algorithm, a business can react almost instantaneously to price movements by competitors. Moreover, because a computer program generates the actual prices for transactions while evaluating complex data with a level of speed and sophistication that a human cannot replicate, the use of pricing algorithms creates a perception that price-setting is entirely machine-driven. But it is the human element in the way that the algorithm is programmed that creates potential anti-trust liability.[38]

United States regulators and enforcers take the view that the legal standard for finding unlawful collusion does not need to change in the context of pricing algorithms, and that independent use of pricing algorithms that interact with each other, without an agreement to fix prices, should not give rise to liability. A key area where competition issues may arise is the risk of collusion. Collusion is a prohibited practice. It arises when competitors in market agree upon the price that they will charge to customers or the price that they are willing to pay to suppliers. This anti-competitive behaviour leads to poor decision-making by competitors and synthetically manipulates supply and demand. Collusion leads to poor economic outcomes. On the other hand, mere 'parallel conduct' is considered a rational response to market conditions, and so is permitted. Parallel conduct occurs when business competitors adopt the same pricing or economic terms or engage in the same conduct. In *Bell Atlantic Corporation v Twombly*,[39] the United States Supreme Court held that parallel conduct, absent evidence of agreement, is insufficient to sustain an anti-trust action under Section 1 of the *Sherman Act*.[40]

The *Sherman Act* prohibits entering into a 'contract, combination or conspiracy' for the purpose of restraining trade. This is a provision that regulates anti-competition. The Supreme Court held that while parallel conduct (actions by competing companies that might be seen as implying some agreement to work together) is 'admissible circumstantial evidence' from which an agreement to engage in anti-competitive behaviour may be inferred, parallel conduct alone is insufficient to prove a *Sherman Act* claim.

Concern has been raised by some about the role that machine learning algorithms will have in the way prices are determined and whether this could potentially lead to collusive outcomes. It is possible that, in the right market conditions, pricing algorithms may engage in and sustain collusion, whether 'tacit' or not.

38　DI Ballard and AD Naik, 'Algorithms, Artificial Intelligence, and Joint Conduct', *Competition Policy International* (May 2017) <https://www.competitionpoli cyinternational.com/wp-content/uploads/2017/05/CPI-Ballard-Naik.pdf>.

39　*Bell Atlantic Corp v Twombly*, 550 U.S. 544 (2007) (Steven J dissenting).

40　The Sherman Antitrust Act of 1890 is a United States federal statute that prohibits activities that restrict interstate commerce and competition in the marketplace. The Sherman Act was amended by the Clayton Act in 1914. The Sherman Act is codified in 15 U.S.C. §§ 1–38.

A profit maximising algorithm could work out the pricing game and using its core logic to achieve maximum profit at the expense of legislation. Coding anti-competition rules into a program that is designed to maximise the way it competes could create design conundrums for developers. To complicate matters further, the development of deep-learning and artificial intelligence may mean that companies will not necessarily know how, or why, a machine came to a particular conclusion.

It is argued that if similar algorithms are deployed by competing companies, an anti-competitive equilibrium may be achieved without contravening competition laws.[41] However, this suggestion that competitors could share the algorithms that are programmed to behave in a way that is competitive also lacks logic. The unilateral use of algorithms can lead to tacit collusion by algorithms.[42] Collusion is more than just price-fixing. Collusion occurs when a few players in the market deliberately behave in a way that will exclude new players. It also includes setting output quota and agreeing to prices paid to suppliers. All of these behaviours are anti-competitive and the possibility of this occurring only increases if shared algorithms are programmed to optimise profits. At this time, authorities lack the ability to address effectively this type of algorithmic anti-competitive conduct. The Australian regulator has warned that firms cannot avoid liability by saying 'my robot did it'.[43]

Algorithmic Bias

Setting aside fraud and other wrong-doing, the riches to be won by disrupting the financial services industry provide more than enough incentive to rush technology into the market. In addition, there are concerns that automation may entrench historical unfairness and promote a financial services monoculture with new opportunities to exploit customers and a greater vulnerability to catastrophic failure than the less coordinated actions of humans working without automated advice.

Industry forecasters believe software programs incorporating automated decision-making will only increase in the coming years as artificial intelligence becomes more mainstream. One of the major challenges of this emerging reality is to ensure that algorithms do not reinforce harmful and/or unfair biases.

Algorithmic bias is a phenomenon that has been observed in various contexts. Despite a widespread belief that software and algorithms that rely on

41 See, R Sims (Conference Chair), 'Can Robots Collude?', *Speech delivered at the ACCC Conference* (16 November 2017) <https://www.accc.gov.au/speech/the-a ccc%E2%80%99s-approach-to-colluding-robots>.

42 K Lee, 'Algorithmic Collusion & Its Implications for Competition Law and Policy', *SSRN* (14 August 2018) <https://papers.ssrn.com/sol3/papers.cfm?abstractid= 3213296>.

43 See, R Sims (Conference Chair), 'Can Robots Collude?', *Speech delivered at the ACCC Conference* (16 November 2017) <https://www.accc.gov.au/speech/the-a ccc%E2%80%99s-approach-to-colluding-robots>.

data are objective,[44] software is not free of human influence. Algorithms are written and maintained by people, and machine-learning algorithms adjust what they do based on people's behaviour. As a result, say researchers in computer science, ethics and law, algorithms can reinforce human prejudices.[45] Since the early 2010s, concerns have been growing about how machines interpret data and then optimise outcomes. For example, pre-programmed prejudices that were present in existing and historical data may inform the way that the particular machine or algorithm will determine a correct outcome or optimise its own functionality. Two legally problematic examples of algorithmic bias in business include discrimination by algorithms and anti-competitive behaviour by self-learning machines.

With the advent of robo-recruiting and the use of data analytics to support criminal sentencing, it is important to test the outcomes produced by the pre-set logic that drives the automation of decision-making. Importantly, recruiters (for example) need to question the outcomes they want to ensure. Concealing personal information on job applications (for example, name, citizenship, phone number, address, languages spoken, religious references and educational institution) can result in fewer minorities actually making it through a first screening round than when that information is front and centre. To improve diversity usually requires a concerted campaign to positively discriminate in favour of those who are under-represented. If an algorithm is only programmed to counter implicit bias, then minorities are even less likely to be recruited and promoted because they are – by definition – either under-represented statistically in the population or in the particular cohort of applicants. In the case of data-driven criminal sentencing, the hope is the court's assessment of whether to grant bail (for example) can be assisted with tools that can help identify patterns of recidivism in defendants. Judging an individual defendant's potential to re-offend has long been a fundamental part of the criminal sentencing and bail application process. Most often, these judgments are made on the basis of some gut instinct. Proponents of using big data and analysis tools in these difficult process can offer a uniform and transparent approach to determine risk.[46]

---

44   CC Miller, 'Can an Algorithm Hire Better Than a Human?', *The New York Times* (25 June 2015) <https://www.nytimes.com/2015/06/26/upshot/can-an-algorithm-hire-better-than-a-human.html?module=inline>; and H Devlin, 'Discrimination by Algorithm: Scientists Devise Test to Detect AI Bias', *The Guardian* (19 December 2016) <https://www.theguardian.com/technology/2016/dec/19/discrimination-by-algorithm-scientists-devise-test-to-detect-ai-bias>.

45   CC Miller, 'When Algorithms Discriminate', *The New York Times* (9 June 2015) <https://www.nytimes.com/2015/07/10/upshot/when-algorithms-discriminate.html>.

46   M Hamilton, 'We Use Big Data to Sentence Criminals, But Can the Algorithms Really Tell Us What We Need to Know', *The Conversation* (6 June 2017) <https://theconversation.com/we-use-big-data-to-sentence-criminals-but-can-the-algorithms-really-tell-us-what-we-need-to-know-77931>.

There is a direct relationship between transparency and trust. In order to trust algorithms, the basis of their behaviour must be made openly available and subject to scrutiny. Trust is a key concern in the design of technology, as it affects its initial adoption and continued use.

Trust is understood as 'an attitude of confident expectation in an online situation of risk that one's vulnerabilities will not be exploited'.[47] Trust in a system requires transparency, but can be lost quickly if expectations are violated (whether the reason for the violation is explained or not). Fulfilling expectations is an important aspect in the maintenance of trust.

A major problem with algorithms, algorithmic bias and technology generally is that in many domains, they are held to a higher standard than humans undertaking similar functions. This is readily understood when thinking about automated vehicles: people will not adopt or trust self-driving vehicles until they can guarantee the safety of passengers and pedestrians. This is stark contrast to the acceptance of human drivers of vehicles, notwithstanding the thousands of road deaths caused globally every year by humans. This expectation also arises in relation to bias. Human decisions have always been skewed by some level of conscious or unconscious bias and yet we reject any algorithm that demonstrates even the slightest hint of bias. This propensity to hold technology to account at a higher standard than humans can manifest as a disproportionate lack of trust in a technology that is actually performing at a superior level to humans. The consequences for government-use of decision-making algorithms means that managing trust in these situations demands particular attention if there is not going to be wider negative consequences for the economic fabric of society.

Anti-competitive Behaviour

Anti-competitive practices are business, government or religious practices that prevent or reduce competition in a market. Standard anti-competitive regulation prohibits contracts, arrangements, understandings or concerted practices that have the purpose, effect or likely effect of substantially lessening competition in a market, even if that conduct does not meet the stricter definitions of other anti-competitive conduct.

Anti-competitive (or 'anti-trust' behaviour) is not allowed in most economies. There seems to be an inherent conflict of interest created by the regulatory requirement not to behave in a way that is anti-competitive, while at the same time competing with others in the market. However, a closer look at different types of anti-competitive behaviour clearly characterises such activity as either deceptive or monopolistic. For example, forming a cartel is a type of anti-

47 RF Kizilcec, 'How Much Information? Effects of Transparency on Trust in an Algorithmic Interface', *Department of Communication, Stanford University* (May 2016) <http://edithlaw.ca/cs889/2018/reading/Experimenting/Paper1.pdf>.

competitive behaviour. Cartels are businesses that make agreements with their competitors to fix prices, rig bids, share markets or restrict outputs. These businesses are breaking laws and stealing from consumers and businesses by inflating prices, reducing choices and damaging the economy. Other examples include collective bargaining and boycotts,[48] exclusive dealing,[49] imposition of minimum resale prices,[50] misuse of market power,[51] a refusal to supply products or services[52] and unconscionable conduct.[53]

While there are many economic advantages, realised and unrealised, in data-driven innovation, there are also potential competition issues. Regulators in a number of jurisdictions are already considering cases where algorithms have been deployed as a tool to facilitate conduct which may contravene competition law.

Price fixing cartels are illegal, irrespective of the means by which they are implemented or operated. Algorithms can be used intentionally to implement, monitor and police cartels. In this scenario, humans agree to collude and machines execute the collusion, acting as mere intermediaries or messengers.

David Topkins, the founder of 'Poster Revolution' (an online seller of posters, prints and other merchandise), was the first senior manager from an e-commerce business to be prosecuted under anti-trust law by the United States Department of Justice. On the day after Easter in 2015, Topkins was served with a complaint filed by the United States Department of Justice's San Francisco division. The complaint charged Topkins with one count of price-fixing, in violation of the *Sherman Act*. The department alleged that Topkins had conspired with other online sellers between September 2013 and January 2014 to fix the prices of certain posters sold on Amazon Marketplace.

48 It is against the law in Australia for businesses to fix prices, restrict outputs or allocate customers, suppliers or territories. But most regulators will grant businesses an exemption providing protection from legal action under the relevant competition and consumer protection laws when such conduct results in benefits to the public.

49 Broadly speaking, exclusive dealing occurs when one person trading with another imposes some restrictions on the other's freedom to choose with whom, in what or where they deal. Exclusive dealing is against the law in Australia, the UK, the USA and other developed economies only when it substantially lessens competition.

50 A supplier may recommend that resellers charge an appropriate price for particular goods or services but may not stop resellers charging or advertising below that price.

51 A business with a substantial degree of power in a market is not allowed to engage in conduct that has the purpose, effect or likely effect of substantially lessening competition in a market. This behaviour is referred to as 'misuse of market power'. It is not illegal to have, or to seek to obtain, market power by offering the best products and services.

52 In most cases, businesses have the right to decide who they do business with. There are a few circumstances, where a supplier's refusal to supply is breaking the law.

53 Unconscionable conduct is generally understood to mean conduct which is so harsh that it goes against good conscience. Under the Australian Consumer Law, businesses must not engage in unconscionable conduct, when dealing with other businesses or their customers.

According to prosecutors, Topkins and his co-conspirators collected, exchanged, monitored and discussed how much to charge for posters that were sold, distributed and paid for on Amazon's auction site. The tool underlying Topkins' apparent misdeeds was an algorithm he had coded to instruct his company's software to set prices. Topkins pleaded guilty and agreed to pay a US$20,000 fine.[54]

What this case indicates and the warning that emerges in relation to the increasing use of automated artificial intelligence is that algorithms will widen instances in which known forms of anti-competitive conduct occurs.

Algorithmic markets will display new forms of anti-competitive conduct beyond just collusion and price fixing. In addition to these traditional forms of anti-competition, algorithms will optimise data capture, data extraction and the way that consumers are co-opted into using certain platforms. The reason why algorithms will succeed in achieving these outcomes is because they are designed to operate in the background, behind the scenes, so that the consumer's user experience makes them feel as though their interaction with the particular website or app is serving their needs (that is, the consumer's needs). A superior user experience hides the reality that the product or service is just a sideline in their vendor's business model, the majority of which trades in data.

Transparency Policies for Code, Data and Algorithms

Big data and data science transform organisational decision-making. We increasingly defer decisions to algorithms because machines have earned a reputation of outperforming us.

Australia's *Digital Service Standard* suggests that programmers should make all new source code open by default.[55] The Standard regards as important the value of making sure that the code is open, so that others can re-use it. Making code 'open source', will reduce the costs of projects (for developers and others), prevent duplication of work, increase transparency and add benefits (including improvement of the code by other developers). Developers are also encouraged to test the code in a *Beta* environment,[56] and to be explicit with users about licensing and how bugs and fixes will be handled.[57]

---

54 J Priluck, 'When Bots Collude', *The New Yorker* (25 April 2015) <https://www. newyorker.com/business/currency/when-bots-collude>.

55 Australian Digital Codes, 'Digital Service Standard – 8 Make Source Code Open' <http s://guides.service.gov.au/digital-service-standard/8-make-source-code-open/>.

56 A beta environment is a test version of a platform that will not affect production data. It is a way running live code in real time, but with minimal risk. They are usually provided for free or significantly reduced rates to low risk users. Automated and manual feedback systems provide reports on bugs and errors that can be fixed to improve the alpha version.

57 Australian Digital Codes, 'Digital Service Standard – 8 Make Source Code Open' <http s://guides.service.gov.au/digital-service-standard/8-make-source-code-open/>.

As algorithms become embedded within organisations, they become more influential and increasingly opaque. Those who create algorithms may make arbitrary decisions in all stages of the 'data value chain', yet these subjectivities are obscured from view. Algorithms come to reflect the biases of their creators, can reinforce established ways of thinking and may favour some political orientations over others. This is a cause for concern and calls for more transparency in the development, implementation and use of algorithms in public- and private-sector organisations.[58] In recent years, scientists have devised a way to test whether an algorithm is introducing gender or racial biases into decision-making.

The challenges automated advice pose to regulators seeking to preserve the integrity of financial markets do not stop there. There are well-known privacy and security challenges that accompany the digitisation of personal financial data.[59]

The Public Policy Council of the United States Association for Computing Machinery propose seven principles for Algorithmic Transparency and Accountability:

1 Awareness: Owners, designers, builders, users, and other stakeholders of analytic systems should be aware of the possible biases involved in their design, implementation, use and the potential harm that biases can cause to individuals and society.

2 Access and redress: Regulators should encourage the adoption of mechanisms that enable questioning and redress for individuals and groups that are adversely affected by algorithmically informed decisions.

3 Accountability: Institutions should be held responsible for decisions made by the algorithms that they use, even if it is not feasible to explain in detail how the algorithms produce their results.

4 Explanation: Systems and institutions that use algorithmic decision-making are encouraged to produce explanations regarding both the procedures followed by the algorithm and the specific decisions that are made. This is particularly important in public policy contexts.

5 Data Provenance: A description of the way in which the training data was collected should be maintained by the builders of the algorithms, and accompanied by an exploration of the potential biases induced by the human or algorithmic data-gathering process. Public scrutiny of the data provides maximum opportunity for corrections. However, concerns over privacy, protecting trade secrets or revelation of analytics that might allow

---

58 J Kemper and D Kolkman, 'Transparent to Whom? No Algorithmic Accountability Without a Critical Audience', *Information, Communication & Society* (Rcvd 4 October 2017, Accepted 11 May 2018, Published online 18 June 2018) <https://www.tandfonline.com/doi/full/10.1080/1369118X.2018.1477967>.

59 T Baker and B Dellaert, 'Regulating Robo Advice across the Financial Services Industry' (2018) Faculty Scholarship at Penn Law 1740, 1742, 715 <https://scholarship.law.upenn.edu/faculty_scholarship/1740>.

malicious actors to game the system can justify restricting access to qualified and authorised individuals.

6   Auditability: Models, algorithms, data and decisions should be recorded so that they can be audited in cases where harm is suspected.

7   Validation and Testing: Institutions should use rigorous methods to validate their models and document those methods and results. In particular, they should routinely perform tests to assess and determine whether the model generates discriminatory harm. Institutions are encouraged to make the results of such tests public.[60]

What all seven of these principles have in common is transparency and human oversight: formal and informal processes to deliver transparency in relation to the code, the data upon which algorithms rely, the way the algorithm is tested and whether it can be audited. All of these functions combine to deliver a more trustworthy system. The emergence of robo advice does not dispense with the role people play in the financial services industry. People design, model, program, implement and market these automated advisors, and many automated advisors operate behind the scenes, assisting people who interact with clients and customers.

While robo advisors have the potential to outperform humans in matching consumers to mass market financial products, they are not inherently immune from the misalignment of incentives that has historically affected financial product intermediaries.[61] A robo advisor can be designed to ignore those incentives, but many consumer financial product intermediaries that develop or purchase robo advisors are subject to those incentives.[62] It would be naive simply to assume that intermediaries will always choose the algorithms and architecture that are best for consumers, rather than those that are best for the intermediaries. This means that regulators should take a more active role in assessing robo advisors as robo advisors grow in scale.

In the case of David Topkins and his business 'Poster Revolution', he and his co-conspirators had adopted specific pricing algorithms that collected competitors' pricing information, with the goal of coordinating changes to their pricing strategies for the sale of posters on Amazon Marketplace. Algorithm-driven (or bot-driven) selling poses a new and formidable challenge to

---

60   'Statement on Algorithmic Transparency and Accountability', *Association for Computing Machinery US Public Policy Council (USACM)* (12 January 2017) <https://www.acm.org/binaries/content/assets/public-policy/2017usacmstatementalgorithms.pdf>.

61   N Fligstein and AF Roehrkasse, 'The Causes of Fraud in the Financial Crisis of 2007 to 2009: Evidence from the Mortgage-Backed Securities Industry' (2016) 81 *American Sociology Review* 617, 625.

62   D Schwarcz and P Siegelman, 'Insurance Agents in the 21st Century: The Problem of Biased Advice', in *Research Handbook In The Law & Economics Of Insurance*, D Schwarcz and P Siegelman eds (Edward Elgar Publishing, 2015), 45.

existing anti-competition (or anti-trust) laws. If the practice has not yet become a full-blown conundrum for prosecutors and regulators, the Topkins case suggests that it soon might.

In capturing a plea, the Department of Justice was apparently able to rely on evidence of a 'meeting of the minds' among co-conspirators. Topkins's algorithm was not an impediment to prosecution, because the seller had otherwise demonstrated a will to collude with other parties and then coded the algorithm to carry out the agreement. But often there is no evidence of a prior agreement when computers are in play, which means that anti-trust prosecutions involving algorithms could be harder to prove in the future.

Similar regulations in other parts of the world may also need to be amended in order to regulate the automaton of decision-making. For example, Australia's 2015 Competition Policy Review was prepared by Professor Ian Harper, Australian economist and current dean of the Melbourne Business School. Professor Harper's Final Report (known as the 'Harper reforms') amended the 'concerted practices' provision to reduce the need to establish a 'meeting of the minds' to prove collusion.[63]

Australia's Competition and Consumer Commission has a Data Analytics Unit that is used in market studies and to support the work of investigations teams and economists. In order to stay abreast of developments, the Australian regulator is engaging with other competition authorities and practitioners about these issues.

Algorithms and artificial intelligence have been a recent focus of the Organisation for Economic Co-operation and Development Competition Committee and the International Competition Network's Unilateral Conduct Working Group, which has been focusing on online competition issues for some time.[64] Given their pervasive nature, the United States Association for Computing Machinery Public Policy Council has also acknowledged that it is imperative to address 'challenges associated with the design and technical aspects of algorithms and preventing bias from the onset'.[65]

It is important to keep in mind that the tech giants depend on users remaining glued to their devices.[66] They design algorithms to keep the

---

63 Prof I Harper, 'Competition Policy Report', *Australian Competition Law* (March 2015) <http://www.australiancompetitionlaw.org/reports/2015harper-report.html#report>

64 See, R Sims (Conference Chair), 'Can Robots Collude?', *Speech to ACCC Conference* (16 November 2017) <https://www.accc.gov.au/speech/the-accc%E2%80%99s-approach-to-colluding-robots>.

65 'Statement on Algorithmic Transparency and Accountability', *Association for Computing Machinery US Public Policy Council (USACM)* (12 January 2017) <https://www.acm.org/binaries/content/assets/public-policy/2017usacmstatementalgorithms.pdf>.

66 G Zichermann, 'I've Worked in Tech for 22 Years – and It's Clear We're Living in an "Addiction Economy"', *Business Insider Australia* (15 December 2017) <https://www.businessinsider.com.au/tech-addiction-product-of-an-addiction-economy-2017-12#oZgDezzCOLBLr8yM.99>.

attention of those who already engaged with their platform. News services achieve this by producing a coloured banner on our screen that reads 'Breaking news'. The news feed in our social media has advertisements that may look like a tabloid story about a famous person. Advertisers post images of things that we searched for only hours earlier. Our attention is constantly being hijacked and this keeps us online.[67] The business of keeping consumers online is known as the 'addiction economy.'[68]

Economist Herbert Simon is credited with coining the concept of the attention economy as early as the 1970s. It is the idea that people's attention is a resource just like time or money, and companies will market their products to compete for that resource. Facebook has been very successful at establishing a platform in which we are always connected online with people we know and – once you are connected to enough 'friends' on Facebook – there is a statistical probability that at any time on any given day, someone is posting something into your news feed that may be interesting. And until you read the post and look at the pictures, you do not know whether you are interested. But the newsfeed has your attention in any event. Meanwhile, advertisements also appear in the feed via paid content from marketers or the sharing and liking of paid content by friends. All of this information and advertising is curated to suit your age, interests, recent posts and past posts. The system is using predictive analytics to decide what you might want to buy. Facebook even re-orders the news feed so as to ensure that most 'liked', active, and connected of our 'friends' are appearing as the most prevalent posts in out feed. This is because they are more likely to inform which advertisements should appear and they provide the most attractive and therefore most valuable statistical data for Facebook, so that it can be used to market Facebook to advertisers. At the heart of this entire business model is our attention and the time we spend on the platform.

Spending our time on Facebook is not in itself something that will cause economic harm or erode our trust in the operators of the platform. Indeed, if Facebook just recommended travel destinations we love, quality kitchen knives and good movies, then all would be well. But a problem arises when the information that is being fed into the news feed is dressed up as news, but is actually propaganda, or is presented as the views of a real person, but is actually a fake account created to engender trust at first and then hatred towards a particular minority group. This sort of activity has been revealed on Facebook and other social media platforms, particularly during the 2016 United States presidential election and the United Kingdom's Brexit referendum.

It now seems that the underlying algorithms were feeding fake news to manipulate the opinions of voters by analysis of posts to determine sentiment.

---

67 J Guszcza et al., 'Why We Need to Audit Algorithms', *Harvard Business Review* (28 November 2018) <https://hbr.org/2018/11/why-we-need-to-audit-algorithms>.
68 G Zichermann, 'I've Worked in Tech for 22 Years – and It's Clear We're Living in an "Addiction Economy"', *Business Insider Australia* (15 December 2017) <https://www.businessinsider.com.au/tech-addiction-product-of-an-addiction-economy-2017-12#oZgDezzCOLBLr8yM.99>.

These sorts of algorithms are being used in a way that negatively impact on our democracies, our justice systems and our well-being. This erodes trust in others and opens up communities and societies to real risks.[69]

The impact of manipulative algorithms is similar to corruption. It introduces a synthetic and irrelevant influence into a decision-making process. As with most processes that occur on global platforms like Facebook, the outcome is amplified. When a confidence trickster stops people in the street or goes door-knocking to target gullible and vulnerable victims, the scale of his or her deception and the amount to be extorted will be minimal compared to an online scam. This is why algorithms used in business, social media and advertising should be treated with a particularly high level of care. Algorithms can be gamed by humans to sow discord. They have the capacity to replicate and amplify human bias. Computer programs are made by humans who bake in certain design goals and draw on certain data sets. Inside all of this are the normal contradictions of humanity: generosity and greed; inclusion and bias; good and evil. Further, this technology is developed by a small handful of companies and, due to their control and the sheer scale of the problem, the public and government do not have the tools or resources to hold algorithms accountable.

Attempts to Regulate Algorithms

A number of countries around the world are working on the problems of accountability of algorithms and the ethical use of artificial intelligence. The New York City mayor's office established a new Artificial Intelligence watchdog panel. Mayor de Blasio observed that as data and technology become more central to the work of city government, the algorithms used to aid in decision-making must be aligned with the city's goals and values.[70] The governments of Canada and France have announced a joint initiative to examine the intersection of Artificial Intelligence and ethics. Interestingly, both countries stressed the need to embed their common values into the behaviour of autonomous systems.[71] The notion of ensuring that the values of the government and society generally are reflected in the way that algorithms behave will resonate with ethicists. However, this presupposes that the designers and developers also hold those values. The values need to be hardwired into the code for the outcomes to be consistent with these expectations.

69 M Surman, 'How to Keep AI from Turning into the Terminator', *CNN.com* (15 January 2019) <https://www.google.com.au/amp/s/amp.cnn.com/cnn/2019/01/15/opinions/artificial-intelligence-ethical-responsible-programming-surman/index.html>.

70 'Mayor de Blasio Announces First-In-Nation Task Force To Examine Automated Decision Systems Used By The City', *NYC.gov* (16 May 2018) <https://www1.nyc.gov/office-of-the-mayor/news/251-18/mayor-de-blasio-first-in-nation-ta sk-force-examine-automated-decision-systems-used-by>.

71 W Knight, 'Canada and France Plan an International Panel to Assess AI's Dangers', *MIT Technology Review* (7 December 2018) <https://www.technologyreview.com/s/612555/canada-and-france-propose-an-international-panel-to-assess-ais-dangers/>.

In Finland, the government is training 1% of the population in Artificial Intelligence basics, such as when it is deployed and the definitions of terms like 'machine learning' and 'neural networks.'[72] The companies participating in the challenge have pledged to train their staff in the basics of Artificial Intelligence.

Recent years demonstrate a growing use of algorithmic law enforcement by online intermediaries. Facilitating the distribution of online content, online intermediaries offer a natural point of control for monitoring access to illegitimate content, which makes them ideal partners for performing civil and criminal enforcement. Copyright law has been at the forefront of algorithmic law enforcement since the early 1990s when it conferred safe harbour protection to online intermediaries who remove allegedly infringing content upon notice under the Digital Millennium Copyright Act. Over the past two decades, the Notice and Takedown regime has become ubiquitous and embedded in the system design of all major intermediaries: major copyright owners increasingly exploit robots to send immense volumes of takedown requests and major online intermediaries, in response, use algorithms to filter, block and disable access to allegedly infringing content automatically, with little or no human intervention.

Algorithmic enforcement by online intermediaries reflects a fundamental shift in our traditional system of governance. It effectively converges law enforcement and adjudication powers in the hands of a small number of mega platforms. The best way to support trust in the law is to enforce it. Accountability refers to the extent to which decision-makers are expected to justify their choices to those affected by these choices, be held answerable for their actions and be held responsible for their failures and wrong-doings. This applies equally to decisions made by humans and algorithms.

72 J Delcker, 'Finland's Grand AI Experiment', *Politico* (2 January 2019) <https://www.politico.eu/article/finland-one-percent-ai-artificial-intelligence-courses-learning-training/>.

13 Trustless Relationships Enabled by Blockchain

Despite its potential for good, the blockchain's recent past has been much maligned due to its part in the illicit trade in drugs and guns, its use as a tax haven and the financial suffering of digital currency investors. Since the October 2013 demise of the anonymous marketplace *Silk Road* and the collapse of the *Mt Gox* bitcoin exchange in February 2014, there has been an emergence of legitimate uses for crypto-currencies and blockchain technology. Despite a relatively 'slow burn' and some considerable hype about blockchain's potential uses, it is now being explored by governments and regulators for its potential to collect taxes, deliver welfare benefits, issue passports, record land registries and assure the quality and supply of goods. Commercial and non-profit organisations are also investigating its ability to manage and track data, assets and value. Most importantly, blockchain technology's cryptographic proof of work can automate the relationship of trust between entities that is so essential for the automation of e-commerce.

The Case for Manufacturing Artificial Trust

Commerce on the Internet has come to rely almost exclusively on financial institutions serving as trusted third parties to process electronic payments. While the system works well enough for most transactions, it still suffers from the inherent weaknesses of the trust-based model: namely, the cost of providing for the trusted intermediary (particularly for small transactions); payments are reversible; and there is an accepted percentage of fraud.[1]

Blockchain technology can manage the performance of a contractual (or non-contractual) exchange while also providing and building trust and reputation. The capacity of humans to place our trust in strangers, not because of a belief in our innate goodness, but because of the systems that humans have made, has been described as 'the true genius of our species'.[2] Those systems

---

1   D Ma, 'Taking a Byte out of Bitcoin Regulation' (2017) 27 *Alberta Law Journal of Science and Technology* 1, 1.

2   Dr A Finkel, 'Artificial Intelligence: A Matter of Trust', *Committee for Economic Development of Australia (CEDA)* (18 May 2018) <https://www.chiefscientist.gov.au/wp-content/uploads/Chief-Scientist-Artificial-Intelligence-speech-to-CEDA.pdf>.

are founded on established standards, rules, conventions, customs and laws. Some of these systems are institutional and some are intuitive.

Blockchain technology is a layer of architecture that operates over the Internet. It is an online record-keeping system that is decentralised and maintained by immutable records of transactions using cryptography to verify the records. This distributed network provides incredible protection capabilities because 'blocks' are not added to the chain without consensus on their validity. When Alice transfers $100 to Bob using traditional online banking, Alice's bank reduces the ledger for her account by $100 and increases Bob's account by $100. Online banking does not need to evidence the balance in Alice and Bob's accounts with proof of cash deposits. Indeed, there are no cash deposits in their accounts. This process is based upon the principles of double-entry booking. When Alice 'transferred' the $100 to Bob, all that happened was the alteration to their ledgers. Nothing more needs to happen, because Alice and Bob trust their respective banks to make sure that the ledgers reflect their arrangement. If Alice withdraws cash from an ATM, the bank will make sure her ledger is changed to reflect this withdrawal. Until Alice withdraws the cash, the bank can use it. If someone tampers with Alice's bank account, then absent any fault on Alice's part, her bank will indemnify her for any losses. With blockchain technology, Alice can send crypto-currency to Bob on a blockchain network, every node on the ledger can see the transaction. This is multiple-entry bookkeeping and all participants on the network share the same interest in the system's integrity. This solves the problem of double-spending. Verification that the transaction should be so recorded and rendered immutable is managed cryptographically. Because of the support that these distributed ledger systems provide to enable trust and the recourse that they enable when trust is broken, the overall cost of trust is lowered.

The Internet, artificial intelligence and blockchain technology present a new challenge for all our economies and their development. How do we trust machines that we do not understand?[3] Machines do not necessarily interact with our standards, rules, conventions, customs and laws in a way that we can readily monitor or assess – either formally or intuitively. If we are to continue to adopt the use of artificial intelligence, then we need to find a way to program trust systems into the code that enable the use of artificial intelligence. Programmable or manufactured trust will need to include the values of the governing entity. In the words of Australia's chief scientist, a system that rewards quality and prioritises ethics will reward the economy in which it functions.[4]

3   V Polonski, 'People Don't Trust AI – Here's How We Can Change That', *The Conversation* (10 January 2018) <https://theconversation.com/people-dont-trust-ai-heres-how-we-can-change-that-87129>.

4   Dr A Finkel, 'Artificial Intelligence: A Matter of Trust', *Committee for Economic Development of Australia (CEDA)* (18 May 2018) <https://www.chiefscientist.gov.au/wp-content/uploads/Chief-Scientist-Artificial-Intelligence-speech-to-CEDA.pdf>.

Blockchain and the Automation of Trust

With its cryptographic signatures and sophisticated algorithms, blockchain technology enables the creation of distributed ledgers that can transform the delivery of public and private services, and enhance a number of existing online applications. It is regarded as a breakthrough in payment systems because it allows for 'cash-like' online transactions. They are cash-like because – for the first time – users can trust that the digital money they are using has a unique currency that cannot be duplicated, counterfeited or misdirected. This innovation is made possible by 'proof of work' via distributed trustless consensus. Trustless consensus means that the distributed ledger records the transaction, the wallets are updated to reflect where the bitcoin file (for example) has moved to on the network, and then a block with that record is stamped with all updated information to reflect that point in time and thereafter cannot be changed. With all users able to see and verify these movements, a hacker would have to break into every node (all of the computers on the network) to tamper with the ledger. Because the technology is managing these processes, the participants do not need to trust each other or another third party to make sure this happens and to get it right. The word 'trustless' reflects the state of not having to trust anyone on the network. In traditional banking, participants are known to each other, but the contents of their ledgers are kept private and known only to the account holder and their bank. In blockchain networks, the participants on the network remain anonymous, while the ledgers are public and transparent.

This is a breakthrough for online payments and removes the need for expensive trusted third parties. Blockchain's cryptographic verification mechanisms can also reduce risk of fraud.

In a trustless relationship, the parties to the agreement or arrangement do not need to rely on the traditional mechanisms that enable social relationships of trust. Rather, the traditional process of establishing trust is circumvented completely by technology. The system is 'trustless' because it does not depend on the intentions, benevolence or goodwill of any party. The technology ensures that all players meet their part of the bargain in any transaction. In order to do business with each other, we need to trust that each party is competent and motivated to put the terms of the agreement ahead of any other competing or personal interests. Any other scenario will not be trustworthy and will undermine the agreement and the potential for any other future relationship. Trust that each party will fulfil their end of the bargain may not always be 100% trust. Sometimes, the parties will assess the risk that the deal will fail and will purchase insurance to offset that risk, or otherwise consider that level of risk acceptable. However, with blockchain technology, the offline bargain is struck between the parties and the online execution of the bargain is managed by the technology. The technology assesses whether each side of the bargain is able to meet its obligation and when all conditions are satisfied, the system handles the transaction or exchange. The record of the transaction is transparent. It can be audited easily. It is immutable and non-reversible. All of these features increase trust in the arrangement and reduce the risk that one of the parties will not be satisfied. 'Trustless' in this case is, therefore, synonymous with 'riskless'.

Trustless Relationships in Smart Contracts

A smart contract is a computer program recorded on a blockchain or distributed ledger system that depends upon consensus from all participants about the effects of any execution of the program and that is recorded on the network. A smart contract may or may not be intended to represent terms in a legal contract, and may or may not be legally recognised. Smart contracts are not restricted to distributed ledger systems. The term may have a different meaning in other contexts. A definition was proposed by Nick Szabo in 1994. Under this definition a smart contract may also run outside of distributed ledger systems as a contract automation tool that could be run on any computer system that records contractual activities and related transactions, which in turn support the automatic execution of certain transactions.[5]

The Recent Proliferation of Blockchain-based Smart Contracts

While articulated and entered into in the form of action, speech or writing, a smart contract is characteristically a computer program built on code.[6] Some smart contracts, however, contain similar logic and characteristics that can be likened to those of conventional contracts, at least from a theoretical viewpoint. Indeed, the smart contract operates with a similar logic to the 'traditional' contracts whereby the will of both parties to enter into the agreement is needed in order for it to be valid.[7] In addition to traditional contract terms and conditions listed in the agreement, smart contracts are capable of a wide range of actions, including collecting data from outside resources and processing it according to the terms specified in the contract, as well as adopting concrete solutions based on the results of this procedure.[8]

The architecture of the smart contract automates the performance of contractual and other obligations. However, smart contracts are more than just

5   N Szabo, 'Smart Contracts: Building Blocks for Digital Markets', *Extropy #16* (1996) <http://www.fon.hum.uva.nl/rob/Courses/InformationInSpeech/CDROM/ Literature/LOTwinterschool2006/szabo.best.vwh.net/smartcontracts2.html>.
6   K Lauslahti, J Mattila and T Seppälä, 'The Research Institute of the Finnish Economy: Smart Contracts – How will Blockchain Technology Affect Contractual Practices?' (9 January 2017) 68 *ETLA Reportit – ETLA Reports* 1, 10.
7   R Koulu, 'Blockchains and Online Dispute Resolution: Smart Contracts as an Alternative to Enforcement' (2016) 13(1) *ScriptEd* 65.
8   *BBVA Research* – 'Digital Economy Outlook October 2015' (23 August 2016), 4 <https://www.bbvaresearch.com/wp-content/uploads/2015/10/DigitalEconom yOutlookOct15Cap1.pdf>.

automated processes for enabling performance – they also have the means to ensure the performance takes place. If performance does not occur, the smart contract will report this failure. This is known to as 'tamper evident' execution. It is this ability to perform 'on its own' which makes the contract 'smart'.[9] In the case of blockchain technology, value may be represented by a digital token, such as bitcoin or other crypto-currency. The engine room of the smart contract is the automation of trust enabled by different cryptographic proofs.

Much of the discussion around blockchain-based smart contracts has focused on whether or not they operate in the same way as legal contracts. However, most contracts are social rather than legal in nature and are entered into because the parties trust each other to perform the agreed exchange. Although some smart contracts may not necessarily be contracts in terms of having a binding intention, they may still give rise to enforceable obligations. These issues may be treated differently from country to country.

Most importantly, blockchain's trust protocol can enable the kind of social contracting that characterised the way exchanges were conducted before the Internet.[10] This is not to say that smart contracts are not or cannot be legal contracts. However, legal contracts are not usually the focus of discussion when exchanges are conducted offline. This disconnect between the treatment of exchanges managed by smart contracts and exchanges in the analogue world is probably due to a combination of factors including the word 'contract' in the term 'smart contract', and also the claim made by many blockchain developers and advocates that this innovative technology can provide and manage trust between the parties.

Smart contracts can manage financial interactions between machines, vehicles, humans, regulators, government and financial service providers. Indeed, many of these processes are already managed online via processes that are automated. However, at this time, some steps along the path still require human intervention.

Transforming smart contracts from an exciting concept to having practical application presents a number of challenges. From a legal perspective, a number of issues need to be considered. What contractual terms should be automated? How should these terms be expressed? How can lawyers validate

---

9   S Farrell, H Machin and R Hinchcliffe, 'Lost and Found in Smart Contract Translation – Considerations in Transitioning to Automation in Legal Architecture', *UNCITRAL.org* (21 February 2017) <http://www.uncitral.org/pdf/english/congress/PapersforProgramme/14-FARRELLandMACHINandHINCHLIFFE-SmartContracts.pdf>.

10 See, PA Ryan, 'Smart Contract Relations in eCommerce' (2017) 7(10) *Technology Innovation Management Review* 10. See also, S Macaulay, 'Non-Contractual Relations in Business: A Preliminary Study' (1963) 28(1) *American Sociological Review* 55; S Macaulay, 'Elegant Models, Empirical Pictures, and the Complexities of Contract' (1977) 11(3) *Law & Society Review* 507; S Macaulay, J Kidwell and WC Whitford, *Contracts: Law in Action* (2nd Ed, LexisNexis, 2003); and S Macaulay and WC Whitford, 'The Development of Contracts: The Law in Action' (2015) 87 *Temple Law Review* 793.

the legal effect of any automated contractual terms that are not expressed in natural language?[11] If the human steps in the performance of a contract or transaction are to be replaced by automated processes, then it is important to ensure that the coded steps emulate the appropriate human interactions.

In any analysis of the performance of blockchain and smart contracts, it is important to keep in mind that in many online transactions, the parties do not need to trust each other. They just need to trust that the transaction that they are entering into will be completed on time and as promised. Smart contracts are also particularly attractive when the parties do not know each other, have no prior dealings and there is no trusted third party or moderator to manage the risk that the transaction will not proceed as agreed. In such a case, the distributed ledger can guarantee correct execution of the contract. In most existing distributed ledger and smart contract systems, the process is managed in a chronological or 'serial' manner. That is, all users have to run a contract before its result can be accepted by the system. Although this approach is easy to implement and manage, it is not scalable and greatly limits the system's ability to handle a large number of smart contracts. This explains why bitcoin transactions are so slow – running at just seven transactions per second (compared to the Visa network, which can manage tens of thousands of transactions per second).[12] There are new technologies being developed to enable a greater level of security and improved volume of transactions on blockchains. These new technologies will involve more complex mathematical models and improved hardware and processing systems (including quantum computing).[13]

Once the management of performance of a blockchain-based smart contract is explained and understood, it is possible to give expression to the way that blockchain manages good faith in online business exchanges. In this way, blockchain solves a significant problem for anyone wanting to do business online.

Attempts to Regulate Blockchain and Crypto-economic Activities

With the combined processing power of personal computers and interconnected devices, the traditional role of third parties and intermediaries is changing. Third parties and intermediaries are being rendered obsolete by peer-to-peer transactions between strangers. Introducing an entirely new medium of exchange, bitcoin and other crypto-currencies remove the need for banks or central clearing houses. These maths-based payments systems have

11 S Farrell and C Warren, 'Smart Derivatives Contracts: From Concept to Construction', *King & Wood Mallesons* (4 October 2018) <https://www.kwm.com/en/au/knowledge/insights/smart-derivatives-contracts-from-concept-to-construction-20181004>.

12 D O'Keefe, 'Understanding Cryptocurrency Transaction Speeds', *Medium* (5 Jun 2018) <https://medium.com/coinmonks/understanding-cryptocurrency-transaction-speeds-f9731fd93cb3>.

13 Z Gao, 'Performance Analysis of Blockchain and Smart Contracts', *Dissertations, University of Houston Libraries* (2017) <https://uh-ir.tdl.org/handle/10657/2879>.

been made possible by the blockchain: distributed ledger technology that enables secure verification, storage and transfer of value or data. This innovative technology gives decentralised marketplaces a platform for conducting business without the need for a third party to authenticate the participants or to guarantee payments.

Blockchain technology is being explored by governments and regulators for its potential to provide transparency and to automate processes, including collecting taxes, delivering welfare benefits, issuing passports, recording land titles and assuring the quality and supply of goods. Commercial and non-profit organisations are also investigating its ability to manage and track data, assets and value. However, these uses contemplate that the relationship between users and a central authority will exist on and off the blockchain. This is problematic as these analogue relationships import with them levels of trust and confidence or agency and control, none of which can be managed or negated by cryptography and consensus.

It is understood in the regulatory regime of most developed countries that a director, secretary, other officer or employee of a corporation must not improperly use their position to gain an advantage for themselves or someone else; or cause detriment to the corporation.[14] This statutory duty reflects, and to some extent refines, the corresponding obligation in Equity. Where a director acts in relation to a transaction in which the director, or a party to whom the director owes a fiduciary duty, stands to gain a benefit without making adequate disclosure of her or his interest, that director acts 'improperly'. However, where the activities of the organisation are operating in an online environment, detecting misconduct, identifying wrong-doers and recovering any losses can be particularly difficult. If that online environment enables the anonymity or pseudonymity of participants, then the difficulties are even more acute. This is the challenge facing regulators since the inception of the world's first and (so far) most successful crypto-currencies, as well as blockchain-enabled smart contracts.

Different jurisdictions are grappling with, enacting or repealing different legislative provisions to regulate the use of distributed ledger technologies and blockchain enabled systems in different contexts. For example, smart contracts that underpin transactions in initial coin offerings (ICOs) may be completely unacceptable in some jurisdictions, while a smart contract that handles intra-institutional banking and other financial transactions may be quite acceptable,

14 For example, in Australia: section 182 of the *Corporations Act 2001* (Cth). In the US for example, Delaware has a statute that permits the stockholders through the certificate of incorporation to exonerate completely or limit the exposure of directors for personal liability to the corporation or the stockholders for monetary damages for breach of fiduciary duty as a director. That statute does not allow exoneration if the director is found to have committed a breach of the duty of loyalty, acts or omissions not in good faith, intentional misconduct, a knowing violation of the law, improper payment of dividends or improper personal benefit (8 Del C, sections 102(b)(7)). Other states in the United States have similar statutes, and many corporations have adopted such charter provisions (see, American Law Institute, Principles of Corporate Governance, s 7.19). In the United Kingdom, the *Companies Act 2006* has codified these obligations in sections 171–177.

within the same jurisdiction or elsewhere. This is important in light of the decentralised, global nature of the Internet and public blockchain networks.

The domain name bitcoin.org was registered in 2008 and in the beginning of 2009 the *genesis block*, the first block in a blockchain, was created. The cryptography that makes bitcoin possible solves a long-standing problem of double-spending, where digital money can be spent more than once. For years, double spending has been one of the main barriers to widespread adoption of digital money. A bitcoin transaction is simply a data record of a transaction that is shared in (almost) real time with everyone on the network. This means it is transparent and any attempt to tamper with this record – or distributed ledger – will be evident to everyone on the system. Data records are stored chronologically in *blocks* that are *chained* together cryptographically. Every node in the network has a copy of the blockchain and in order for a transaction to be added to a blockchain, there has to be a consensus among the nodes in the network.

The result is that peer-to-peer transactions become possible, without the need for a centralised certifying authority, such as a bank, which usually takes a small commission to carry out the work. If third parties are no longer necessary and organisations or consumers can do transactions peer-to-peer, which are also processed nearly instantly, that is a paradigm shift and that is why the blockchain is so important.

Bitcoin is a digital, decentralised, partially anonymous currency, not backed by any government or other legal entity, and not redeemable for gold or other commodity. It relies on peer-to-peer networking and cryptography to maintain its integrity. It can be seen as both a digital currency for transacting, and a commodity akin to digital gold. It can be used as a medium of exchange between currencies and it can also be invested in (like any speculative asset).

Bitcoin and other crypto-currencies were created to circumvent the control of the payments and monetary systems by banks and central banks, but groups including the World Economic Forum have been advising central banks not to be passive in their approach to crypto-currencies, given the profound and disruptive impact in how trust is being built in the new digital economy.[15]

The regulation of crypto-currencies – like bitcoin – presents unique challenges for governments and their agencies. This is particularly so in the case of agencies that need to support innovation, but at the same time want to provide guidance to the community about how to characterise transactions involving crypto-currencies. For example, in Australia, the taxation office treats payments to workers in bitcoin as a payment of a fringe benefit that may be a taxable event. However, using bitcoin to purchase goods and services is treated as equivalent to 'spending money' (as opposed to 'buying bitcoin'). This is

---

15 J Eyers and V Poljak, 'RBA Governor Philip Lowe Says Bitcoin Is a "Speculative Mania"', *AFR* (12 December 2017) <http://www.afr.com/technology/rba-gov ernor-philip-lowe-says-Bitcoin-is-a-speculative-mania-20171212-h02zf0>

important, because buying bitcoin would impose Goods and Services Tax on that transaction, whereas spending it does not.

In some countries, the use of bitcoin and other crypto-currencies is illegal,[16] while others tolerate their use without setting down particular regulation to control or exploit their use. In South America, there is a diverse patchwork of individual approaches from different countries, ranging from outright bans to openly embracing crypto-currencies.[17]

It is legal to use crypto-currencies in the European Union, but member states are not allowed to introduce their own digital currencies. The regulatory environment also varies from one country to the next, with some nations delegating all crypto-regulation to the European Union and others taking a more hands-on approach.

Many African countries have yet to issue a ruling either way, but reasonable concerns around terrorist funding, tax evasion and other criminal uses have led to outright bans in some countries and tight regulations in others. The most bitcoin-active African nations are South Africa, Nigeria, Zimbabwe, Kenya and Ghana.[18] The South African government has established a working group to explore the regulation of crypto-assets. Its terms of reference include clarification of the tax status of crypto-currencies.[19]

Several countries across the Middle East (including Iran, Turkey and Bahrain) are planning to develop a regulatory framework for crypto-currencies and have indicated a positive interest in exploring the use of blockchain technology.[20] In December 2018, Saudi Arabia and the United Arab Emirates announced the launch of a joint cross-border crypto-currency. The digital currency is not targeted at consumers. It will be strictly for banks and to be used between the central monetary authorities.[21] Meanwhile, in Qatar,

---

16 For example, bitcoin and other crypto-currencies are banned in Algeria, Bahrain, Bangladesh, Bolivia, China, Ecuador, Egypt, Iceland, Iraq, Ireland, Morocco, Namibia, Nepal, Pakistan, Qatar and Saudi Arabia. See, 'Is Bitcoin Legal? Crypto-currency Regulations Around the World', *Finder.com* <https://www.finder.com.au/global-cryptocurrency-regulations#country>

17 These regional summaries are from 'Where Is Bitcoin Banned? Where Is Bitcoin Legal?', *Finder.com* (12 November 2012) <https://www.finder.com.au/global-cryptocurrency-regulations#country>.

18 F Akeredolu, 'The Top 5 African Countries That Are Embracing Bitcoin', *bitcoinAfrica.io* (7 December 2018) <https://bitcoinafrica.io/2018/12/07/african-countries-embracing-bitcoin/>.

19 A Zmudzinksi, 'South African Government Establishes Crypto Assets Regulatory Working Group', *CoinTelegraph.com* (2 January 2019) <https://cointelegraph.com/news/south-african-government-establishes-crypto-assets-regulatory-working-group>.

20 S O'Neal, 'From Qatar to Palestine: How Cryptocurrencies Are Regulated in the Middle East', *CoinTelegraph.com* <https://cointelegraph.com/news/from-qatar-to-palestine-how-cryptocurrencies-are-regulated-in-the-middle-east>.

21 J Aki, 'UAE and Saudi Arabian Central Banks to Jointly Launch a Cross Border Cryptocurrency', *CoinTelegraph.com* (December 2018) <https://www.ccn.com/uae-and-saudi-arabian-central-banks-to-jointly-launch-a-cross-border-cryptocurrency/>.

Egypt, Oman, Jordan, Kuwait, Lebanon and Iraq, crypto-currencies are banned.[22]

Many countries around Asia were some of the earliest and most enthusiastic crypto-currency adopters, but government responses vary. China is clamping down on the sector. In China, crypto-currencies are not legal tender. The banking system is not accepting crypto-currencies or providing relevant services. The government has cracked down on activities related to crypto-currencies in the interests of investor protection and financial risk prevention. Those measures include announcing that initial coin offerings are illegal, restricting the primary business of crypto-currency trading platforms and discouraging bitcoin mining. In the meantime, China's central bank is reportedly considering issuing its own digital currency.[23]

The reason why many governments have banned crypto-currencies is a lack of trust. Powerful institutions are wary of bitcoin because it offers an alternative to the conventional, state-sanctioned banking system. The fact that powerful institutions are so distrustful of crypto-currencies is enough to concern regulators. The price is volatile because of speculation and manipulation.[24] It is also possible that the network itself is bloated due to over-activity. When these factors are combined, it is possible to see how governments might be concerned that its economy should not have to rely on something so apparently nebulous. Authoritarian governments may want to ban crypto-currencies because it undermines the authority they exert over their fiat (government-issued and government-backed) denomination.

Most of the countries that permit crypto-currency markets to operate impose taxes upon their use as an asset or other investment product. However, the tax treatment of income generated from a crypto-currency transaction varies depending on how it is categorised. For instance, in Argentina a transaction of this nature would be taxed in a manner similar to revenue generated from the sale of securities and bonds, whereas in Switzerland crypto-currency is categorised as a foreign currency for tax purposes. Some of the countries do not levy taxes on crypto-currency transactions (for example, Belarus and Jersey).[25]

In October 2018, Japan's Financial Services Agency gave the crypto-currency industry self-regulatory status. This approval gives the industry association rights to set rules to safeguard customer assets, prevent money laundering

22 S O'Neal, 'From Qatar to Palestine: How Cryptocurrencies Are Regulated in the Middle East', *CoinTelegraph.com* <https://cointelegraph.com/news/from-qatar-to-palestine-how-cryptocurrencies-are-regulated-in-the-middle-east>.

23 The Law Library of Congress, Global Legal Research Center, 'Regulation of Cryptocurrency – China', *United States Library of Congress* (June 2018, update 12 July 2018) <https://www.loc.gov/law/help/cryptocurrency/china.php>.

24 Securities and Exchange Commission (Release No. 34–80206; File No. SR-BatsBZX-2016–30); See also, J Naughton, 'Why Bitcoin Scares Banks and Governments', *The Guardian* (7 April 2013) <https://www.theguardian.com/technology/2013/apr/07/bitcoin-scares-banks-governments>

25 The Law Library of Congress, Global Legal Research Center, 'Regulation of Cryptocurrency – China', *United States Library of Congress* (June 2018, update 12 July 2018) <https://www.loc.gov/law/help/cryptocurrency/china.php>.

and give operational guidelines. The Japan Virtual Currency Exchange Association will be required to police and sanction exchanges for any violations.[26]

Many of the countries that permit crypto-currency markets to operate have enacted laws subjecting participating organisations to rules designed to prevent money-laundering, terrorism financing and organised crime. These include Australia, Belarus, Canada, Gibraltar, Japan, Jersey and Switzerland. While a bill that would have the same effect is working its way through the Brazilian legislative process, countries like Argentina, France and Mexico have yet to follow suit.[27]

Research shows that the strength of any economy is based on the trust that exists in its economic transactions.[28] A peer-to-peer model that completely eliminates trust removes itself from any historical context and presents new challenges to the present-day regulatory scheme.[29] Blockchain and bitcoin are concepts that defy the traditional notions of money. Read in this light, it is understandable that regulators would initially baulk at supporting something so radical and something that threatens to upend such a fundamental component of a vital human system. However, with the development and testing of new regulatory models, many governments around the world are embracing the potential for crypto-currencies to operate as alternatives to traditional government-issued paper monies. Paper money lacks the traceability of digital payments. Digital payments lack the trustworthiness of transactions conducted with crypto-currencies.

The regulation of crypto-currency exchanges has been particularly decisive in most jurisdictions. Without foreign currency exchanges, it is not possible to redeem local currencies in exchange for foreign ones. The same applies to crypto-currencies. Crypto-currency exchanges operate online and using traditional bank accounts, they buy and sell crypto-currencies in exchange for fiat currencies.

There are three main crypto-currency exchange activities that have attracted regulatory control. Firstly, the exchange must be registered with the Australian Securities and Investments Commission (ASIC). Secondly, large financial transactions conducted by the exchange must be reported. In Australia and the United States, any transaction above AU\$10,000 or US\$10,000 (respectively) must be reported to the relevant local financial authority. In Europe, the reportable figure is Euro 10,000. In the United Kingdom it is UK£10,000. In Australia the government agency that monitors these types of transaction is the Australian Transaction Reports and Analysis Centre (AUSTRAC). AUSTRAC

---

26 T Uranaka, 'Japan Grants Cryptocurrency Industry Self-Regulatory Status', *Reuters* (24 October 2018) <https://www.reuters.com/article/us-japan-cryptocurrency/japan-grants-cryptocurrency-industry-self-regulatory-status-idUSKCN1MY10W>.

27 The Law Library of Congress, Global Legal Research Center, 'Regulation of Cryptocurrency – China', *United States Library of Congress* (June 2018, update 12 July 2018) <https://www.loc.gov/law/help/cryptocurrency/china.php>.

28 PJ Zak and S Knack, 'Trust and Growth' (2001) 111 *Economic Journal* 295, at 295.

29 D Ma, 'Taking a Byte out of Bitcoin Regulation' (2017) 27 *Alberta Law Journal of Science and Technology* 1, 3.

has been given the authority to monitor local crypto-currency exchanges to combat the threat of serious financial crime. This move was spurred on by the global watchdog Financial Action Task Force, in an effort to combat international money laundering and terrorism financing. It is important to note that Australia's anti-money laundering framework has been found to be particularly deficient.[30] Finally, crypto-currency exchanges must not engage in misleading and deceptive conduct. Any breaches of these prohibitions are regulated in Australia by its anti-competition (anti-trust) watchdog – the Australian Competition and Consumer Commission (ACCC).[31]

ASIC and the ACCC have joined forces to regulate initial coin offerings (ICOs), also known as token generation events (TGEs) or token crowd sales.[32] An ICO is a type of funding using crypto-currencies. Mostly the process is done by crowdfunding, but private ICOs are becoming more common. The Australian laws applicable to a crypto-asset or ICO may differ depending on whether the crypto-asset or ICO is (or is not) a financial product.[33]

The United States has also been comprehensive in its response to the popularity of crypto-currencies and ICOs. US laws have already been tested in the courts. In the matter of *Tomahawk Exploration LLC and David Thompson Laurance,* the Securities and Exchange Commission (SEC) brought proceedings against the respondents pursuant to Section 8A of the *Securities Act of 1933* ('Securities Act') and Sections 15(b) and 21C of the *Securities Exchange Act of 1934* ('Exchange Act'), for their failure to register the stocks they had offered through an ICO.

---

30 For example, in 2017, the Commonwealth Bank of Australia (CBA) was found to have been chronically deficient in its anti-money laundering practices. The bank's procedural shortcomings came to light when eleven people were jailed and dozens more arrested in Australia and overseas for using the CBA's lax funds transfer systems for money laundering, drug dealing, and receiving the proceeds of crime – *Chief Executive Officer of the Australian Transaction and Analysis Centre v Commonwealth Bank of Australia Limited ACN 123 123 124* (NSD1305/2017) <http://www.fedcourt.gov.au/data/assets/pdffile/0003/45075/NSD1305-2017-Statement-of-Claim.pdf>.

31 In 2017, the ACCC received 1,289 complaints related to bitcoin scams, with reported losses totalling AU$1,218,206. In response, the corporate regulator, ASIC, issued a warning to would-be investors that crypto-currencies are high-risk speculative products. See, L Hobday, 'More Than 1,200 People Complain to ACCC About Bitcoin Scams', *ABCNews.net.au* (20 February 2018) <https://www.abc.net.au/news/2018-02-19/more-than-1200-people-complain-to-accc-about-bitcoin-scams/9462240>.

32 ASIC received a delegation of power from the ACCC that enables ASIC, in coordination with the ACCC, to take action where there is potential misleading or deceptive conduct. 'Initial Coin Offerings and Crypto-currency', *ASIC* (2018) <https://asic.gov.au/regulatory-resources/digital-transformation/initial-coin-offerings-and-crypto-currency/>.

33 'Initial Coin Offerings and Crypto-currency', *ASIC* (2018) <https://asic.gov.au/regulatory-resources/digital-transformation/initial-coin-offerings-and-crypto-currency/>.

The company offered a 'Bounty Program,' whereby Tomahawk dedicated 200,000 TOM tokens to pay third parties, offering between 10 and 4,000 TOM tokens in exchange for various activities including marketing efforts; making requests to list TOM tokens on token trading platforms; promoting TOM tokens on blogs and online forums such as Twitter or Facebook; creating professional picture file designs; YouTube videos, other promotional materials; and online promotional efforts that targeted potential investors and directed them to Tomahawk's offering materials.

According to the SEC's Cease-and-Desist Order, between July and September 2017, Tomahawk issued more than 80,000 TOM crypto-tokens as bounties to approximately forty wallet holders on Tomahawk's decentralised platform in exchange for the promotional activities it sought to reward. Based on these specific facts and circumstances, the SEC reasoned that the TOM tokens were securities (or investment contracts), because 'the TOM tokens were offered in exchange for the investment of money or other contributions of value'. The representations in Tomahawk's online offering materials created an expectation of profits derived from the efforts of others, namely from the oil exploration and production operations conducted by Tomahawk and Laurance and from the opportunity to trade TOM tokens on a secondary trading platform.[34]

The SEC found that notwithstanding 'the lack of monetary consideration for purportedly 'free' shares,' the issuance of the TOM tokens as a 'gift' of a security through the Bounty Program constituted a 'sale' or 'offer to sell' within the meaning of the Securities Act.[35]

Consequently, the SEC found that the Respondents violated the securities registration provisions that prohibit the sale or offering of a security through any means or instrument of transportation and communication in interstate commerce or the mails without an effective registration statement or qualifying exemption. The SEC also found violations of its anti-fraud provisions arising from materially false and misleading statements found on Tomahawk's ICO website and in its white paper. Importantly, *Tomahawk* is a new application of the principle that the issuance of 'free' securities for some economic benefit would still constitute a sale of, or an offer to sell, securities.[36]

---

34 *SEC v. W.J. Howey Co.*, 328 U.S. 293 (1946), and its progeny, including the cases discussed by the SEC in its *Report of Investigation Pursuant to Section 21(a) Of The Securities Exchange Act Of 1934: The DAO* (Exchange Act Rel. No. 81207) (July 25, 2017).

35 See, *SEC v. Sierra Brokerage Servs., Inc.*, 608 F. Supp. 2d 923, 940–43 (S.D. Ohio 2009), aff'd, 712 F.3d 321 (6th Cir. 2013).

36 In the *Vanderkam & Sanders* No-Action Letter, SEC No-Action Letter 1999 WL 38281 (27 January 1999), the SEC opined that 'the issuance of securities in consideration of a person's registration on or visit to an issuer's Internet site would be an event of sale' and therefore the sale of those stocks needed to be registered. See also, United States Securities and Exchange Commission, Rule 144 (under section

These responses by the Australian regulators in relation to crypto-economic activities and the United States SEC in *Tomahawk* highlight the potential legal consequences for dealing in crypto-currencies and crypto-assets in exchange for an expectation that they will operate in the same way as traditional currencies or securities. Governments and their regulators are not just protecting their own role in the generation and management of money, they are fulfilling an obligation to protect consumers and investors from misconduct, to maintain trust and integrity in the financial system.

5 of the Securities Act of 1933) <https://www.sec.gov/fast-answers/answersru le144htm.html>.

Part III

Legal Relationships of Trust in Digital and Crypto Economies

14 Introduction

A social relationship of trust in business is predicated upon the existence of key intangibles: the expectation of competency; and the benevolence of operators of businesses. The expectation of competency is fulfilled when the business person has the requisite experience and/or skills to deliver particular products and services or to manage the affairs of others. Benevolence is the quality of selflessness with which a business operator manages their side of a bargain. Businesses and professionals operate for profit. In exchange for a customer's (a promisee's) undertaking to pay for their products and services, a business (a promisor) must fulfil their promise as agreed. While intangible in quality, these requirements for the existence of trust are fundamental in both social relations of trust and in the administration of Trusts. These expectations apply equally to purely commercial relation and Trusts. Trustees and fiduciaries manage assets on behalf of others in personal and business arrangements. This Part focuses on Trustees and fiduciaries who manage assets on behalf of others in business or commercial arrangements.

There are particular challenges for Trustees and fiduciaries as they manage assets that are transacted digitally or verified with cryptography. Trustees are charged with managing and investing prudently. In a commercial context, this duty has presented concerns for futures traders since the 1980s. The complexity of effective speculation in the futures market and legal restrictions on investments by fiduciaries, such as the requirement that plan assets be invested prudently, caused speculative activity to be limited to those plans which were very large and had the ability to develop or retain advisers with expertise in futures trading.[1] This is the nature of managing Trusts in commercial arrangements.

In all cases where fiduciary relationships arise, one person voluntarily allows another to exercise discretion in making choices that will affect the interests of the first person or at least interests that the first person cares about. This feature of all fiduciary relationships is a 'reliance on discretion'.[2] The constructive trust imposed on accessories to a breach of fiduciary duty is remedial in

1 TA Russo, SG Bachelder and BE Grala, 'Employee Plan Trading in Commodity Futures' (1980) 37 *Washington and Lee Law Review* 811.
2 See, M Harding, 'Trust and Fiduciary Law' (2013) 33(1) *Oxford Journal of Legal Studies* 81.

nature.[3] However, rather than being a remedy affording the beneficiary specific restitution (because Trust property need not pass into the accessory's hands), it is essentially a means of calculating the accessory's liability as if they themselves are a Trustee (or fiduciary) in breach of duty. In the case of the fiduciary in breach, they have been referred to as a 'constructive fiduciary'.[4] Sometimes, each party to a fiduciary relationship relies on the discretion of the other, but more often reliance on discretion is a one-sided affair. Resulting, constructive and bare express trusts are fiduciary relationships.[5]

If reliance on discretion is a feature of all fiduciary relationships (including with Trustees), then it may render fiduciary relationships fertile ground for 'thick trust'.[6] In thick-trust relationships, there is no room for betrayal, bad faith or incompetency. Instead, in these contexts, 'over-trust' prevails. Trust decisions tend to be made subconsciously rather than consciously. People in thick-trust relationships often refuse to process specific information that indicates distrust might be in order. Negative traits can be turned into positive ones, as for example when a person's failure to complete work on time is viewed as a commitment to getting the job done properly.[7]

Provided that a Trustee acts honestly and does not breach other duties (such as the duty to comply with the terms of a Trust instrument and the duty to act with reasonable care), the determination of what serves the interests of the beneficiaries is very much a matter for the subjective judgement of the Trustee. It is noted, however, that beneficiaries may be entitled to relief if what the Trustee has done, or proposes to do, clearly cannot be justified as serving their interests. In two important types of case, however, statute imposes what apparently is meant to be a higher, and presumably objective, standard. The two particular types of case to which this higher standard might apply are where a Trustee acts for reward; and where a Trustee holds itself out as having particular expertise in the administration of Trusts.[8]

3   D Hayton, 'Personal Accountability of Strangers as Constructive Trustees' (1985) 27 *Malaya Law Review* 313 at 313–4; RP Austin, 'The Melting Down of the Remedial Trust' (1988) 11 *University of New South Wales Law Journal* 66 at 79; M Halliwell, 'The Stranger as Constructive Trustee Revisited' (1989) *Conveyancer & Property Lawyer* 328, 335.

4   *Markwell Bros Pty Ltd v CPN Diesels Queensland Pty Ltd* [1983] 2 QdR 508, 525. See also, P Podzebenko, 'Redefining Accessory Liability: *Royal Brunei Airlines Sdn Bhd v Tan*' (1996) 18(2) *Sydney Law Review* 234, 238.

5   See Lionel Smith, 'Constructive Fiduciaries?' in Peter Birks (ed), *Privacy and Loyalty* (Clarendon Press, 1997), 249, 262–264.

6   See, M Harding, 'Trust and Fiduciary Law' (2013) 33(1) *Oxford Journal of Legal Studies* 81.

7   DJ McAllister, 'The Second Face of Trust: Reflections on the Dark Side of Interpersonal Trust in Organizations' (1997) 6 *Research On Negotiations In Organisations* 87, 99. See also, CA Hill and EA O'Hara, 'A Cognitive Theory of Trust' (2006) 84 *Washington University Law Review* 1717, 1763.

8   *Bartlett v Barclays Trust Co (No 1)* [1980] 1 Ch 515, 533. See also, JRF Lehane, 'Delegation of Trustees' Powers and Current Developments in Investment Funds Management' (1995) 7(1) *Bond Law Review* 36.

A number of key statutory instruments regulate the conduct of solicitors,[9] Trustees[10] and directors.[11] Each act has its own approach to determining liability for innocent or fraudulent breach of Trust, or for breach of Trust-like and fiduciary duties. In the case of solicitors, the common law also imposes obligations in relation to the management of a bare Trust. A bare Trust arises when a solicitor (or other Trustee) has been given title and control over a client's assets or property for the purposes of assisting in a commercial transaction. In such a case, the solicitor owes fiduciary duties to the client and must discharge them in accordance with the particular instructions from the client. This chapter will include a discussion of the liability that may be imposed on a solicitor who misdirects assets or property in breach of their duty or the client's instructions.[12]

Whether charged with the administration of a bare Trust or an investment Trust, a Trustee's experience, knowledge and practices in a digital world where investors expect to make money from their investment tend to suggest that the 'prudent man rule' can, at times, be counterproductive.[13] It is possible that there is a lack of knowledge in many contexts and use-cases as to what amounts to 'prudent' investment decision-making. In the United States, for example, legislators moved early to set minimum standards for most voluntarily established retirement and health plans in private industry to provide protection for individuals.[14]. Under this regulatory framework, the fiduciary standard requires trustees to act with the prudence of an expert for the exclusive purpose and sole benefit of the plan's participants. Although the Act imposes a high standard of care on pension plan Trustees, it nevertheless allows corporate representatives to serve as pension plan Trustees and permits them to invest up to 10% of the plan's assets in the 'sponsoring corporation's' stock.[15] These rules accommodate the changing nature of a Trustee's role as profit starts to rank ahead of preservation. It also accommodates the delegation of investment and custodial duties to

9 For example, in New South Wales, solicitors are regulated by the *Legal Profession Uniform Law Application Act 2014* (NSW), known in Victoria as *Legal Profession Uniform Law Application Act 2014* (Vic).

10 For example, in Queensland, the *Trusts Act 1973* (Qld); and in South Australia, the *Trustee Act 1936* (SA).

11 In Australia, the *Corporations Act 2001* (Cth); and, in the United Kingdom, the *Companies Act 2006* (UK).

12 PA Ryan, 'Examining Breaches of Fiduciary Duty by Solicitors in Commercial Arrangements' (2016) 31 *Australian Journal of Corporate Law* 209, 210.

13 M Kovalcin, 'Prudence Redefined: Finding the Happy Medium between Prudence and Risk for the Uniform Prudent Investor Act' (2018) 27 *Widener Commonwealth Law Review* 249, 256.

14 See, the *Employee Retirement Income Security Act of 1974* (ERISA).

15 EJ Buck, 'Making a Prudent Response to a Tender Offer: The Corporation Trustee's Dilemma under ERISA' (1983) 32 *American University Law Review* 839, 841.

commercial experts. This expertise includes the need to understand how investments are managed at a technical level.

Digital or online trading platforms have been the preferred mode for trading in stocks since the 1990s. Prior to the Internet, investors placed their orders through stockbrokers either in person or via telephone. The brokerage firms would then enter the order into their system, which was linked to trading floors and exchanges. Since 2013, a new type of Exchange Traded Fund (ETF) has entered the investment market: the crypto-asset investment fund, for example, the Winklevoss brothers' proposed bitcoin Asset Trust and their Gemini exchange.

Structure of This Part

This chapter provides a summary of the nature of Trusts and the duties of Trustees and fiduciaries, with a particular focus on how the advent of digital economies and crypto-currencies has impacted on the way that Trusts will be administered and regulated in the future. The maturation of commercial Trusts as investment vehicles and the advent of crypto-currency exchanges have both revolutionised the legal relationship of Trustees with their beneficiaries – from common law and regulatory perspectives. In the light of these developments, three particular issues are explored in this Part.

The first issue that is explored in this Part is the higher standard of 'prudence' that may be imposed on Trustees who profit from their role, whether this is in investments markets; and whether the duty to act prudently can be discharged to the requisite standards where Trustees of crypto-assets delegate their custodial duties to blockchain-based networks (Chapter 15).

Chapter 16 deals with the particular challenges that face regulators of the Statutory Trustees who manage estates in bankruptcy, proceeds of crime, registered securities, solicitors acting as Trustees in commercial arrangements, and Trustees of digital assets in estate planning.

The third issue examined in this Part is the personal liability that may be imposed on operators of failed schemes and scams. This liability can extend to strangers or third parties who receive misapplied Trust (or Trust-like) funds. To this end, Chapter 17 first reviews some recently collapsed Ponzi schemes and financial scams, as well as some examples of spectacular losses resulting from the mismanagement of crypto-currency exchanges. In all of these cases, the way that the operators of these schemes managed the assets of their clients and customers gave rise to fiduciary duties that – when breached – imposed personal obligations upon the fiduciaries. Chapter 18 will explain how these personal obligations could then be imposed upon third parties and strangers who either received some of the misapplied assets from the collapsed fund, or who may be made liable for knowingly or dishonestly assisting in the wrong-doing that led to the collapse.

The Nature of Trusts

A Trust is an institution developed by Equity and recognised in the court of Equity as imposing obligations enforceable in Equity.[16] A Trustee holds property on Trust for the beneficiaries for a particular purpose.[17]

The primary vehicle in property protection strategies in England from the early 1600s was the Trust. It is in this setting that infant, illiterate, elderly, infirm, naive or absent property owners relied on Trustees to protect their interests. Such arrangements exposed beneficiaries to the risk of their property being exploited or misused, particularly during the process of administration of a deceased's estate. These are not the only circumstances in which beneficiaries were exposed to such risk. Charities and charitable estates controlled by trustees were similarly vulnerable.[18]

Until the 18th century, private Trusts remained relatively simple affairs, established to ensure that real property remained in the family. As a result of the socio-economic changes that marked the late Victorian era and the Industrial Revolution, the nature of Trusts, banking and the roles of women began to shift. The mid to late 1800s were a time of new wealth, social mobility and travel. However, with no systems of telecommunication, domestic and international trade and business relied on Trustees, agents and advisors to manage the affairs of absent investors and landholders.[19] This dramatic change to the society that the Courts of Chancery served meant that it had to contend with a greater variety of disputes.[20]

The South Sea Company's collapse in 1720 was the first significant event to cause the English legislature to intervene in the administration of Trusts. The South Sea Company was a British joint-stock company founded in 1711, created as a public-private partnership to consolidate and reduce the cost of national debt. That debt was partially due to the cost of warring with Spain. The company was granted a monopoly to trade with the king of Spain in South America and nearby South Sea islands (hence its name). Confidence in the South Sea Company's stock was fuelled by a combination of the reputation and trading history of the East India Company (founded in 1600), the success

---

16 JD Heydon and M Leeming, *Jacobs' Law of Trusts in Australia* (7th edn, Butterworths 2006), 1.

17 JD Heydon and M Leeming, *Jacobs' Law of Trusts in Australia* (7th edn, Butterworths 2006), 10.

18 For example, *Charity* [1667] EngR 32; (1667–1744) 2 Eq Ca Abr 190; 22 ER 163, which in enquired into the question of what will be a good charitable use and what conduct should constitute a breach or 'misemployment' of a charity – concluding that anyone receiving the benefit of a breach of trust should pay costs (Eq Ca Abr, 199). Also, in *Attorney-General v Cradock* [1837] EngR 611; (1837) Donn Eq 231; 47 ER 340, Cradock intermeddled with the property of a charitable estate, knowing that it was trust property and without authority to so act.

19 For example, *Harrison v Pryse* [1740] EngR 46; (1740) Barn C 324; 27 ER 664 was one of the authorities cited in *Eaves v Hickson* (1861) 30 Beav 137.

20 F Burns, 'The Court of Chancery in the 19th Century. A Paradox of Decline and Expansion' (2001) 21(2) *University of Queensland Law Journal* 198, 199.

of Robert Harley's previous national fund-raising efforts and exaggerated tales of the riches being exploited in the South Seas. What came to be known as a mania struck investors from all walks of life in England and abroad. The trading activity and price volatility of the South Sea Company stocks was similar to that seen previously in the Dutch tulip mania of the 17th century and then revisited 300 hundred years later with bitcoin.

In order to halt trading in the South Sea Company, the English Parliament passed the *Bubble Act 1720* (also, *Royal Exchange and London Assurance Corporation Act 1719*). It forbade all joint-stock companies not authorised by royal charter. One of the reasons for the Act was to prevent other companies from competing with the South Sea Company for investors' capital.

After successfully passing the *Bubble Act*, Parliament turned its attention to constructing a regime of company law to serve the frenetic increase in enterprise. This development presaged major developments in Trust law. By the end of the 1700s, *Keech v Sandford* [21] had been applied in numerous cases in Chancery and the obligations that attach to fiduciaries had become entrenched in equitable principle.[22]

Interestingly, an unintended consequence of the *Bubble Act* was that businesses turned to alternatives to the corporate form to run their businesses. Trading Trusts became popular and businesses became more dependent upon lawyers, who in turn developed their skills in business organisation and administration. In the era of the *Bubble Act,* businesses increasingly called upon lawyers to construct complicated forms of unincorporated business organisations that could perform most of the desirable functions of incorporated bodies, while remaining *Bubble Act*-compliant. Paradoxically, an Act that was designed to suppress the use of unincorporated business associations resulted in encouraging their proliferation, through the use of Trusts.[23]

A traditional Trust will typically govern the ownership-management of property for a group of potential beneficiaries over a lengthy number of years. If the Trustee makes an unauthorised disposal of the Trust property, the obvious remedy is to require them to restore the assets or their monetary value. It is likely to be the only way to put the beneficiaries in the same position as if the breach had not occurred. It is a real loss, which is being made good.[24] As Lord Wilkinson-Browne observed in *Imperial Group Pension Trust*

21　*Keech v Sandford* [1726] EngR 954; (1726) Sel Cas T King 61; 25 ER 223, 223 (ER).

22　For example, *Addis versus Clement* [1728] EngR 1; (1728) 2 P Wms 456; 24 ER 811; *Rakestraw v Brewer* [1728] EngR 343; (1728) 2 P Wms 511; 24 ER 839; *Blewett v Millett* [1774] EngR 49; (1774) 7 Bro PC 367; 3 ER 238; and *York Buildings Co v McKenzie* [1795] EngR 4112; (1795) 8 Bro PC 42; 3 ER 432.

23　LE Talbot, 'Enumerating Old Themes – Berle's Concept of Ownership and the Historical Development of English Company Law in Context a Paper Delivered to the Symposium: In Berle's Footsteps – A Symposium Celebrating the Launch of the Adolf A Berle Jr Center on Corporations', Law & Society (2009–2010) 33(4) *Seattle University Law Review* 1201, 1209.

24　*AIB Group (UK) Plc v Mark Redler & Co Solicitors* [2014] UKSC 58 (5 November 2014).

v Imperial Tobacco, [25] the traditional trust is one under which: 'The settlor, by way of bounty, transfers property to Trustees to be administered for the beneficiaries as the objects of his bounty ... The beneficiaries have given no consideration for what they receive.'[26]

For the purposes of the discussion of Trusts in digital economies, it is important to note two significant developments in the history of the legal relationships of the Trust:

1 The imposition of the obligations that traditionally attached only to Trustees onto other fiduciaries; and
2 The imposition of fiduciary relationships in otherwise purely commercial relationships.

With respect to the first development – that is, the expansion of Trustee duties onto other fiduciaries – a fiduciary relationship is a 'Trust-like' relationship and a fiduciary is a person whose position is 'Trustee-like'.[27]

The duties owed by a fiduciary do not flow from the title, but from the position in which the fiduciary finds themselves. It is the fact that they have assumed responsibility for the property or affairs of others that renders them liable for their careless performance of what they have undertaken to do, not the description of the trade or position which they hold.[28]

Commercial and Trading Trusts

In the last 40 years or so, English, Australian and other Common Law courts have come to recognise fiduciary obligations in commercial arrangements. It is this feature that has seen the extension of the trust relationship into commercial arrangements. Identifying when a commercial arrangement gives rise to a Trust relationship is a key consideration for the determination of whether a breach of duty will result in an order to restore the Trust monies or an order for compensation.

A Trustee or custodial fiduciary has control over their principal's funds or assets. Using the label 'Trustee' to describe a manager of another's property in this way reflects a general recognition of fiduciary obligations in modern commercial arrangements. Here, the term 'Trustee' reflects the personal and fiduciary obligations owed to a client or principal with respect to assets or other property, which are analogous to the personal obligations owed by a Trustee with respect to Trust property. This arrangement is particularly common in modern commercial and banking relationships. For example, in addition to

---

25 *Imperial Group Pension Trust v Imperial Tobacco* [1991] 1 WLR 589.
26 *Imperial Group Pension Trust v Imperial Tobacco* [1991] 1 WLR 589, 597
27 P Birks, 'Equity in the Modern Law, An Exercise in Taxonomy' (1996) 26 *University of Western Australia Law Review* 1. 17.
28 *Henderson v Merrett Syndicates Ltd* [1994] UKHL 5; [1995] 2 AC 145, 205.

contractual obligations, directors are said to have Trustee-like responsibilities in respect of company property.[29] By contrast, finance companies and directors manage assets, money and property on behalf of their principals for short periods of time or pursuant to objectives other than merely preserving the corpus of the trust. Modern commercial Trust arrangements can arise out of very different relationships and expectations among the key players to the Trust.[30]

This expansion of Trust and Trust-like relationships into commercial arrangements is important when considering the relationships that arise in digital economies and the way that money and assets are managed online, on behalf of clients and customers.

The Duties of Trustees and Fiduciaries

The legal relationship of Trust is fiduciary in nature. A fiduciary is someone who acts on behalf of another based on a relationship of trust and confidence. The paradigm fiduciary relationship is that of the Trustee and beneficiary. It is recognised by the decisions of the courts that there are other classes of persons who normally stand in a fiduciary relationship to one another, for example, partners, principal and agent, director and company, employee and employer, solicitor and client.[31]

The essence or the characteristics of the relationship between Trustees and fiduciaries has been described in terms of 'relationships of trust and confidence'. The critical feature is that 'the fiduciary undertakes or agrees to act for or on behalf of or in the interests of another person in the exercise of a power or discretion, which will affect the interests of that of another person in a legal or practical sense' giving the fiduciary 'a special opportunity to exercise the power or discretion to the detriment of that other person who is accordingly vulnerable to abuse by the fiduciary of his position'.[32]

The express Trustee is the paradigm custodial fiduciary. Most custodial fiduciaries are Trustees or executors.[33] Trustees are under a duty to account for the Trust fund.[34] As Rickett notes, this duty arises immediately upon receipt of

---

29 *Youyang Pty Ltd v Minter Ellison Morris Fletcher* [2003] HCA 15; (2003) 212 CLR 484.
30 *Imperial Group Pension Trust v Imperial Tobacco* [1991] 1 WLR 589.
31 *Hospital Products Ltd v United States Surgical Corporation* (1984) 156 CLR 41, 68 per Gibbs CJ; 96 per Mason J.
32 *Hospital Products Ltd v United States Surgical Corporation* (1984) 156 CLR 41, 96–97 per Mason J.
33 CEF Rickett, 'Equitable Compensation: Towards a Blueprint?' (2003) 25 *Sydney Law Review* 31, 47.
34 'Custodial fiduciary' is a term used in Steven Elliott, *Compensation Claims Against Trustees* (DPhil thesis, University of Oxford, 2002) Ch II, 'Fiduciaries and Claims' at 1. The Custodial Fiduciary Relation. Dr Elliott states: 'A custodial fiduciary may be tentatively defined as any person who receives property in circumstances binding him in equity to apply it for the benefit of another.'

the relevant property.[35] When an agent, a solicitor (or attorney) or other fiduciary receives its client's or its principal's property for the purposes of assisting in a transaction or commercial arrangement with another party, this non-Trust (but Trust-like) property is held pursuant to the agent's contractual arrangement with the client, as well as their fiduciary duties to the client. If a fiduciary misdirects their principal's property, it is important for the purposes of deciding which remedy to impose that the Court determines the nature of the obligations that the fiduciary owed, for example, whether the property was the subject of legal or equitable obligations, or both.[36]

As well as owing contractual, professional and statutory duties, solicitors, agents, employees and partners, can also owe fiduciary duties. The obligations of fiduciaries have found expression in the workplace, the duties of agents and other directors and in commercial transactions and relationships. For example, the role of the solicitor has changed significantly over the past 200 years. The work that modern solicitors do can now include acting as a Trustee in relation to traditional express trusts or assuming Trust-like obligations in relation to their client's assets when facilitating commercial transactions.

Digital and Crypto Assets

Digital assets and crypto assets are not the same. They both function online and utilise programmable applications to enable transactions. But the distinctions between the two are important when considering the role of trustees. The different ways that these two type of assets are recorded and stored is significant in light of the obligations that Trustees owe to their beneficiaries and that fiduciaries owe to their principals or (in commercial arrangements) their clients.

Digital assets come in the form of content that is shared on social media and via email, audio and video files, images and music, computer programmes and software code, personal records and publications, as well as licences, usernames and passwords. Meanwhile, a crypto-asset may have similar qualities or uses as a digital asset, but they utilise cryptography to ensure their validity and they reside on peer-to-peer networks, without the intervention of third parties or intermediaries. The advantage of crypto-assets is that they facilitate decentralisation. They do this by incentivising a key process that replaces trusted third parties and intermediaries. For example, without an intermediary, it is necessary to validate transactions and prove that promised obligations have been fulfilled. The key benefit of decentralisation is reduced cost. If a trusted third party is needed to certify these steps and to provide assurance against risk,

---

35 CEF Rickett, 'Equitable Compensation: Towards a Blueprint?' (2003) 25 *Sydney Law Review* 31, 35.
36 See, P Millett: 'Tracing the Proceeds of Fraud' (1991) 107 *Law Quarterly Review* 71, 82.

each transaction and the whole system becomes more expensive. By mathematically automating these processes, costs are reduced.

Whether crypto-assets are in the form of currencies (like bitcoin and Dash) or other types of tokens designed for transactions on other platforms, they all enable fast and transparent payments across borders.

Blockchains present special challenges for Trustees and fiduciaries because they are different from conventional databases and computer platforms. Blockchains and other distributed ledger technologies are not owned and operated by a single party. Instead, blockchains are operated by a collective that jointly ensures the integrity of the data stored on the blockchain. Trustees and fiduciaries owe duties of prudence and loyalty to beneficiaries and clients. Fulfilling these important obligations via an app is a challenge that crypto-currencies and crypto-assets facilitate. Traditionally, when two parties engaged in a business relationship, that relationship was facilitated by a trusted third party providing services such as bookkeeping, escrow, payment or exchange. With a blockchain, these services may be provided by new technology, implemented by blockchain software and operated jointly by many independent parties.

Trustee and Fiduciary Duties in Digital and Crypto Economies

Potential commercial uses of blockchain technology contemplate that the relationship between users and a central authority may exist both on and off a blockchain network. An off-chain relationship can satisfy regulatory requirements and help to manage investment and other external risks. An on-chain environment is relatively self-sufficient and self-regulating. This of itself can be problematic as the combination of analogue and digital relationships imports levels of trust and confidence or agency and control that cannot be managed or negated by cryptography and consensus.

It is important for Trustees, fiduciaries and other participants in financial transactions and commercial arrangements being conducted on blockchain networks to be aware of the circumstances that can give rise to liability for breach of Trust or breach of fiduciary duty. These actors may include advisers and agents or government agencies, malicious strangers or other participants who are ostensibly innocent, but may be fixed with liability because they were on notice of certain facts that should have put them on notice of wrong-doing. It is also possible for operators of crypto-currency businesses to be under a misapprehension that – because of the widely touted claim that blockchain networks are 'trustless' – they (the operators of the business) do not owe 'trust-like' or other legally enforceable duties in relation to the management of crypto-assets on their network. This is important because the 'trustless' nature of crypto-currency is limited to the technical on-chain verification of transactions, and does not describe the on- or off-chain relationships between administrator, miner, exchanger and user.

A good example of an off-chain risk is data protection. Personal data could be stored off-chain and merely linked to the blockchain through a technical connection known as a 'hash pointer'.[37] Data-management solutions are currently being developed that combine blockchain and off-chain storage to construct a personal data management platform focused on privacy.[38] Developers working on such solutions must, however, be careful to ensure that meta-data is also treated appropriately as it can reveal personal information even where personal data is not directly stored on-chain.[39] These are important issues for Trustees to consider when the assets in the corpus of the Trust are stored on a blockchain.

There are many ways that risk could arise on-chain, including the loss of crypto-currency and other assets due to mismanagement of the private and public keys that are needed in order to control and transfer crypto-assets; the manipulation of the value of a crypto-currency by exchange operators running 'pump and dump' schemes; and the discovery that the proceeds of a crypto-currency transaction are misapplied funds from a Trust.

The appointment of a Trustee to manage crypto-assets that are held on Trust is important and demanding. A bitcoin owner may choose to appoint a Trustee to manage the bitcoin for asset protection purposes – that is, to insulate the bitcoin from creditors, while meeting any tax obligations. The Trustee will naturally be someone other than the named beneficiary. In this case, the Trustee would need to be someone who is familiar with bitcoin or at least aware of the processes involved in securing, accessing and using bitcoins.[40]

Trustees are charged with preserving the corpus of the Trust that they administer, while meeting any investment expectations of the beneficiaries.[41] This can be a tricky line to walk when so many trading and commercial Trusts are an alternative to the corporate form.

The common law Trust can allow businesses to obtain many of the same doctrinal advantages as the corporate form, entity shielding, capital lock-in, tradable shares, legal personhood in litigation and a sensible scheme of fiduciary powers. The Trust offers these features in a format that is cheaper and easier to access than the corporation. While the Trust is never a completely perfect substitute for the corporate form, and it may be burdened by legislative

---

37 M Finck, 'Blockchains and Data Protection in the European Union' (2018) *European Data Protection Law Review* 17, 23.

38 G Zyskind et al., 'Decentralizing Privacy: Using Blockchain to Protect Personal Data' (IEEE Security and Privacy Workshops, 2015), 180 <http://ieeexplore.ieee.org/document/7163223/>.

39 J Smith et al., 'Applying Blockchain Technology in Global Data Infrastructure', *Technical Report ODI-TR-201 6–001, Open Data Institute* (2016) <https://data.gov.ru/sites/default/files/documents/315354748-applying-blockchain-technology-in-global-data-infrastructure.pdf>.

40 AK Noonan, 'Bitcoin or Bust: Can One Really Trust One's Digital Assets' (2015) 7 *Estate Planning & Community Property Law Journal* 583, 589–90.

41 Unlike directors of companies who are charged with risk the company's capital in order to maximise profits, a Trustee must be prudent. Prudence means that a Trustee's exercise of discretion should be based on knowledge of critical quantitative measurement of risk. See, PJ Collins, 'Prudence' (2007) 124 *Banking Law Journal* 29.

acts that made the Trust illegal or otherwise less appealing than the corporate form, it is remarkably effective in offering the key features of the corporate form.[42]

Seen from the Trustee's perspective, the most significant difference in the administration of a Trust and the management of a company is that Trustees must be prudent in their investment decisions so as to preserve the corpus of the Trust, while a company director can use his or her business judgement to risk the company's capital in order to maximise its profits. A Trust containing bitcoins – for example – will require different investment approaches that will necessarily depend upon the Trustee's skills and the Trust's purpose, while protecting and preserving the user's bitcoins; and the beneficiary's needs.[43]

In terms of liability for breach of Trust and breach of fiduciary duty, there is an important distinction between the way that the courts treat Trustees and third parties. When a Trust fund is found to be deficient, the Trustee must account for that shortfall. In Australia, there is no requirement for a causal inquiry as to whether the shortfall was the fault of the Trustee.[44]

Absent any fraud or dishonesty, the Trustee may be indemnified by the Trust's insurance policy, but the strict obligation to regularise the accounts falls to the Trustee.[45] With respect to the liability of third parties, they can only be made liable if the relevant breach by the Trustee or fiduciary was a breach of one of their fiduciary duties. In Australia, for example, this would be the duty not to profit from their position and the duty not to let their interests conflict with those of their client.[46] It is of the essence of a Trust that the Trustee holds property subject to an obligation to administer it in the interests of others – the beneficiaries.[47] Trustees and fiduciaries can owe many non-fiduciary duties to their client. For example, a fiduciary may have entered into a contract that includes an undertaking as to confidentiality. A breach of this duty alone would not give rise to the liability of third parties as it is not a fiduciary duty.

---

42 J Morley, 'The Common Law Corporation the Power of the Trust in Anglo American Business History' (2016) 116(8) *Columbia Law Review* 2145 <https://columbialawreview.org/content/the-common-law-corporation-the-power-of-the-trust-in-anglo-american-business-history/>.

43 See, A Ullal, 'Understanding the Proposed Bitcoin ETF: 5 Key Questions', *NASDAQ* (November 11, 2014, i1:09 AM) <http://www.nasdaq.com/article/understanding-the-proposed-bitcoin-etf-5-key-questions-cm 412799>. See also, AK Noonan, 'Bitcoin or Bust: Can One Really Trust One's Digital Assets' (2015) 7 *Estate Planning & Community Property Law Journal* 583, 590.

44 *Youyang Pty Ltd v Minter Ellison Morris Fletcher* [2003] HCA 15; (2003) 212 CLR 484. This is to be distinguished from the position in the United Kingdom where a causal inquiry is applicable in cases where there has been an innocent breach of fiduciary duty. See, *Target Holdings v Redferns* [1996] 1 AC 421.

45 *Re Dawson; Union Fidelity Trustee Co Ltd v Perpetual Trustee Co Ltd* [1966] 2 NSWR 211, 220 (Street J).

46 See, *Breen v Williams* [1996] HCA 57; (1996) 186 CLR 71, [27] (Gaudron and McHugh JJ).

47 JRF Lehane, 'Delegation of Trustees' Powers and Current Developments in Investment Funds Management' (1995) 7(1) *Bond Law Review* 36, 38.

15 Duties of Trustees and Fiduciaries in Digital Economies

Trustees are obliged to exercise their powers in the best interests of present and future beneficiaries of the Trust, and treat different classes of beneficiaries impartially.[1] This duty is paramount.[2] Trustees must also obey the law. However, subject to the law, they must put the interests of their beneficiaries first. When the purpose of the Trust is to provide financial benefits for the beneficiaries, as is usually the case, the best interests of the beneficiaries are usually their best financial interests. For example, in the case of a power of investment, the power must be exercised so as to yield the best return for the beneficiaries, judged in relation to the risks of the investment in question; and the prospects of the yield of income and capital appreciation both have to be considered in judging the return from the investment.[3] In any discussion of a duty to act in the best interests of beneficiaries, the established duties are to have regard, in exercising fiduciary powers, to the interests of the beneficiaries and not to extraneous considerations; and to act with reasonable care and prudence.[4]

Prudence means that a Trustee's exercise of discretion should be based on knowledge of critical quantitative measurement of risk.[5] Three issues arise from this edict that directly impact the duties of Trustees. Firstly, in the case of 'professional Trustees',[6] (notwithstanding the adjective 'professional') the necessary types or levels of skill expected of a Trustee must be judged in the absence of a professional qualification or established standard. Secondly, Trustees who administer crypto-assets that are recorded on blockchain networks need to apply specialist skills to manage storage and transactions. Determining whether a Trustee's duties have been discharged prudently may be difficult when the requisite skill is new and specialist. In such a case, there may be no

---

1   A Trustee also has duties as to the fair treatment of beneficiaries among themselves, whether the beneficiaries form one class or several classes. See PD Finn, *Fiduciary Obligations* (The Law Book Company, 1977), chapters 12, 13.
2   See, JRF Lehane, 'Delegation of Trustees' Powers and Current Developments in Investment Funds Management' (1995) 7(1) *Bond Law Review* 36, 36.
3   *Cowan v Scargill* [1985] Ch 270.
4   *Cowan v Scargill* [1985] Ch 270, 288.
5   See, PJ Collins, 'Prudence' (2007) 124 *Banking Law Journal* 29.
6   Professional Trustees are so-called because they are remunerated for their services.

precedent against which to measure the Trustee's level of skill and care. Thirdly, the Trustees of bitcoin (and other crypto-currencies) in exchange traded funds (ETFs) may be subject to novel obligations if the custodial duties are characterised by the courts as having been delegated to a blockchain network (or other distributed ledger technology). These three issues are explored in this chapter.

This chapter will also explore the circumstances where an asset management arrangement – although not necessarily subject to a Trust – gives rise to fiduciary duties. Although a Trustee is the paradigm fiduciary, not all fiduciaries are necessarily Trustees. Exchange operators and fund managers who use their clients' funds to make investments owe fiduciary duties to their clients (unless they have expressly and successfully contracted out of the fiduciary-principal relationship).[7]

The feature that marks the fiduciary out for special scrutiny is the obligation of loyalty reflected in various aspects of the relationship, the most important of which are the duty to avoid a conflict of duty and interest and the duty not to misuse the fiduciary position.[8] What lies at the heart of the fiduciary obligation is a standard of conduct that requires the fiduciary to act selflessly and with undivided loyalty in the best interests of the other party. The fiduciary's standard of conduct is set at a very high level. The effect of the standard is to limit the way in which the fiduciary may use a discretion or power over another party.[9] Whether such standards are imposed turns on whether the relationship meets the criteria for characterisation as fiduciary in nature. This is why commercial transactions falling outside the accepted traditional categories of fiduciary relationship often do not give rise to fiduciary duties. It is not that they are commercial in nature; rather, it is that they do not meet the relevant criteria.[10]

---

7 In *ASIC v Citigroup Global Markets Australia Pty Ltd* (2007) 160 FCR 35; [2007] FCA 963, Jacobson J's decision is authority for the proposition that, as between contracting parties, a fiduciary relationship, and associated duties and proscriptions, may be excluded entirely by agreement. His Honour said at [280], without qualification, that 'there appears to be no restriction in the law to prevent a fiduciary from contracting out of ... his or her fiduciary duties, particularly where no prior fiduciary relationship existed and the contract defines the rights and duties of the parties'.

8 See, *Breen v Williams* [1996] HCA 57; (1996) 186 CLR 71 at [27] (Gaudron and McHugh JJ), citing Lord Hershell in *Bray v Ford* (1896) AC 44 at 51–52, that 'it is an inflexible rule of a Court of Equity that a person in a fiduciary position is not unless otherwise expressly provided, entitled to make a profit; he is not allowed to put himself in a position where his interest and duty conflict.' See also, *Chan v Zacharia* [1984] HCA; (1984) 154 CLR 178, 198–199.

9 M Cope, 'A Comparative Evaluation of Developments in Equitable Relief for Breach of Fiduciary Duty and Breach of Trust' (2006) 6(1) *Queensland University of Technology Law and Justice Journal* 118.

10 *John Alexander's Clubs Pty Ltd v White City Tennis Club Ltd* [2010] HCA 19; (2010) 241 CLR 1 at [90] (French CJ, Gummow, Hayne, Heydon and Kieffel JJ). See also, PA Ryan, 'Examining Breaches of Fiduciary Duty by Solicitors in Commercial Arrangements' (2016) 31 *Australian Journal of Corporate Law* 209.

The special obligations of fiduciaries are important to note when considering the relationship between those who are doing business online, particularly where one party manages the assets of the other. This is a regular occurrence in the case of crypto-currency exchanges and ETFs. All duties arising out of the assumption of responsibility for another's property or affairs have a fiduciary character. It is not necessary for the fiduciary to know that they are in this special position or that it has a name. This is important in light of the arrangements that bitcoin exchanges enable in relation to their customers, and that managers of crypto-tokens create when they launch a new coin (known as 'initial coin offerings' or 'ICOs'). It is not unusual to see websites run by such businesses expressly disclaiming responsibility for the types of duties that are imposed by statute and the common law, and which therefore cannot be avoided.

Professional Trustees and the Prudence Paradox

The term 'Professional Trustee' refers to Trustees who are remunerated for their efforts. Professional Trustees such as pension scheme managers, lawyers, accountants, banks and investment firms, due to their expertise, play a large role in managing trust investment trusts.[11] Despite the use of the adjective 'professional', there is no formal requirement for a qualification in order to undertake this role. This is despite a lot of regulation setting out the obligations of Trustees and the rights of beneficiaries to the trust that they administer.[12] In the United States, for example, the various states consistently require, as a basic standard of conduct, the care and skill of a prudent person. However, there is no such consistency of approach among the states to the question of whether professional trustees should be held to a higher standard of care.[13]

Since the mid-20th century, a significant portion of the funds invested in the modern securities market have derived from the assets of various types of trust accounts.[14] As early as 1936, courts recognised the logic of requiring Professional Trustees to utilise their expertise in managing the funds entrusted to them.[15] Due to the large volume of business they manage for their many clients, judicial decisions have endorsed the particular skills of professional and corporate Trustees as being better equipped than other individuals to manage and keep track of Trust account investments.[16] However, unlike directors of

---

11 LD Laurino, 'Investment Responsibility of Professional Trustees' (1977) 51 *St John's Law Review* 717, 717.
12 B Maton, 'The Paradox of Professional Trustees', *Financial Times* (21 March 2001) <https://www.ft.com/content/83762314-33f1-11df-8ebf-00144feabdc0>.
13 DA Steele, 'Exculpatory Clauses in Trust Instruments' (1995) 14 *Estates & Trusts Journal* 216
14 LD Laurino, 'Investment Responsibility of Professional Trustees' (1977) 51 *St John's Law Review* 717, 717.
15 *In re Church's Will*, 221 Wis. 472, 266 N.W. 210 (1936)
16 LD Laurino, 'Investment Responsibility of Professional Trustees' (1977) 51 *St John's Law Review* 717, 728.

companies who are charged with risking the company's capital in order to maximise profits, a Trustee must be prudent. Herein lies the paradox: the Professional Trustee is not necessarily professionally qualified.

This lack of professional qualifications could be problematic in light of the duties imposed on Trustees to manage investments with skill and care. Most modern trust instruments give Trustees a wide power to make investment decisions as they see fit. Trustees have an overriding duty to exercise their investment powers with care and prudence. Trustees must establish a suitable level of risk and diversification across portfolios. Most common law jurisdictions have statutes regulating Trustees and set standard investment criteria that they must consider, both when making an investment decision and also when reviewing investments.

There are arguments in favour of holding a Professional Trustee to a higher standard of care. For example, in *In re Estate of Beach*, a California court suggested that the present executor, The Bank of California, was something other than 'a man of ordinary judgement'. This is because a bank is a Trust company, a professional in its field. Trust companies solicit business through advertisements and invitations in which they claim greater expertise than individuals. They employ staff of Trust officers, securities analysts, property managers, accountants and attorneys. A rule of care phrased for individual executors is inappropriate for measuring the conduct of Trust companies in their executorship role. In light of this, the California court observed: 'A banker, a doctor, a lawyer, may not gain business as a specialist and then expect to defend their mistakes as a layman.'[17]

The United Kingdom's *Uniform Prudent Investor Act* clearly explains that non-Professional Trustees should be held to a lower standard of care than professionals, and the delegation rules provide that the status of a Trustee is a critical factor in determining whether the Trustee properly delegated and performed its duties. It has been claimed in the United Kingdom that the use of exemption clauses by Professional Trustees is unconscionable. On this, Shinn poses the rhetorical question:

> Should not the colorful advertising on the part of trust companies, representing to the public that their officers are skilled specialists in the business of investing and protecting trust estates, cause the courts to regard any act that falls short of closely superintending the trust as gross negligence which an exoneration clause will not excuse?[18]

Whereas the usual approach to assessing the level of skill that a Trustee must exercise is measured against the degree of care and skill that a person of

---

17 Paraphrasing here from, *In re Estate of Beach* 116 Cal. Rptr. 418 (1974), modified, 15 Cal. 3d 623, 542 P.2d 994, 125 Cal. Rptr. 570 (1975).
18 HA Shinn, 'Exoneration Clauses in Trust Instruments' (1933) 42 *Yale Law Journal* 359, 374.

ordinary prudence would exercise in the management of his or her own private affairs, Shinn's suggestion has merit in light of the expectation that such claims would create in the investors. Conversely, the Ontario Law Reform Commission has recommended that no term in a trust instrument should be valid to the extent that it purports to exonerate Trustees from liability for failure to exercise the degree of care, diligence and skill that a person of ordinary prudence would exercise.

While not needing to be an expert, the modern Professional Trustee must therefore have a broad understanding of the way the available investment markets operate and must be able critically to assess the worth of any recommendations; and a Trustee needs to know when and how they can delegate their duties to others with impunity.[19] A consequence of a failure to set minimum standards for the conduct and prudence of Professional Trustees extends beyond just the tests to be applied in courts. The immediate and practical result is that if the more experienced and sophisticated Trustees retreat from novel investments, there is a danger that the more exotic portfolios and products will be left in the hands of those with less experience. Furthermore, it would not be an answer for Trustees to delegate their investment responsibilities to others and assume that this will eliminate any risk of liability.

Trustees of Crypto-currency Exchanges and Asset Trusts

Crypto-currency exchanges enable the exchange of crypto-currencies to and from fiat currencies (for example, selling bitcoin for euro); and exchange between different crypto-currencies (for example, selling bitcoin for ether). Meanwhile, crypto-currency asset Trusts invest crypto-currencies on behalf of their investor clients. The objective of a crypto-currency asset Trust is for the value of the Trust's shares to reflect the combined value of the crypto-currencies owned by the Trust (less the cost of running the Trust and any liabilities). It is common for physical asset Trusts to be registered to operate as an ETF. Investors in an ETF own shares in the underlying asset that is being traded by the fund. However, at this time, no crypto-currency asset Trusts have succeeded in an application to operate as an ETF.

Crypto-currency Asset Trusts

In the case of speculative or hazardous investments, a Trust deed would need to stipulate that it is anticipated that this sort of investment will be undertaken by the Trustee. This would apply – for example – in the case of a 'bitcoin asset Trust'. The objective of an asset Trust is for the value of the Trust's shares to reflect, at any given time, the value of assets owned by the Trust at that time, less the Trust's expenses and liabilities. The Trust's shares are listed and traded on an exchange. Each share represents a fractional undivided beneficial interest

19 *Speight v Gaunt* (1883) 22 ChD 727, 739 (per Jessel MR).

in the net assets of the Trust. As the shares are bought and then sold at increasingly higher prices, the value of the corpus of the Trust's assets increases. A bitcoin asset Trust would be hazardous because its price fluctuates, which in turn is caused by speculation and uncertainty. The price of bitcoin in its first decade ranged in price per bitcoin from less than US$0.10 in January 2009, to almost US$20,000 in December 2017, retreating back to US$6,000 in December 2018.[20] Throughout this period, unsuccessful attempts were made to register more than one bitcoin asset Trust as an ETF with the United States Security and Exchange Commission (SEC). The SEC rejected these applications largely due to the volatility of the price of bitcoin, the ease and secrecy with which the price can be manipulated, and the vulnerability of the blockchain network to malicious attack.[21]

Operating an ETF offers unique advantages to bitcoin exchange operators. They are inexpensive, with low management fees, and they are tax efficient. Unlike other funds, an ETF can be sold at any time through the trading day. The disadvantages of ETFs include a lack of diversification in stocks and the untested nature of many of the types of stocks. Both of these disadvantages apply in relation to bitcoin ETFs. Furthermore, the SEC said in relation to bitcoin that the near anonymity (or pseudonymity) of participants would make it difficult for the ETFs to meet their surveillance-sharing obligations.[22] The SEC found that the proposed surveillance-sharing agreements were not sufficient, particularly in light of bitcoin's disreputable history.[23]

The Winklevoss brothers have twice attempted to register their Winklevoss *Bitcoin Asset Trust* as an ETF, but on both occasions the regulator deemed the crypto-currencies too risky for registration as an ETF. In March 2017, the SEC rejected a first attempt by Cameron and Tyler Winklevoss to launch a bitcoin asset trust, after more than three years of amended applications. Their second attempt failed in July 2018. The SEC said that it disapproved the application and rejected any suggestion that 'bitcoin markets are uniquely resistant to manipulation'. It also highlighted problems with potential fraud and investor protection.[24] Although the Winklevoss brothers assured the SEC that detailed

20 'Bitcoin Price Index', *CoinDesk* (2019) <https://www.coindesk.com/price/bitcoin>.
21 'Document Filing', *United States Security and Exchange Commission* (8 February 2018) <https://www.sec.gov/Archives/edgar/data/1579346/000119312517034708/0001193125-17-034708-index.htm>.
22 Under section 6(b)(5) of the *Securities Exchange Act of 1934* (the Exchange Act), the rules of a national securities exchange are designed to prevent fraudulent and manipulative acts and practices and to protect investors and the public interest. Surveillance sharing between reputable entities ensures that conduct on the market place complies with the regulatory framework.
23 W Hu et al., 'What Do the SEC's Recent Bitcoin Disapproval Orders Really Mean for Investors?', *Harvard Law School Forum on Corporate Governance and Financial Regulation* (27 April 2017) <https://corpgov.law.harvard.edu/2017/04/27/what-do-the-secs-recent-bitcoin-disapproval-orders-really-mean-for-investors/>.
24 K Rooney and B Pisani, 'Winklevoss Twins Bitcoin ETF Rejected by SEC', *CNBC* (26 July 2018) <https://www.cnbc.com/2018/07/26/winklevoss-twins-bitcoin-etf-rejected-by-sec.html>.

risk warnings would be provided on their EFT website, the application was refused for being too risky. The SEC and other regulators are still uneasy with the volatile and largely unpoliced crypto-currency market.[25]

Keeping bitcoin asset trusts from operating ETFs has not put a stop to the provision of other commercial crypto-currency services, the most popular crypto-currency exchanges. Some exchanges operate as Trusts, holding their clients' bitcoin or ether in deposit accounts (an exchange's equivalent to a bank account) or in common Trust funds (which the operator then uses to invest or speculate in crypto-currencies).

The Winklevoss brothers' Gemini exchange was launched in August 2017. It offers digital asset exchange and custodial services for crypto-currency investors. The exchange describes itself as a 'New York Trust Company' with the tag line, 'Every Revolution Needs Rules'. In similar terms as the Grayscale bitcoin Trust, the Gemini exchange describes its service offering with language that suggests dramatic and almost violent change. The word 'revolution' connotes force, overthrowing of a government and social disorder, all in favour of a new system. With this careful choice of language, users would be in no doubt as to the novelty and riskiness of this investment product.

The Grayscale bitcoin Trust is an exchange. It operates under the tag line 'A bold opportunity in the era of bitcoin gold'.[26] The use of the word 'bold' in this context suggests that this investment will be better suited to brave investors: those with an appetite for risk. Promoting its services in this way may help the Trustees to defend their investment decisions and to prove that they have satisfied a requisite standard of care (that is, by putting their prospective customers or investors on notice of the risks involved).

The operators of the Gemini and Grayscale exchanges may be strategically using language that warns investors of 'bold' and 'revolutionary' investments so as to establish a line of defence in the face of any litigation about whether the Trustees discharged their duties to invest prudently. Rather than reassuring potential investors that they can rely on skill and expertise of the Trustee, the decisions seem to support a shift in onus to the client or beneficiary to accept an extraordinary level of risk. This shift could be significant in the course of any litigation because when considering an action for breach of duty in relation to investment, the Court is able to take into account whether the Trustees invested according a strategy developed by them in response to their duty to invest prudently. These stark 'warnings' that investors need to be bold and revolutionary in their appetite for risk seems to be setting up a defence that this is the 'investment strategy' of the Trustee.[27] In such a case, the demand for

---

25 B Fung, 'Winklevoss Twins Bitcoin Fund Rejected by SEC', *AFR* (27 Jul 2018) <http s://www.afr.com/news/world/
winklevoss-twins-bitcoin-fund-rejected-by-sec-20180727-h1386c>.

26 'Grayscale Bitcoin Trust', *Grayscale.co* (2019) <https://grayscale.co/bitcoin-trust/>.

27 Similarly, extreme warnings of risk have also been used in advertising by cigarette companies. By warning consumers that 'smoking kills', cigarette companies have

prudence in the Trustee seems to be outweighed by the investors' acceptance of unreasonable risk.

Custodial Duties of Trustees of Crypto-assets

The assets of an asset Trust are usually in physical form. This could be resources like gold, silver, nickel and copper. For example, in the JP Morgan Physical Copper Trust, the Trust's copper is held in one or more warehouses maintained by a warehouse-keeper.[28] However, in the case of a bitcoin asset Trust, the underlying asset is not something physical; it is a virtual currency that is identifiable only because of a unique record that can be identified or 'tokenised' on a blockchain network. The fact that the underlying asset is not in physical form, but is instead just programmable code, presents an interesting custodial challenge for secure storage or 'warehousing' of these assets.

Blockchains are not stand-alone systems; rather, they are only components in broader systems. For example, the parties that transact on a blockchain are normally represented by the public keys, and so key management must be performed outside the blockchain. Blockchains do not have user interfaces, and do not have a native connection to physical systems, and so must be integrated with other components connecting to human users and 'Internet of Things' (or 'IoT') systems.

Once a relationship of Trust is established in relation to crypto-assets, a Trustee must exercise the full suite of obligations in relation to those 'funds'. These obligations are custodial, fiduciary and statutory. This presents challenges that are peculiar to crypto-assets, including the virtual nature of digital records and the sensitivity of keeping secure the private and public keys that are needed to access and manage the assets. To secure crypto-currency purchased from an exchange, a Trustee would need to request the exchange to transfer that crypto-currency to an address directly controlled by the Trustee. When investing with a bitcoin asset Trust, the Trustee manages the crypto-currency in wallets and stores the private and public keys on behalf of the investors. For example, the website for the Grayscale bitcoin Trust assures potential investors that: 'BTC Trust enables investors to gain exposure to the price movement of bitcoin through a traditional investment vehicle, without the challenges of buying, storing, and safekeeping bitcoins.'[29]

Good key management practices are critical for crypto-asset management. Private keys should not be exposed to computers that are connected to the Internet. This can be facilitated by what is known as 'cold storage' of secure hardware wallets or paper wallets. Key management encompasses the

created a clear line of defence against claims by dying plaintiffs that they suggested otherwise.

28 JP Morgan Physical Copper Trust, 'Company Description' (since withdrawn, on 22 December 2014) <https://www.nasdaq.com/markets/ipos/company/jpm-xf-physical-copper-trust-839821-65466>.

29 Grayscale Asset Trust, *Grayscale.co* (2019) <https://grayscale.co/bitcoin-trust/>

generation of encrypting and decrypting keys as well as their storage, distribution, cataloguing and eventual destruction. These functions may be handled centrally, distributed among users, or managed by some combination of central and local key management.[30]

Crucially, if trust is to be ensured when crypto-assets are held on Trust, there will need to be transparency in relation to the fulfilment of the Trustee's obligations. This means that prudence in relation to investment and integrity of key management must be disclosed and reported in a way that protects the security of the relevant assets and the privacy of the beneficiaries. According to the 'User Agreement' of Gemini, the user enters into a custody agreement with Gemini Trust Company, LLC. The exchange offers to trade in a number of crypto-currencies, it offers custody accounts for two types of crypto-currency: bitcoin and ether. Gemini describes itself on its website as:

> A custodian that is licensed to custody your digital assets in trust on your behalf. As a New York trust company licensed by the New York State Department of Financial Services, Gemini is:
> (i)   a Qualified Custodian;
> (ii) a fiduciary under §100 of the New York Banking Law; and
> (iii) held to specific capital reserve requirements and banking compliance standards.[31]

This 'User Agreement' stipulates that 'Digital Assets custodied in a Depository Account are pooled together in one or more of our Digital Asset wallets'. Under New York law, Trust companies are formed for the purpose of managing assets with fiduciary powers. The Trust company shall neither accept deposits nor make loans except for deposits and loans arising directly from the exercise of the fiduciary powers specified in Section 100 of the state's Banking Law. The principal businesses of Trust companies comprise a diverse range of activities under the fiduciary umbrella, such as corporate trust, transfer agency, securities clearance, investment management and custodial services. Because of size considerations, the institutions tend to focus on one or two of these business lines.[32] In the case of the Gemini Trust Company, its fiduciary obligations are particularly important in light of the pooling and reinvesting of investors' fiat money and crypto-currencies in 'common trust funds'.[33]

---

30 D Bernard Jr and WS Hein Co. Reams Inc, 'Law of E-SIGN: A Legislative History of the Electronic Signatures in Global and National Commerce Act' (2000) *Public Law No.* 106.

31 Custody Services, *Gemini* (as at 19 November 2018) <https://gemini.com/custody-services/>. It is noted that the use of the word 'custody' as a verb is grammatically unusual, but has been transcribed faithfully here.

32 New York State, 'Banking Industry', *Department of Financial Service* (2019) <https://www.dfs.ny.gov/banking/iaus1b.htm>.

33 Under §100 of the New York Banking Law, when moneys are held in a common trust fund, the trust company, either alone or in conjunction with one or more

These arrangements could lead to some confusion for investors, particularly with regard to their expectations about whether their assets are being held on Trust by a Trust company. For example, the two options for types of accounts on offer are Deposit accounts and Custody accounts. The nature of a Trust company and the use of the term 'Custody' could lead investors to think that their funds are being held on Trust – no matter which type of account they are in. This assumption could be significant if any of the funds are lost and not recoverable, because only funds that are lost pursuant to a breach of trust or breach of fiduciary duty may be recoverable from the Trustee's operators personally. Furthermore, only a breach of Trust or breach of fiduciary duty will give rise to a cause of action against any third parties for their knowing participation in a dishonest breach. For this reason, whether a custodian is a Trustee and owes fiduciary duties will be critical in the case of a breach, and does not turn on whether the Trustee or fiduciary thinks they are in that position.

Curiously, Gemini characterise the deposit into the Custody account as a 'bailment'. The terms and conditions stipulate that funds place into the Custody Account are 'a bailment and remain the property of the investor (or customer)'. Characterising a deposit that will be in the custody of Gemini as a 'bailment' is contrary to the established convention that a deposit of funds into an account is a loan. For example, bank accounts are contracts of lending or borrowing only. A fixed deposit of $100 for one year at 3% interest means that the customer is lending $100 to the bank for that period and in exchange will be repaid the $100 plus $3 interest. Bailments involve goods or tangible assets. In banking, what may seem like a bailment to a depositor, the law transforms into a loan. What may look like a bailor-bailee arrangement, the law says is a creditor and a debtor relationship. Title to the deposited funds passes from the depositor to the bank.[34]

To support its claim that the deposit is a bailment, Gemini refers to the deposit of 'digit assets'. This begs the question, can non-physical assets or goods can be the subject of a bailment? If this is answered in the positive, then confusion may still arise from reference in the Gemini User Agreement to users 'opening an account';[35] the bases upon which an account may be 'suspended and all accounts beneficially owned by you'; and Gemini's right to 'freeze/lock the funds and assets in all such accounts' under certain circumstances.[36] This

other persons acting with it in any fiduciary capacity, may invest and reinvest such moneys or any part thereof by adding the same to any such common trust funds and short term investment common trust funds.

34 TC Harker, 'Bailment Ailment: An Analysis of the Legal Status of Ordinary Demand Deposits in the Shadow of the Financial Crisis of 2008' (2014) 19(3) *Fordham Journal of Corporate & Financial Law* 543, 543.

35 'You agree and understand that by signing up to Gemini and opening an account, you are agreeing to enter into this user agreement'. See, 'User Agreement', *Gemini* (2019) <https://gemini.com/user-agreement/#account-closure>.

36 'You agree and understand that we have the right to immediately (i) suspend your account and all accounts beneficially owned by you and any members of your household or for which you are a representative or authorized signatory and, in the

section of the User Agreement adopts the language used in bank accounts, not the bailment of goods and assets. Indeed, in August 2013, a federal judge ruled that for purposes of United States securities regulation, bitcoin is indeed 'money'.[37] If this is correct, then a deposit of bitcoin into the Custody account is unlikely to constitute a 'bailment'. However, there is always the possibility of contention and change when it comes to defining and characterising crypto-currencies.

If the funds in the Custody account were indeed a bailment, then if Gemini (as the bailee) fails to return the funds to the bailor in accordance with the bailment agreement, then Gemini would be guilty of larceny. The law of bail-ment does not operate within the same strict liability as the law of Trusts. However, once a bailee accepts delivery of any assets or goods, they become responsible for their safekeeping, no matter what. Usually, if a bailee exercises due care, then absent any fraud, the bailee is not liable for loss. However, there are some jurisdictions that align with the school of thought that this is only the case if the bailment was for the benefit of the bailor.

If a bailee is a professional or 'for profit' organisation or service, then an extraordinary level of care may be owed. Bailees may try to disclaim their lia-bility for loss or damage. However, many courts refuse to honour the dis-claimers, unless the bailee has given clear notice of the disclaimer and the legal effects intended by the disclaimer. In the case of the Gemini Trust Company, it may be that the notice provided on their website satisfies this requirement. The relevant wording in the Gemini Custody Agreement reads:

> By entering into this Custody Agreement, you agree that you intend to create a bailment of Assets with us, and you agree you intend that we be the bailee ... You agree and understand that in the event of a market dis-ruption, we may, in our sole discretion, do one or more of the following:
> (i) suspend access to our custody services; or
> (ii) prevent you from completing any actions via our custody services. We are not liable for any losses suffered by you resulting from such actions. Following such an event, when custody services resume, you agree and understand that the prevailing market prices may differ significantly from the prices prior to such event.[38]

The warning here that 'you agree and understand that the prevailing market prices may differ significantly from the prices prior to such event' suggests that if Gemini is unable to return the bailed assets in full, then Gemini says that this

---

case of entities, any affiliates (each, a "Related Account"), (ii) freeze/lock the funds and assets in all such accounts ...'. See, 'User Agreement', *Gemini*<https://gem ini.com/user-agreement/#account-closure>.

37 *Sec. and Exch. Comm'n v. Shavers*, No. 4:13-CV-416, 2013 WL 4028182, at *2 (E.D. Tex. Aug. 6, 2013) ('Bitcoin is a currency or form of money').

38 Custody Agreement, *Gemini* (as at 19 November 2018) <https://gemini.com/custody-agreement/>.

outcome is agreed to by the parties. However, such an agreement or disclaimer may offend the exception that applies to all 'bailees for business'. In the case of bailees-for-business, even if it can be proven that the bailor has read the disclaimer and understood it, courts are likely to make the bailee liable on grounds of public policy.[39]

Most Trustee legislation sets out the rules in relation to the delegation of custodial services. The core duties of loyalty and fidelity entitle a beneficiary to the single-minded loyalty of the fiduciary. Fiduciary duties of loyalty and fidelity are usually owed by custodial fiduciaries *in addition to* duties of trust and confidence. When it comes to Trustees and the delegation of custodial duties to third parties, it is a common position across many jurisdictions that custodial obligations must be delegated prudently.[40]

Exclusion of Trustee Liability

When a Trustee is in breach of their duties to the Trust and the beneficiaries, the Trustee, their insurer and any third parties who may have participated knowingly or dishonestly in the breach may seek to have the Trustee exonerated. A Trustee's liability for breach of Trust may be excluded completely; or liability may be limited by an express provision to that effect in the Trust instrument.[41] Such exclusion of liability provisions takes effect as equitable provisions and not as contractual provisions.[42]

In the English decision in *Armitage v Nurse*, [43] the court considered the effect of a clause that exonerated a Trustee from their 'own actual fraud'. This was construed to mean dishonesty so as to connote:

> an intention on the part of the Trustee to pursue a particular course of action either knowing that it is contrary to the interests of the beneficiaries or being recklessly indifferent whether it is contrary to their interests or not.[44]

In *Armitage v Nurse*, Millett LJ reflected on the permitted scope of such clauses, and indicated that an exemption clause could exclude liability for wilful default as well as for ordinary negligence and want of probity as well as gross

---

39 In the United States, it is unlikely that any court in any of the States would uphold a disclaimer by a bailee for business – see, *Restatement (Second) of Contracts* (1979, copyright 1981), Section 195(2)(b).

40 For example, section 53 of *Trustee Act 1925* (NSW).

41 *Armitage v Nurse* [1998] Ch 241; *Taylor v Midland Bank Trust Co* (2000) 2 ITELR 439; *Bogg v Raper* (1998) The Times, 22 April; *Wight v Olswang* (1999) The Times, 18 May.

42 *Re Duke of Norfolk Settlement Trusts* [1982] Ch 61, 77.

43 *Armitage v Nurse* [1998] Ch 241; [1997] 3 WLR 1046, ALL ER 705.

44 *Armitage v Nurse* [1998] Ch 241; [1997] 3 WLR 1046; ALL ER 705, 711 per Millett LJ.

negligence.[45] As *Armitage v Nurse* establishes, Trustees can exclude liability for duties of skill and care and prudence and diligence. The Trustees in *Armitage v Nurse* were not liable for negligence, because they acted in good faith and in the honest belief that they were acting in the best interests of the beneficiary.[46] But liability for the 'irreducible core of obligations owed by Trustees' cannot be excluded.[47] It appears from *Armitage v Nurse* that the losses which Trustees can negotiate out of are those which arise from a breach of an equitable duty of care and skill, not those which arise from misapplication of Trust assets or undisclosed conflicts of duty and interest, which are surely part of the irreducible core.[48]

Trustees have a statutory indemnity in respect of costs 'reasonably incurred in or about the execution of the trusts or powers'.[49] The right to an indemnity extends to former Trustees. In this case, the Trust Deed includes a trustee indemnity clause. A new Trustee will demand the right to an indemnity that to a former Trustee.[50]

The term 'trading trust' refers to an entity (the Trust) that is conducting a business under the authority of a Trust instrument. While the ordinary Trust is for the holding and conservation of particular property with incidental powers of sale and investment, the business Trust is a medium for the conduct of a business and the sharing of its profits.

Trust structures can create confusion and legal issues for trade creditors. Often, trade creditors may not even realise they are trading with a customer as Trustee of a Trust. This could be a problem that will face the operators of crypto-currency exchanges and crypto-currency asset Trusts. They might assume that they can decide upon the nature of the relationship, without realising that the arrangement will in fact dictate whether they are a Trustee, a fiduciary, a bailee or a debtor.

The minimum necessary and sufficient duty to give substance to a Trust is the duty of the Trustee to perform the Trust 'honestly and in good faith for the benefit of the beneficiaries'. To this minimum standard, one can add the duties of skill, prudence and diligence. However, in the case of crypto-currencies, it will be necessary for the operators of exchanges and asset Trusts to define their purpose and properly characterise the nature of the relationship. In

45 *Armitage v Nurse* [1998] Ch 241; [1997] 3 WLR 1046; ALL ER 705, 713 per Millett LJ.
46 *Armitage v Nurse* [1998] Ch 241, [1997] 3 WLR 1046; ALL ER 705, 714 per Millett LJ.
47 *Armitage v Nurse* [1998] Ch 241, [1997] 3 WLR 1046; ALL ER 705, 717. Cf *Reader v Fried* [2001] VSC 495.
48 K Barnett, 'Equitable Compensation and Remoteness: Not So Remote From the Common Law After All' (2012) 38(1) *University of Western Australia Law Review* 48.
49 *Butterfield v Public Trust* [2017] NZCA 367, [121].
50 D Loxton, 'In With the Old, Out With the New. The Rights of a Replaced Trustee Against Its Successor, and the Characterisation of Trustees' Proprietary Rights of Indemnity' (2017) 45 *Australian Business Law Review* 285.

the event of litigation, the courts will ultimately assess whether there was a Trust in place and the type of breach that occurred, if any.

In addition to the question of the Trustee's liability, the characterisation of a bailee, custodian or contractor as a Trustee or fiduciary means that not only will the Trustee or fiduciary be personally liable for any losses to the Trust, but the liability of third parties will be enlivened.

16 Statutory Trustees of Crypto-assets

Regulatory frameworks in many countries provide for official Trustees to manage assets on behalf of others, under certain circumstances. Three of these types of Trustee arrangements are explored in this chapter: Trustees in bankruptcy; Trustees of proceeds of crime; and Trustees of digital assets in estate planning. These arrangements give rise to particular obligations and it is these statutory obligations that distinguish official or statutory Trustees from other professional Trustees. Statutory and official Trustees who are charged with managing crypto-assets face unique challenges when discharging their duties to satisfy a bankrupt's creditors, court orders or beneficiaries under a will. There can be more than one Trust element in each of these scenarios. The Trustee in bankruptcy may face a claim by creditors that the funds they claim are the subject of a Trust within the bankrupt's estate. Meanwhile, the bankrupt may have moved their assets into a Trust, so as to avoid their creditors. Trustees of proceeds of crime may be faced with a Trust into which the ill-gotten gains of the defendant have been transferred for the specific purpose of avoiding creditors or prosecutors. Finally, an executor who is charged with the administration of the testator's will may be required to distribute proceeds that are held on Trust. In all of these situations, the Trustees must discharge their duties according to any Trust deeds and in compliance with the law.

Trustees in Bankruptcy

When a company files for bankruptcy, creditors and their counsel often look for scapegoats. Wiser directors or more capable managers would have avoided the economic calamity that now confronts the disappointed creditor constituency.

A key determination that must be made in the administration of a trading Trust where the bankrupt was the Trustee is the separation of Trust creditors from the non-Trust creditors. In one such case,[1] the assets of the Trust were insufficient to pay the creditors of the Trust. There were creditors of the

---

1 *Lane (Trustee), in the matter of Lee (Bankrupt) v Deputy Commissioner of Taxation* [2017] FCA 953.

bankrupt estate who were not creditors of the Trust. The court decided that the non-trust creditors were entitled to priority in the bankrupt estate in preference to Trust creditors until non-Trust creditors had received a dividend equal to the dividend that Trust creditors would receive out of the trust funds. While this case did not involve crypto-assets, it is important to be mindful of the obligation to separate types of creditors, particularly in the case of a crypto-currency exchange, where some of the assets may be held on trust for creditors and some may sit outside the trust arrangement.

In the United States, applications for bankruptcy are filed under Chapter 11 of the Bankruptcy Code. In Australia, bankruptcy is filed under section 120 of the *Bankruptcy Act 1966* (Cth). In response to these applications for bankruptcy, claims made against the directors and officers of the insolvent company are often pursued by a Trust established for the benefit of the unsecured creditors. The circumstances under which a Trustee in bankruptcy is appointed may be stressful for the directors of a company and there may be tension or even hostility felt by officers and managers of the bankrupt company towards the Trustee.

In Australia, the specific duties of a Trustee of the estate of a bankrupt include: notifying the bankrupt's creditors of the bankruptcy; determining whether the estate includes property that can be realised to pay a dividend to creditors; reporting to creditors within three months of the date of the bankruptcy on the likelihood of creditors receiving a dividend before the end of the bankruptcy; giving information about the administration of the estate to a creditor who reasonably requests it; determining whether the bankrupt has made a transfer of property that is void against the Trustee; taking appropriate steps to recover property for the benefit of the estate; and exercising powers and performing functions in a commercially sound way.[2]

In the case of bankrupt estates that include crypto-assets, some of these obligations may be problematic. This is because liquidating crypto-currencies (for example) requires specific information and some expertise. The assets themselves are under the control of a blockchain. The Trustee will need to know the private and public keys to transfer the assets from the virtual wallet in which they are stored. In order to meet any expectations that creditors be satisfied in fiat currency, the crypto-currency or virtual asset will need to be exchanged for the local currency. This raises a question of whether and if so how the Trustee can comply with their obligation to exercise powers in a way that is both controlled by the Trustee and also commercially sound.

Claims for breach of the duty of loyalty are not limited to cases of conflict of interest. Delaware courts have held that the fiduciary duty of loyalty is not limited to cases involving a financial or other noticeable fiduciary conflict of interest. It also encompasses cases where the fiduciary fails to act in good faith. Demonstrating good faith in pseudonymous transactions conducted online may not be readily possible. This raises a question about how much a Trustee

---

2   Division 42 of the *Insolvency Practice Rules* – subsection 19(1).

should reasonably allocate from the corpus of the Trust to ensure transparency of conduct. Where directors fail to act in the face of a known duty to act, thereby demonstrating a conscious disregard for their responsibilities, they breach their duty of loyalty by failing to discharge that fiduciary obligation in good faith.[3]

In addition to these challenges, Trustees will need to release the bitcoin, ether or other crypto-token in accordance with their non-custodial duties. When the administration of the Trust is being managed online using virtual wallets, it is harder to scrutinise the Trustee's activities. Trustees need to consider when they should act personally, and when and how far they may delegate matters to staff. Insolvency and bankruptcy practitioners will need clear guidance as to best practice for the sale of crypto-currencies in order to satisfy creditors. For example, existing claim forms used by creditors to claim against the bankrupt should be amended to reflect the possibility that proving losses against crypto-currencies will require information that is not currently sought on the proof of claim form.

Possible ways to address the issues that will be faced by Trustees of bankrupts and seized assets that are crypto-assets may include simply treating crypto-assets the same way as any other assets and apply existing processes in the same way (where possible) or by analogy (for example, crypto-currency could be treated the same way as foreign currency). Another approach could be to observe and adopt the way that other jurisdictions are managing these challenges. Alternatively, countries can make their own new policies and laws that will prescribe for authorities and practitioners the best practice for managing crypto-assets.

What remains uncertain is whether creditors can be satisfied with crypto-currency (rather than fiat currency). Some jurisdictions have ruled on this point, but not necessarily consistently. In October 2017, the Moscow Arbitration Court ruled in the case of a Russian citizen (Ilya Tsarkov) that crypto-currency cannot be used to pay creditors in his bankruptcy. Tsarkov's crypto wallet was with Blockchain.info, and (despite admitting these assets) he opposed the seizure of his crypto-currencies, citing that 'Russian legislation does not consider crypto-currency assets as property, [so] it is impossible to foreclose on them'. Tsarkov's representative stressed that crypto-currency is not part of the Russian Civil Code asserting, 'The legal regime of the crypto-currency is not given in any legal act, the cryptocurrency is information that cannot be included in the bankruptcy mass.'[4] On this occasion, the argument succeeded and Tsarkov was able to keep his crypto wallet separate from the funds to be distributed to his creditors.

---

3   *Stone v Ritter*, 911 A.2d 362, 370 (Del. 2006).
4   'Moscow: Court Refuses to Collect Cryptocurrency as Debt Payment From Bankrupt Person', *Crime Russia* (28 February 2018) <https://en.crimerussia.com/gromkie-dela/moscow-court-refuses-to-collect-crypto-currency-as-debt-paym ent-from-bankrupt-person/>.

While Leonov 'insisted on the inclusion of digital currency in the bankruptcy assets', the publication elaborated that 'the court noted that the laws of the Russian Federation do not recognise cryptocurrency as property'. The court therefore 'refused to include cryptocurrency discovered on the accounts of insolvent Ilya Tsarkov in the bankruptcy assets'. The court indicated in its decision that the concept of crypto-currency is not set out in the current legislation and is therefore not permitted to recognise digital money as property and, thus, include it in the bankrupt's assets. However, in May 2018, this decision was considered at a policy level and the Russian regulator deemed that in such a case, the crypto-asset could be liquidated in order to satisfy creditors.[5]

In the wake of the 2014 collapse of the popular bitcoin exchange, Mt Gox, the Japanese regulator sought to liquidate the remaining bitcoin so as to satisfy the creditors of the failed exchange. In November 2014, Kraken (a San Francisco-based bitcoin exchange) announced that it had been selected to support the Mt Gox investigation to retrieve its missing bitcoin and with the distribution of any remaining assets to the creditors. The duties that the Japanese Trustee in bankruptcy delegated to Kraken also included a duty to exchange bitcoin to fiat currency, as needed.[6]

In an interesting development, the remaining bitcoin that the Trustee in bankruptcy of Mt Gox has been distributing to its creditors has dramatically increased in value since its 2014 collapse. When the liquidation process began, the Trustee fixed the price of the bitcoin for each claimant at the 2014 value, which was $483 per bitcoin. Since then, the price of bitcoin skyrocketed to just over US$17,000 (in December 2017).[7] In March 2018, the price of one bitcoin was US$10,000. This has resulted in sufficient remaining value to satisfy the claims made by Mt Gox's corporate creditors, who had previously been excluded from the pool of creditors. One commentator described this as a 'bizarre upside-down bankruptcy'.[8] What makes this situation particularly odd is that in most bankruptcy or insolvency processes, creditors are satisfied *pari passu*. Under the *pari passu* principle, all unsecured creditors in insolvency processes share equally any available assets of the company or individual, or any proceeds from the sale of any of those assets, in proportion to the debts due to each creditor. It is important to note, however, that *pari passu* is only one of

---

5   W Woo, 'Russia: Court Rules Bitcoin Is Property in Landmark Bankruptcy case', *Bitcoinist* (8 May 2018) <https://bitcoinist.com/russian-court-rules-bitcoin-property/>.

6   T Kasai, 'Bitcoin Exchange Kraken to Help in Mt Gox Bankruptcy', *Reuters* (November 2014) <https://www.reuters.com/article/bitcoin-mt-gox-kraken-idINKCN0JA0RB20141126>.

7   'Bitcoin Price Index', *CoinDesk* (2019) <https://www.coindesk.com/price/bitcoin>.

8   A Jeffries, 'Inside the Bizarre Upside Down Bankruptcy of Mt Gox', *The Verge* (22 March 2018) <https://www.theverge.com/2018/3/22/17151430/bankruptcy-mt-gox-liabilities-bitcoin>.

the many rules of priority (one of which is the claim that funds were held on trust and therefore rank above all other creditors).

There is an expectation that, when a bankrupt's assets are transferred into the hands of a Trustee, the distribution of assets will be achieved efficiently, fairly and transparently. Crypto-currencies introduce new hurdles to meeting these expectations.

Trustees of Proceeds of Crime

In 2016, global accounting giant Ernst & Young sold $16 million in con-fiscated bitcoin at auction in Sydney.[9] The 24,518 bitcoins were seized as proceeds of crime in 2015. For the auction, they were divided into 11 lots of 2,000 coins and one lot of approximately 2,518.[10] Bidders were required to register their interest. Eligibility to bid relied on the ability to transact with a rigorous registration process that required a substantial deposit up front.

The more common approach to dealing with large quantities of seized property, especially liquid assets such as currency or shares, is off-market sales. However, in the case of a volatile crypto-currency like bitcoin, simply going through the process of putting them through public exchanges would push the price down. For this reason, an exclusive auction of the twelve parcels of bit-coin was preferred.

This bitcoin sale process was the first of its kind in Australia and only the second globally. The United States Marshals Service conducted several sales during 2015 following the arrest and conviction of Ross Ulbricht, the mas-termind behind online drug marketplace Silk Road.

While bitcoin transactions are all visible in the public ledger, it has had a reputation as the payment method of drug dealers, money launderers, tax avoiders and dark online vendors. Money laundering is the process of making illegally gained proceeds appear legal.[11] Money laundering is typically accom-plished through a three-step process: (a) depositing the dirty money into the financial system; (b) layering or mixing it with other funds so that it is a removed from its origin; and (c) integration: where clean money re-enters the financial system in a seemingly legitimate state.[12] Crypto-currencies make it easier for money launderers to move illicit funds faster, more cheaply and more discretely than ever before. Within the bitcoin system, both legitimate and illegitimate users are able to transfer money very quickly to anywhere in the world, at little to no cost, while remaining virtually anonymous. While bitcoin

---

9   J Sier, 'Ernst & Young to Sell $16 Million in Confiscated Bitcoin at Auction in Sydney', *AFR.com* (27 May 2016) <http://www.afr.com/technology/ernst–young-16-million-Bitcoin-auction-20160527-gp53i0>.
10 In 2016, the value of one bitcoin was about AU$654.
11 See, D Bryans, 'Bitcoin and Money Laundering: Mining for an Effective Solution' (2014) 89 *Indiana Law Journal* 441,442.
12 See, D Bryans, 'Bitcoin and Money Laundering: Mining for an Effective Solution' (2014) 89 *Indiana Law Journal* 441,442.

moves more slowly than credit card transactions, it is much quicker than the alternative method when laundering money. Furthermore, bitcoin transfers are much faster than traditional international money transfers. The user's ability to exchange bitcoin for other virtual and real currencies, to obfuscate by transferring bitcoin through an endless number of nodes (addresses) and to exchange bitcoin for fiat currency frustrates anti-money laundering efforts. For these reasons, it is necessary to devise a framework for the disposal of seized bitcoin that is not vulnerable to exploitation or that lacks transparency and accountability.

With the increasing popularity of blockchain-enabled crypto-currencies and crypto-tokens, authorities with power to take custody and control of the proceeds of crime need to re-think some of the processes and mechanics for managing that custody and control. It is possible that an accused may be prepared to divulge the private and public key information that is needed to access a virtual wallet and transact in bitcoin. With these keys, it is possible for the seized bitcoin to be auctioned or sold.

If a court orders the sale of proceeds of crime, it will be important for the court order to reflect the likely fees and costs involved in the process (including exchange rate losses and fluctuating value of crypto-currencies). This will be important for strict compliance to be achieved and to avoid any unexpected losses being made the responsibility of the Trustee or relevant authority.

In light of the threat that crypto-currencies pose to the global effort to combat money laundering and terrorism financing, international regulators are strengthening their financial crimes legislation. For example, in the United States, at the federal level, the Bank Secrecy Act and the USA Patriot Act require money transmission businesses to operate under a licence and money transmitters must keep records of their customers and report suspicious transactions and other data. In Canada, the Proceeds of Crime (Money Laundering) and Terrorist Financing Act has been amended to capture persons and entities that deal in virtual currencies. These regulations enhance client identification, record keeping and registration requirements for money transmitters and exchange providers. Furthermore, bitcoin businesses are required to register with the Financial Transactions and Reports Analysis Centre of Canada (FINTRAC). Similar legislation has been passed in Australia with AUSTRAC managing transactions and reports analysis.

Digital Assets in Estate Planning

Proper supervision by informed regulatory bodies will ensure continued progress towards a more mature crypto-economy. This maturing requires that the community trusts the issuer of the token and the asset itself. There are many legal contexts in which it is important to identify and deal with digital or crypto assets, including (for example) identifying digital assets upon the death of the owner or custodian (sometimes referred to as 'the digital asset dilemma').

Digital assets may include computing hardware, such as computers, external hard drives or flash drives, tablets, smartphones, digital music players, e-readers, digital cameras and other digital devices; information or data that is stored electronically, whether stored online, in the Cloud or on a physical device; and online accounts, such as email and communications accounts, social media accounts, shopping accounts, photo and video sharing accounts, video gaming accounts, online storage accounts, websites, blogs and intellectual property. Once these digital assets have been identified, a digital executor can be provided with necessary login details so that they can readily access online information and accounts.

Many digital assets, such as bitcoin and commercial domain names, have an ascertainable value that must be included as part of the administration of the estate of an incapacitated individual or a decedent. For an estate subject to federal or state estate taxes, the value of such property may need to be determined and included on the pertinent estate tax returns. Likewise, such property may need to be separately listed on any required inventories of a deceased's estate. Many other forms of digital assets have no extrinsic economic value, but may have tremendous sentimental value. For example, most photographs are now created by digital cameras and stored in some digital form, often within a user's account with an online provider such as Facebook and Instagram. All of these digital assets could fall within the purview of estate planning, but just as photo albums are valued differently to bank accounts, there is a difference between how they will be regarded by beneficiaries, tax regulators and the courts (in the case of litigation).

Estate planning to ensure that crypto-currencies and other crypto-assets can be identified and realised is a little more complicated. Estate planning to preserve bitcoins should be managed as any other asset. They need to be included in any estate planning documents or framework. This applies despite the volatility of their price.[13] Digital executors will need to store the public and private crypto-keys securely. The executor and heirs will need to know the number of wallets and the value in each. In the case of communicating how to access assets, funds and bank accounts, it may be useful to keep this information in cold storage (offline, hard copy and in a safe). In the case of bitcoin and other crypto-currencies, key locations and access controls need to be provided to the digital executor. Access controls are things like PINs, passphrases, multi-signature or time-lock requirements.

Wills with provisions from the United States *Uniform Fiduciary Access to Digital Assets Act* can allow fiduciaries, personal representatives and trustees to access and control digital currency. The *Revised Uniform Fiduciary Access to Digital Assets Act* is a law developed primarily by the Uniform Law Commission to provide fiduciaries (like executors) with a legal path to managing the

---

13 See 'Bitcoins and Estate Planning: Bequeathing Cryptocurrency', *Estate Planning Massachusetts* (5 March 2014) <http://www.estateplanninginmassachusetts.com/2014/03/bitcoins-and-estate-planning-bequeathing-cryptocurrency/>.

digital assets of deceased or incapacitated people. Exchanges and other custodians of bitcoin accounts can be compelled to provide a fiduciary with records of the digital assets and access to such accounts.[14]

Trustees of deceased estates face novel challenges as they seek to discharge their duties in line with their fiduciary or statutory duties. Crypto-currencies were designed to disrupt traditional banking frameworks and to operate without trusted third party intermediaries. They enable anonymity (or pseudonymity) for users on the network. These features mean that identifying the existence of virtual wallets and their contents is an additional burden upon executors and the Trustees of deceased estates.

In December 2018, circumstances arose that brought into sharp focus the precarious nature of wallet security and digital estate planning for operators of crypto-currency exchanges. In a sworn affidavit filed 31 January 2019 with the Nova Scotia Supreme Court, Jennifer Robertson, identified as the widow of QuadrigaCX founder Gerald Cotten, said the exchange owes its customers roughly CA$250 million (US$190 million) in both crypto-currency and fiat money. However, she is unable to access the funds because – according to her affidavit – her husband died in December 2018 and no one know how to access the public and private keys.

QuadrigaCX is also filing for protection from creditors, a step taken to avoid bankruptcy. This step has been taken to 'address' financial issues. In its application, QuadrigaCX is asking the Nova Scotia Supreme Court to appoint professional services firm Ernst & Young to act as an independent third party to oversee its proceedings.[15]

The exchange had been facing issues for some time before Cotten's death, with customers complaining about withdrawal problems with both fiat and crypto-currencies on social media. The exchange's problems with fiat withdrawals were caused in part by a legal battle against its bank – the Canadian Imperial Bank of Commerce (CIBC). The CIBC froze QuadrigaCX's funds in 2018.

The dispute between QuadrigaCX and CIBC stemmed from CIBC's claim that it was unable to determine whether the exchange or individuals who deposited funds to purchase crypto-currencies owned the money in the accounts. QuadrigaCX maintained that it owned the funds in the account opened by Costodian, Inc. The bank sought clarity from the Vancouver courts in a determination as to whether the proper owner of the funds was QuadrigaCX (the exchange), Costodian Inc (the payment processor) or the 388 individuals whose funds had been deposited into the account in exchange for the issue of crypto-currency. The amount frozen by CIBC was CA$28 million

---

14 MS McKeever, 'Bitcoin and Blockchain: What You Need to Know' (November/December 2018) 21(6) *Nebraska Lawyer* 15.

15 N De, 'Crypto Exchange QuadrigaCX Files for Creditor Protection', *CoinDesk* (31 January 2019) <https://www.coindesk.com/crypto-exchange-quadrigacx-files-for-creditor-protection>.

(about US$21.6). It is impressive that the individuals who claimed an interest in those frozen funds had each invested on average more than CA$70,000.

The sheer volume of transactions into the account would have been sufficient to cause concern for the bank. Regulators require that financial institutions report large transactions that exceed the 'reportable' amount. In Canada, this is CA$10,000.[16] Reportable transactions are not just where the amount in any single transfer is CA$10,000 or more. They also include the receipt of two or more cash amounts of less than $10,000 that total $10,000 or more (24-hour rule). In Australia, these types of transactions are known as 'structured transfers'. They are structured or divided into smaller transfers to conceal the total (reportable) amount.

Because the exchange could not access the frozen funds in the CIBC accounts, some customers faced delays when attempting to withdraw their money from the platform. Many of the investors took to social media to air their grievances about the exchange. A Reddit account purporting to represent the exchange commented that 'it is frightening how much power the banks have … we find it particularly troubling when they attack crypto companies and then create their own competing crypto projects'.[17] However, there is no suggestion at the time of the Reddit post that CIBC is launching or embracing any crypto-currencies. Indeed, according to CIBC, it is not convinced and has decided to watch with interest any developments with crypto-currencies but –for now – 'staying on the sidelines'.[18]

As at 31 January 2019, there were roughly 115,000 users with balances signed up on QuadrigaCX, with CA$70 million in fiat and CA$180 million in crypto owed overall, according to the filing. It is not clear what portion of the exchange's crypto holding were kept in cold storage, versus its hot wallet. In the affidavit, Robertson explained that 'only a minimal amount of coins' were stored in the hot wallet, but specifics were not provided. According to Robertson's evidence, her husband would move the majority of the coins to cold storage as a way to protect the coins from hacking or other virtual theft. Cotten maintained sole responsibility for handling the funds and coins. Cotten reportedly died of Crohn's disease in Jaipur, India in early December 2018. This was announced on the exchange's website in January. A death certificate was included in the list of exhibits filed with the affidavit.

According to Robertson's affidavit, Cotten was diagnosed with Crohn's disease when he was 24 years old. He left a will that makes Robertson the sole

---

16 'Large Financial Transactions', *FINTRAC* (29 Jun 2017) <http://www.fintrac-ca nafe.gc.ca/reporting-declaration/Info/rptLCTR-eng.asp>.
17 QuadrigaCX, 'Globe and Mail Reports on Legal Battle Between QuadrigaCX and CIBC', *Reddit* (9 October 2018) <https://www.reddit.com/r/QuadrigaCX/ comments/9mmtzl/globe_and_mail_reports_on_legal_battle_between/c7fzluy/>.
18 L de la Durantaye, 'Bitcoin: Real Currency or Speculative Investment?', *CIBC Private Wealth Management* (26 May 2018) <https://www.cibc.com/en/priva te-wealth-management/insights/bitcoin-real-currency-or-speculative-investment. html>.

executrix of his estate. She also asserts that the keys to access the crypto-assets are securely locked away in cold storage. In short, it is Robertson's evidence that her husband failed to plan for his demise with respect to the assets of his business, but had made a will in relation to his personal property.[19] That Cotten – who died aged 30, apparently while he was with Robertson on their honeymoon – had prepared a will at such a young age is understandable in light of his earlier diagnosis and continuing illness. However, his failure to appoint a digital executor will be frustrating for his customers. Probate usually requires publication of the death of the testator so that any claims can be made by any creditors. The consequence of Cotten's failure to ensure that the crypto-assets could be accessed meant that he failed to meet the reasonable expectation that he would conduct the affairs of QuadrigaCX competently. Trusting in the competency and benevolence of any business that takes money on account and then keeps assets in custody is essential to securing and maintaining trust. This must include planning for succession.

19 N De, 'QuadrigaCX Owes Customers $190 Million, Court Filing Shows', *Coin-Desk* (1 February 2019) <https://www.coindesk.com/quadriga-creditor-protection-filing>.

17 Good Faith and Competence in Crypto-economies

The usual formulation for good faith in business demands care and loyalty of directors and officers of companies. A freestanding duty of good faith can apply to situations that do not implicate a director's duty of loyalty. Breach of the duty of good faith can espouse various formulations to the good faith requirement in the 'business judgment rule'. The general effect of the business judgment rule is to allow a court to:

> review the substance of a business decision made by an apparently well-motivated board for the limited purpose of assessing whether that decision is so far beyond the bounds of reasonable judgement that it seems essentially inexplicable on any ground other than bad faith.[1]

The Delaware courts have ruled that egregious decisions are beyond the protections of the business judgment rule, as are decisions that cannot 'be attributed to any rational business purpose', or decisions that constitute 'a gross abuse of discretion'.[2] The Delaware jurisprudence on the business judgment rule 'reflects a general reluctance by Delaware courts to assume responsibility for the substance of business decisions'. Even in the more fraught contexts, the Delaware courts use the business judgment rule to 'mark the point at which their responsibility for evaluating the decision ends'.[3] The Australian authorities support this approach to the business judgment rule, noting that courts begin with an assumption in favour of the impugned decision,[4] and the onus of proving that the decision was not in the best interests of the business falls to the party who is attacking it.[5]

---

1 T Rivers, 'How to Be Good: The Emphasis on Corporate Directors' Good Faith in the Post-Enron Era' (2005) 58 *Vanderbilt Law Review* 631.
2 See, for example, *In re JP Stevens & Co S'holders Litig*, 542 A.2d 770, 781 n.5 (Del. Ch. 1988).
3 *Kahn v M&F Worldwide Corp*, Supreme Court of the State of Delaware, No. 334, 2013.
4 *Australian Metropolitan Life Assurance Co Ltd v Ure* (1923) 33 CLR 199 (see, Knox CJ at 220 and Isaacs J at 221).
5 *Richard Brady Franks Limited v Price* (1937) 58 CLR 112.

The expectations of customers and investors with respect to what conduct and decision-making by directors and officers should reasonably fall within the protection of the business judgment rule seems to align with the findings of the courts. The combination of business judgement and good faith is particularly important when doing business with a company that takes its customers' money and assets on a promise that they can be returned (subject to the terms and conditions of the investment outlook and the costs charged by the business for their services). This expectation is consistent with the investment framework and relationship offered by crypto-currency exchanges.

In some jurisdictions, it is recognised that anyone who makes a profit from an act of fraud, or who knowingly takes advantage of a fraud, may be fixed with the personal liability of constructive trusteeship. Knowledge at the time of receipt that the assets received are traceable to a breach of fiduciary duty is required, if the personal liability of constructive trusteeship is to be imposed on the recipient. Importantly, an unknowing recipient may at first be innocent, but once he or she knows they have the advantage of a fraud, it must be refunded. If the recipient refuses to return the property or repay the funds, then the recipient also becomes a party to the fraud and is liable to the jurisdiction of the Court of Equity.[6] This will also apply where a third party has an equitable interest in the property and the transferee has obtained the property by duress or undue influence. Only if the transferee holds the property as a bona fide purchaser for value without notice will they be excused.[7]

The use of the 'constructive trust' as a remedial device for restoring property acquired by mistake, fraud, duress or undue influence is a specific category in which general principles are applied to justify charging the holder of title to property as a constructive trustee of the property.[8] Once a recipient is on notice or is shown to have known of the breach of trust, then they will not be entitled to the defence of 'change of position' and they may be made liable as a constructive trustee. The knowing recipient must disgorge or return his or her

6   *Black & Black v S Freedman & Company* (1910) 12 CLR 105, where Griffith CJ (at 109) cited Sir George Jessel in *Re Hallett's Estate* (1879–80) 13 Ch 696. See also, *El Ajou v Dollar Land Holdings Plc* [1994] 2 All ER 685, per Hoffmann LJ at 700; and *Heperu Pty Limited v Belle* (2009) 76 NSWLR 230 at [92], per Allsop P.

7   M Cope, 'The Constructive Trust as a Remedy for Mistake, Fraud, Duress and Undue Influence' (1987) 3 *Queensland Institute of Technology Law Journal* 111, 127.

8   M Cope, 'The Constructive Trust as a Remedy for Mistake, Fraud, Duress and Undue Influence' (1987) 3 *Queensland Institute of Technology Law Journal* 111, 111. It is not clear whether the principles outlined above also apply where a thief has stolen or misappropriated property and it is not clear whether the holder of the proceeds of stolen property or property purchased out of the stolen property is chargeable as a constructive trustee. A suit to recover the property by way of a constructive trust could be defeated on the ground that the thief has not acquired title to the property. See, M Cope, 'The Constructive Trust as a Remedy for Mistake, Fraud, Duress and Undue Influence' (1987) 3 *Queensland Institute of Technology Law Journal* 111, 127.

benefit and restore it to the plaintiff. The restitutionary lawyers would say that this remedy is enlivened because the knowing recipient purported to enrich himself or herself at the plaintiff's expense.[9]

Dishonesty and Mismanagement in Crypto-currency Exchanges

In the past eight years, more than a third of all crypto-currency exchanges have been hacked. The total losses exceed US$1 billion. Because crypto-currencies are almost untraceable, the rate of recovery after a hack is very low. This rising risk for bitcoin holders is compounded by the fact there is no depositor's insurance to absorb the loss, even though many exchanges act like virtual banks.

Profitability is a big problem for bitcoin exchanges, with many of them unable to generate enough volume to keep afloat. Bitcoin exchanges overall could be launched for as low as $100,000 up to $1 million. That is a fraction of what United States' Forex exchanges are required to put up. A key factor tied to the risk posed by exchanges is whether customers are reimbursed after closure or after the loss of bitcoins following a hack. Because of its irreversible nature, bitcoin requires near perfect security.[10]

As well as these systemic risks that beset the management of bitcoin exchanges, speculation, price volatility and greed have also been endemically problematic. Some start out as deliberate scams or Ponzi schemes, while others might have set out with the best intentions to act in good faith. However, when exchange operators run out of money, attempts to trade their way out of trouble can soon descend into an apparently unavoidable but criminally corrupt Ponzi scheme.

Bitcoin Savings and Trust was a Ponzi scheme that collapsed in 2012 with the loss of 700,000 bitcoin. Trendon Shavers, who operated Bitcoin Savings and Trust, was ordered by United States District Judge Lewis Kaplan in Manhattan to forfeit $1.23 million and pay restitution in the same amount for operating what the judge called a 'classic Ponzi scheme'. Shavers, who pleaded guilty in September 2015 to one count of securities fraud and who now supports himself as a cook, said in court he had 'royally messed up', and had lost friends and embarrassed his family as a result of his fraud.[11]

---

9   In property cases, relief may also flow from the breach of a legally recognised duty of inquiry. It could be argued that the unintended recipient of *trust* property might be treated in a like way to the unintended recipient of *legal* property. However, Lord Millett suggests that the unintended recipient of *trust* property holds it on a proprietary constructive trust; and the unintended recipient of *legal* property holds it on a resulting trust. See, Lord Millett, 'Restitution and Constructive Trusts' (1998) 114 *Law Quarterly Review* 399; and Lord Millett: 'Tracing the Proceeds of Fraud' (1991) 107 *Law Quarterly Review* 71, 82.

10   Reuters, 'Risk of Bitcoin Hacks and Losses Is Very Real', *Fortune.com* (29 August 2016) <http://fortune.com/2016/08/29/risk-of-bitcoin-hacking-is-real/>.

11   N Raymond, 'Texan Gets 1–1/2 Years in Prison for Running Bitcoin Ponzi Scheme', *Reuters* (22 July 2016) <https://www.reuters.com/article/bitcoin-fra ud-texas-idUSL1N1A7270>.

Named after Charles Ponzi, a Ponzi scheme is a fraudulent investment operation that pays returns to its investors either from the investors' own money or the money paid by subsequent investors, rather than from any actual profit earned by the enterprise.[12] Charles Ponzi first used the technique in 1920. Irrespective of the type and nature of fraud, there are generally three prerequisites necessary for a fraud to occur: (1) motivation (such as financial pressure); (2) opportunity (such as weak internal controls, management styles or corporate culture); and (3) rationalisation (the attitude that justifies the fraud).[13] Since its launch in October 2013, bitcoin has featured in numerous spectacular exchange collapses.

Bitcoin Savings and Trust is not the only bitcoin exchange that has collapsed in disgrace. The Australian bitcoin exchange Igot.com was registered in South Australia in 2014. Igot bought and sold bitcoin on behalf of customers while keeping the funds in the company's wallets and accounts. Allegations later surfaced that the company did not use all the money it collected to buy bitcoins for clients.[14] By May 2016, it stopped honouring requests from customers to sell their bitcoin or refund their money. Its owner Rick Day (whose real name is Raghav Dayma) admitted to ABC News that he was struggling to pay customers. It may be that Igot was simply attempting to trade its way out of trouble. If this was the case, then recovery was unlikely as the trade in bitcoin requires payment of a fee. In order to attract new customers, Igot would need to compete with other exchanges to offer the most competitive rate. This would drive down Igot's profits. Meanwhile, if investors want their money back, but the price of bitcoin has dropped, Igot would be unlikely to have the funds to honour that repayment request. Since May 2016, Igot has not operated in Australia and its domain name is for sale.

In 2018, it was reported that Gelfman Blueprint Inc was running a bitcoin scam. Led by its founder, Nicholas Gelfman, the business claimed to have a high-frequency trading computer program that could mine profits from bitcoin. Gelfman claimed his clients typically earned '7–11% monthly return on their bitcoins'. He collected more than $600,000 from at least 80 eager investors from 2014 to 2016. However, Gelfman and his Staten Island-based company presented fake performance reports to investors and paid some of them using other investors' money—the hallmark of a Ponzi scheme. Gelfman and his firm were ordered by the Commodity Futures Trading Commission to pay fines and restitution totalling US$2.5 million. It was the first bitcoin-

---

12 JJ Johnson, 'Fleecing Grandma: A Regulatory Ponzi Scheme' (2012) 16 *Lewis & Clark Law Review* 993, 1000.
13 MA Gillen and SM Packer, 'While Markets Continue to Fall, Fraud Activity Continues to Rise' (2009) 3 *New Jersey Law* 66
14 J Sturmer and A McClymont, 'Igot: Bitcoin Investors "Owed Thousands Of Dollars" by Struggling Australian Exchange', *ABC News* (12 April 2016) <https://www.abc.net.au/news/2016-04-11/australian-bitcoin-exchange-igot-on-verge-of-collapse/7315894?fbclid=IwAR2twho7KF6BeCxGLeppysQwtoJ7GGW6NhK4UyQdz76tS98BocSsrNBUfoo>.

related fraud case for the CFTC. In the settlement, Gelfman admitted to the charges against him and his firm and he agreed not to appeal the decision by the Southern District of New York. The CFTC said – however – that Gelfman's victims may not receive restitution because he did not have sufficient funds.[15]

According to CNN, the bitcoin gold (BTG) wallet duped investors out of US$3.2 million in 2017 by promising to allow them to claim their bitcoin gold. The website allegedly used links on a legitimate website (Bitcoin Gold) to get investors to share their private keys or seeds with the scam. By the time the scam had run its course, the website operators were able to get their hands on $107,000 worth of bitcoin gold and more than US$100,000 in other crypto-currencies[16]

A closer look at some of the bitcoin exchange collapses reveals dishonesty, mismanagement and vast quantity of bitcoin hidden away in secret wallets and apparently irretrievable. This chapter surveys the ten years of crypto-currency exchange collapse and includes a discussion of how the exchange operators and the regulators responded to the circumstances leading up to and in the wake of the dramatic insolvency of each business.

The Mt Gox Collapse

Mt Gox was a website for fantasy gamers who traded bitcoin to defeat dragons, discover lost scrolls and to buy new wizard powers. On 19 June 2011, a security breach of the Mt Gox bitcoin exchange caused the nominal price of a bitcoin to fraudulently drop to one cent on the Mt Gox exchange. This occurred after a hacker allegedly used credentials from a Mt Gox auditor's compromised computer to transfer a large number of bitcoins illegally to his or her own wallet. Despite this attack, within two years, Mt Gox was the biggest bitcoin exchange in the world.

On 7 February 2014, Mt Gox paused its operations. claiming that it was merely temporary. After a number of weeks of uncertainty, on 24 February 2014, the exchange suspended all trading and the website went offline. That same week, a leaked corporate document claimed that hackers had raided and removed from the Mt Gox exchange 744,408 bitcoins belonging to Mt Gox customers. A further 100,000 bitcoins belonging to the company were also stolen. As a result, the exchange was declared insolvent. On 28 February 2014, Mt Gox filed for bankruptcy protection in Japan, and in the United States two weeks later.

---

15 G Dobush, 'First Bitcoin Fraud Case Results in $2.5 Million Fine for Ponzi Scheme That Promised Outrageous Returns', *Fortune* (19 October 2018) <http://fortune.com/2018/10/19/bitcoin-ponzi-scheme-scammer/>.

16 F Memoria, 'CNN, the Bitcoin Gold (BTG) Wallet Duped Investors Out of $3.2 Million', *CNN* (24 November 2017) <https://www.ccn.com/bitcoin-gold-wallet-scam-nets-fraudsters-3-2-million-after-stealing-users-private-keys/>.

At the time of its demise, Mt Gox was handling 70% of all bitcoin transactions. When the 850,000 bitcoins mysteriously went missing, the losses were then valued at more than US$450 million.[17]

Curiously, the operator of Mt Gox (Mark Karpeles) both apologised that the exchange had been hacked and also promised to repay customers. This suggests that his personal wealth could underwrite the losses. However, as the scale of the claims became apparent, Karpeles retreated from this position. Then, about six months after the collapse, Karpeles found some bitcoin that he claimed he had forgotten about. The regulator was able to distribute some of those bitcoin to aggrieved customers. It is interesting that despite blockchain's status enabling peer-to-peer decentralised trustless (that is, riskless) transactions, Mt Gox failed due to the misconduct or mismanagement of a person (not the technology). This level of mismanagement and the consequences fall outside of the potentially excusable defence found in application of the business judgment rule. Under Karpeles' control, a leading bitcoin exchange eventually filed for bankruptcy. The Mt Gox disaster highlighted precisely the dangers of concentrating powers in the hands of one market player not otherwise subject to regulation.[18]

Prior to its collapse, Mt Gox had already started to experience problems with lawsuits and regulators in the United States. In 2013, Mt Gox was investigated by numerous United States Government departments after customers reported delays withdrawing their money. These regulatory issues caused more trouble for Mt Gox. Eventually, the exchange was effectively frozen out of the United States' banking system because of its regulatory problems. The close relationship between and interdependence of Silk Road and Mt Gox meant that as soon as Silk Road was dismantled in October 2013, time was ticking for Mt Gox.

In the wake of Mt Gox, Japanese regulators introduced rules for cryptocurrency exchanges to improve governance and security. So as to bring virtual currency exchanges in line with international anti-money laundering and counter-terrorism financing measures, Japanese lawmakers enacted the *Amended Settlement Act*. Under these new laws, all exchanges operating in Japan must register and comply with rules. These rules include knowing their customers, employing sufficient staff, keeping balance sheets, and (critically) must keep all customers' deposits in 'cold storage' (that is, on a computer hard drive that is not accessible via the Internet). These new laws mean that when an exchange is hacked or collapses, operators can be made liable for the way that they managed their customers' funds.[19]

---

17 YB Perez, 'Mt Gox: The History of a Failed Bitcoin Exchange', *Coindesk* (4 August 2015) <http://www.coindesk.com/mt-gox-the-history-of-a-failed-Bitcoin-exchange/>.

18 Y Zhang, 'The Incompatibility of Bitcoin's "Strong" Decentralization Ideology and Its Growth as a Scalable Currency' (2017) 11 *New York University Journal of Law and Liberty* 556, 583.

19 PA Ryan, 'What the Coincheck Hack Tells Us About How Australian Regulators Will Handle a Crypto-Currency Hack', *The Conversation* (30 January 2018) <https://the

The DAO Attack

At the beginning of May 2016, a few members of the Ethereum community announced the inception of *The Decentralised Autonomous Organisation* (known as The DAO; it was also known as Genesis DAO). The DAO was meant to operate like a venture capital fund for the crypto and decentralised space. It was one of the earliest investment tokens. The DAO was an unincorporated organisation that issued DAO Tokens to represent an interest in a venture capital fund.

The DAO was built as a smart contract on the Ethereum blockchain. The coding framework was developed by the *Slock.It* team, but it was deployed by members of the Ethereum community. Anyone was allowed to send Ether to a unique wallet address in exchange for DAO tokens. The creation period was an unexpected success. It managed to gather US$150 million in token sales, making it the biggest 'crowdfunding' project ever. When the price of Ether was trading at $20, the total Ether from The DAO was worth over $250 million.

In essence, the platform allowed anyone to pitch an idea to the community and potentially receive funding from The DAO. Anyone with DAO tokens could vote on plans, and would then receive rewards if the projects turned a profit. If approved, by DAO token-holders, the project would commit itself to the code via another smart contract. This in turn would remit payments to the project's creator, once certain milestones were reached. The same smart contract would ensure that any profits were distributed on a pro rata basis to DAO token-holders.[20]

In June 2016, a nefarious actor exploited a vulnerability in the smart contract code of The DAO that allowed him to drain funds from The DAO to his own wallet US$67 million.[21]

In the first few hours of the attack, 3.6 million Eth were stolen, the equivalent of $70 million at the time. Once the hacker had done the damage he intended, he withdrew the attack.[22] With millions of dollars of other people's money on the line, it was time for some important decision to be made quickly by a relatively small group of people. Some have suggested that their role in managing the custodial relationship between The DAO and its token-holders imposed fiduciary duties upon the decision-makers (whether they were the team at Slock.it or Ethereum). Consistent with this analysis, the token-

conversation.com/what-the-coincheck-hack-tells-us-about-how-australian-regulators-will-handle-a-cryptocurrency-hack-90842>.

20 See, P De Filippi and A Wright, *Blockchain and the Law: The Rule of Code*, electronic book (Harvard University Press, 2018), location 2658.

21 J Vollmer, 'The Biggest Hacker Whodunnit of the Summer', *Motherboard* (15 July 2016) <https://motherboard.vice.com/en_us/article/pgkzqm/the-biggest-hacker-whodunnit-of-the-summer>.

22 S Falkon, 'The Story of the DAO – Its History and Consequences', *Medium* (24 December 2017) <https://medium.com/swlh/the-story-of-the-dao-its-history-and-consequences-71e6a8a551ee>.

holders would be investors. Notably, the core developers and big miners have been making similarly consequential decisions since the blockchain's creation – the hard fork drama just makes this more transparent.[23]

Even before the attack, several lawyers raised concerns that The DAO overstepped its crowdfunding mandate and ran afoul of securities laws in several countries. Lawyers also pointed to its creators as potentially liable for any problems that may occur, and several expressed concern that token holders of The DAO were accepting responsibility they were likely unaware of. The DAO – it seems – exists in a grey area of law and regulation.

The attacker exploited a previously unknown vulnerability in the code of The DAO to siphon the eth away to a separate entity, known as a 'child DAO'. The illicit cache worth US$600 million dropped in value after news of the attack sparked an ether sell-off. Within weeks it plummeted to US$50 million.[24]

One proposal for regulatory reform in response to The DAO suggests that the United States legal system must clarify the legal status of these organisations and as such should classify The DAO as a general partnership. Assuming The DAO is a general partnership, the question arises as to whether shareholders in The DAO have interests that would be classified as securities under United States securities laws. Given its structure, The DAO and similar decentralised organisations should be classified as general partnerships under United States law, with the partnership interests classified as securities subject to securities regulation.[25]

An inherit weakness in the proposal to introduce securities or other legislation to apply in relation to any blockchain-based crowd-funding projects is that it offends the originating premise that these organisations or platforms are decentralised and self-regulating. An argument in favour of legislation is the oversight, certainty and consistency that this will bring to future projects. However, this could also be achieved with self-imposed standards or clearer statements about the terms upon which the projects will function and how disruptions or hacks will be managed. Either way, any risk of loss will undermine trust in the product or investment model.

---

23 A Walch, *In Code(rs) We Trust: Software Developers as Fiduciaries in Public Block-chains* (OUP, forthcoming) abstract available at <https://papers.ssrn.com/sol3/papers.cfm?abstract_id=3203198>. A counter-argument suggests that public blockchain developers are open source coders not fiduciaries. However, this particular article focuses on a 'legal duty of care', confusing the fiduciary relationship with tort law and contracts. See, A Quentson, 'Call Public Blockchain Developers What They Are: Open Source Coders Not Fiduciaries', *CCN* (11 August 2016) <https://www.ccn.com/call-public-blockchain-developers-what-they-are-op en-source-coders-not-fiduciaries/>.

24 BP Eha and T Macheel, 'What the Attack on the DAO Means for Banks', *AmericanBanker* (17 June 2016) <https://www.americanbanker.com/news/what-the-a ttack-on-the-dao-means-for-banks>.

25 L Metjahic, 'Deconstructing the DAO: The Need for Legal Recognition and the Application of Securities Laws to Decentralized Organizations' (2018) 39 *Cardozo Law Review* 1533.

The Bitfinex Hack

In August 2016, Bitfinex suffered an alleged security breach with losses running to 120,000 bitcoin, valued at the time at US$72 million.[26] The way that Bitfinex responded was modelled on the 'bail-in' solution that was applied to the 2012 banking crisis in Cyprus.

By way of background, on 28 June 2012, Cyprus became the fifth government to request an economic bail-out from the Eurozone, after losing access to international capital markets. Less than a year later, a €10 billion second rescue deal was agreed upon – an unprecedented agreement that bailed in creditors of Cyprus' two largest banks, and triggered an economic crisis from which the nation is still struggling to recover. The 'bail-in' solution involved restructuring the bank's debt and the monies owed to all customers so that the debt was converted to equity in the bank. The upshot was that the bank remained in operation without having to liquidate any assets and no public bail-out was required.

Bitfinex adopted this model and made all of its investors share-holders in Bitfinex. Within a year of this restructuring, Bitfinex announced that it had bought back all of the remaining cryptographic tokens it used to reimburse investors who lost funds in August 2016. Citing increased equity conversions and strong operating results, Bitfinex reduced its internal reserves to purchase the remaining tokens at their $1 face value.

Despite these efforts to recover their position and restore the faith of their customers in the future of their business, Bitfinex fell fowl of the regulator in the United States. The main problem stemmed from the fact that Bitfinex was not registered with the Commodity Futures Trading Commission (CFTC).

In the years preceding the Bitfinex hack, the CFTC had been active in enforcing regulations on bitcoin exchanges that offer bitcoin-based trading products. Several sites offer leveraged trading, and a few sites offer future contracts on bitcoin. However, American retail investors that use these websites may be in contravention of CFTC regulations.[27] The CFTC states that American retail investors can buy leveraged or margined derivative products on a regulated exchange, but not outside of an exchange. If this CFTC regulation applies to bitcoin derivatives, then off-exchange margined trades would be illegal.

After an investigation into the way that Bitfinex was advertising to and transacting with its customers, it was decided that during the time that Bitfinex was promoting and selling its investment tokens, it was in breach of the *Commodity Futures Trading Commission, Commodity Exchange Act* (1936) (the Act). Importantly, it did not actually deliver bitcoins purchased on a leveraged, margined or financed basis to the traders who purchased them, within the

---

26 S Higgins, 'The Bitfinex Bitcoin Hack: What We Know (And Don't Know)', *CoinDesk* (3 August 2016) <http://www.coindesk.com/bitfinex-Bitcoin-hack-know-dont-know/>.

27 *Commodity Futures Trading Commission, Commodity Exchange Act* (1936) <http://www.cftc.gov/files/ogc/comexO6O6Ol.pdf>.

meaning of the relevant section of the Act.[28] Instead, Bitfinex held the purchased bitcoins in bitcoin deposit wallets that it owned and controlled. Therefore, Bitfinex engaged in illegal, off-exchange commodity transactions and failed to register as a futures commission merchant, in violation of the regulations.[29] Bitfinex has since ceased doing business with US-based customers.[30]

Observers of the Bitfinex hack and the way that other crypto-currency exchanges have responded to malicious attacks on the code and the assets do not expect the investigations into the Bitfinex hack will reveal any insights on how to improve protection. What is more obvious is the community's willingness to lay blame for the hack at the victims, while discarding an industry-wide solution. Suggested solutions include third party independent custodial services for wallet and key management, multi-signature security over the private keys themselves and standardised audit processes. The options for adoption of these proposed measures are self-regulation or government imposed and supervised legislation. Self-regulation seems a better cultural fit for an otherwise decentralised network.

However, government imposed and supervised regulation may be needed in order to support competition and market liberalism. Otherwise, there will be a temptation for start-ups and struggling exchanges to avoid the costs associated with compliance. Industry-wide adoption of standards and regulation of compliance can be catalysts to improve the reputation of crypto-assets and exchanges. They can also foster competition and greater acceptance of new business models and philosophies enabled by blockchain and distributed ledger technologies.

The Coincheck Hack

At US$547 million, the monetary impact of the Japanese Coincheck hack in January 2018 dwarfs the US$480 million Mt Gox collapse in 2014.[31] And the circumstances that enabled the Coincheck hack have put the operators of the exchange in breach of the regulations that were put in place after Mt Gox.

In their online apology, the operators of Coincheck have admitted that the hacked deposits were not in cold storage, as required under Japanese legislation. Instead, the deposits and the keys to the virtual wallets were connected to the Internet and this provided the gateway access to the thieves. In their

---

28 2(c)(2)(D)(ii)(III)(aa) of the *Commodity Futures Trading Commission, Commodity Exchange Act* (1936).

29 Sections 4(a) and 4d of the Act, 7 U.S.C. §§ 6(a) and 6d of *Commodity Futures Trading Commission, Commodity Exchange Act* (1936).

30 Scott D. 'Hughes, Cryptocurrency Regulations and Enforcement in the US' (2017) 45 *Washington State University Law Review* 1, 13.

31 'Do Japan's New Regulations Signal the Death of Crypto Scams?', *Bitcoin* (26 October 2018) <https://bitcoin.com.au/new-crypto-regulations-japan/>. By volume Mt Gox remains the worst of all hacks. The Coincheck hack has the biggest dollar value due to the sharp increase in the price of bitcoin between the two events. At the time of the Mt Gox hack (in February 2014) one bitcoin cost US $565. When Coincheck was hacked four years later, one bitcoin cost US$10,000 <https://www.coindesk.com/price/bitcoin>.

defence, Coincheck's directors said that the failure to keep the deposits in cold storage was due to 'staff shortages'. Both of these failures to comply will give the Japanese authorities good reason to prosecute.

Coincheck also lacked multi-signature security, a measure requiring multiple sign-offs before funds can be moved. Close scrutiny of the accounts will be likely to reveal other irregularities. But this is little comfort for Coincheck's investors. Coincheck has promised to return 90% of the lost NEM (its native crypto-currency) to its customers, but has yet to say how or when this will happen.[32]

Since the Coincheck hack, Japan's Financial Service Agency (FSA) has unveiled plans to allow the crypto industry to self-regulate. Notorious for two of the biggest crypto hacks to date, Japan is working to improve the security of the sector.

The FSA announced in October 2018 that the crypto industry would be self-regulated, as recommended by the Japanese Virtual Currency Exchange Association (JVCEA). The JVCEA has been charged with developing the guidelines for self-regulation. From handling disputes to holding digital currencies, the new guidelines will offer greater stability within Japan's crypto exchanges.[33]

The question still remains if this new association will impact the decentralised nature of the crypto industry. Some argue that attempts to regulate crypto-currency may hamper revolutionary technology developments.[34]

Regulating What?

Crypto-currency's decentralised environment is often touted as a practical barrier to regulation. The argument runs that because crypto-currencies reside on networks that cross all borders simultaneously, the code is not 'at home' in any one place or on any single server.[35] However, this approach to the question of regulation suggests that it is the technology that needs to be or will be regulated.[36] This is not necessarily correct. Most regulation targets the way that we use it.

32 PA Ryan, 'What the Coincheck Hack Tells Us About How Australian Regulators Will Handle a Crypto-Currency Hack', *The Conversation* (30 January 2018) <http s://theconversation.com/what-the-coincheck-hack-tells-us-about-how-australia n-regulators-will-handle-a-cryptocurrency-hack-90842>.
33 'Do Japan's New Regulations Signal the Death of Crypto Scams?', *Bitcoin* (26 October 2018) <https://bitcoin.com.au/new-crypto-regulations-japan/>.
34 C Gamble, 'The Legality and Regulatory Challenges of Decentralised Crypto-Currency: A Western Perspective' (2017) 20 *International Trade and Business Law Review* 346.
35 C Gamble, 'The Legality and Regulatory Challenges of Decentralised Crypto-Currency: A Western Perspective' (2017) 20 *International Trade and Business Law Review* 346, 355.
36 C Gamble, 'The Legality and Regulatory Challenges of Decentralised Crypto-Currency: A Western Perspective' (2017) 20 *International Trade and Business Law Review* 346, 355.

Different jurisdictions have implemented laws to regulate the way that blockchain networks are used. For example, with its General Data Protection Regulation, the European Union has taken a firm stance on data privacy, implementing stringent regulations that have notable implications for blockchain. Some Japan and Korea have until recently taken a 'business first, regulation later' approach. In September 2017, China abruptly banned initial coin offerings (ICOs). South Korea soon followed suit. Japanese regulatory bodies have restricted their restricted acceptance of crypto-currencies to bitcoin only, and are reviewing their stance in relation to blockchain-powered businesses. The United States, Canada and Australia have each focused their legislation on how to characterise types of crypto-currency transactions. In all of these cases, it is the use of blockchain that is being regulated, not the technology itself.

The law has been regulating human exchanges and relationships for centuries. The fact that there is a new way of representing value, hosting transactions and managing business exchanges should not be a barrier to making sure that the fundamentals of contract, good faith and business judgment can be applied in decentralised environments, as well as ones that are intermediated by trusted third parties. Indeed, this situation is not novel. In the 1990s, similar questions were posed in relation to the Internet. In a research paper presented to the Australian Parliament in 1995, the author identified key findings to be considered on the question, *Can the Internet Be Regulated?* They included: the Internet can enhance democracy; the self-regulatory culture of the Internet; the Internet lacks centralised control; encryption is widely used on the Internet; the world-wide nature of the Internet; and anonymity and pseudonymity hide the identity of the sender. These features resonate with the emergence of blockchain technology and crypto-currencies.[37]

The regulation of 'good faith' in contract and business is a feature of many modern economies.[38] Furthermore, consumer protection and professional licensing laws ensure that there is an avenue for redress for victims of business that have been mismanaged by directors and officers who incompetent. These existing laws may need modification to protect potential investors from crypto-currency scams and schemes, but ultimately, they regulate relations in business.

---

37 H Roberts, *Can the Internet be Regulated?*, Parliament of Australia, Research Paper 35 (1995–1996) <https://www.aph.gov.au/About_Parliament/Parliamentary_Departments/Parliamentary_Library/pubs/rp/RP9596/96rp35>.

38 For example, *Unfair Terms in Consumer Contracts Regulations 1993* (UK); *Consumer Rights Act 2015* (UK) The Office of Fair Trading acts as the UK's official consumer and competition watchdog; Australian Consumer Law (ACL) is set out in Schedule 2 of the *Competition and Consumer Act 2010* (Cth); Australia's watchdog is the Australian Competition and Consumer Commission; in the United States: *Uniform Deceptive Trade Practices Act 1966*; and the *Federal Trade Commission Act 1914*.

If and when regulation and contract fall short in providing causes of action for plaintiffs who have suffered losses at the hands of Trustees, fiduciaries and custodians, Equity offers a suite of powerful remedies that can empower victims to recover misapplied assets from errant fiduciaries, as well as any knowing or dishonest participants in the relevant scheme or scam.[39]

---

39 For example, injunctions, specific performance of contracts, declarations, rescission, account of profits, equitable compensation and the proprietary remedy of the constructive trust.

18 Liability of Third Parties in Digital and Crypto Economies

The liability of third parties for the wrong-doing of another is well established in the criminal and civil jurisdictions. As well as common law accessorial liabilities, professional and statutory obligations require solicitors and other professional advisers not to assist their clients in any breaches of their obligations. A number of key statutory instruments regulate the conduct of fiduciaries – in particular, solicitors,[1] Trustees[2] and directors.[3] Determining liability for innocent or fraudulent breach of Trust or for breach of Trust-like and fiduciary duties always turns on the circumstance of the case and the list of agents and custodians who may be classed as fiduciaries not closed. Solicitors, banks and other professional Trustees and fiduciaries must take care when advising and assisting their Trustee and director clients not to assist them in a breach of their fiduciary or Trust duties and not to become recipients of funds misapplied as a result of such a breach.

Equity intervenes on behalf of the plaintiff if the conduct of a defendant makes it unconscionable for them to assert a common law or proprietary right.[4] Equitable principles have a distinctive ethical quality, reflecting as they do the prevention of unconscionable conduct.[5] The notion that Equity will grant relief in respect of conduct that is against good conscience resonates through centuries of legal history.[6]

---

1   For example, in New South Wales, solicitors are regulated by the *Legal Profession Uniform Law Application Act 2014* (NSW); known in Victoria as *Legal Profession Uniform Law Application Act 2014* (Vic).
2   For example, in Queensland, the *Trusts Act 1973* (Qld); and in South Australia, the *Trustee Act 1936* (SA).
3   In Australia, the *Corporations Act 2001* (Cth); and, in the United Kingdom, the *Companies Act 2006* (UK).
4   P Parkinson, 'The Conscience of Equity' in P Parkinson (ed), *The Principles of Equity* (LBC, 1996), 28.
5   ICF Spry, *Equitable Remedies* (4th edn, LBC, 1990), 1.
6   Lord Walker, 'Dishonesty and Unconscionable Conduct in Commercial Life – Some Reflections on Accessory Liability and Knowing Receipt' (2005) 27 *Sydney Law Review* 187, 190.

Over the past 40 years, the superior courts of the United Kingdom, Australia and Canada have heard and decided some significant disputes where a third party has been made liable for a breach of fiduciary duty by their client.

This chapter is concerned with how this type of accessorial liability has arisen in some businesses that were particularly reliant on their operational platform in digital and crypto-economies. It begins with a definition and review of the liability for third parties. It then explores three examples of third party liability emanating from online international financial transactions, high volume trading in the stock market and the provision of banking services to crypto-currency exchanges. The first example is a United Kingdom statute that imposes liability on solicitors and bankers who help their clients to launder money. The second example is the liability of recipients of the proceeds from Madoff's collapsed Ponzi scheme. The third example is the unsuccessful accessorial liability claim made against Mitsuri Bank for apparently assisting the Mt Gox bitcoin exchange. All three of these examples reflect the changing nature of the way that businesses operate, that fraud is executed and the risk that this can create for unsuspecting associates, agents and service providers who trusted them. This chapter concludes with a look at the challenges facing plaintiffs and regulators who attempt to trace missing crypto-currencies into the hands of wrong-doers and knowing participants in that wrong-doing.

Establishing the Liability of Third Parties

Participants in the modern commercial community are aware that special care must be taken when undertaking activities on behalf of others, in particular those who are properly appointed to act on behalf of individuals, funds or companies. Parties closely associated with those activities need to be aware of the rules that – if breached – may attribute liability to them as accessories. While the common law protects contractual rights against third parties by the tort of inducing breach of contract, Equity imposes liability on third parties partaking in equitable wrongs.[7]

There are four main bases upon which a breach of a Trustee's fiduciary duties can give rise to the liability of third parties or strangers: those who knowingly receive misapplied assets misapplied; those who assisted the wrong-doer with knowledge of a dishonest or fraudulent design; those who procure the breach; and strangers who intermeddle with Trust funds. The liability that attaches to these participants in a breach of a Trustee's fiduciary duty is a personal liability known as constructive trusteeship. In this case, the expression 'fiduciary duty' is properly confined to those duties which are peculiar to fiduciaries and the breach of which attracts legal consequences differing from those consequent upon the breach of other duties. Only breaches of these particular duties may give rise to constructive trusteeship being imposed on third parties

---

7 R Meagher, JD Heydon and M Leeming, *Meagher, Gummow and Lehane's Equity, Doctrines and Remedies* (Butterworths, 2002), [41–110].

to a breach of fiduciary duty. Unless the expression is limited in this way, it will lack any practical utility.[8] In this sense it is obvious that not every breach of a duty by a fiduciary is a breach of fiduciary duty.[9]

The categories of fiduciary relationships are infinitely varied and the duties of the fiduciary vary with the circumstances that generate the relationship.[10] Underlying all cases of fiduciary obligation is the notion that inherent in the nature of the relationship itself is a position of disadvantage or vulnerability on the part of one of the parties which causes him to place reliance upon the other and requires the protection of Equity acting upon the conscience of that other.[11]

The relation of trust and confidence is nowadays usually thought to consist in a cluster of duties emanating from the core requirement of loyalty.[12] The definition of the fiduciary relationship changes depending upon the specific obligation being considered.[13]

In most common and civil law jurisdictions, legislation regulating corporations imposes positive fiduciary-like obligations upon directors. For example, Australia's Corporations Law provides that directors of companies must act with care and diligence[14] and in good faith.[15] However, unlike other jurisdictions,[16] there are no prescribed or positive fiduciary duties under the Common Law in Australia. Fiduciary duties in Australia are expressed in terms of the injunctions against fiduciaries profiting from their position and against allowing their own interests or the interests of third parties to conflict with the duties they owe to their principal.[17]

8   *Bristol and West Building Society v Mothew* [1998] Ch 1, 16 and 17.
9   *Bristol and West Building Society v Mothew* [1998] Ch 1, 18. In his judgment in *Bristol and West Building Society v Mothew*, Millett LJ (at 18), endorsed the observations of Southin J in *Girardet v Crease & Co* (1987) 11 BCLR (2d) 361, 'The word "fiduciary" is flung around now as if it applied to all breaches of duty by solicitors, directors of companies and so forth … That a lawyer can commit a breach of the special duty [of a fiduciary] … by entering into a contract with the client without full disclosure … and so forth is clear. But to say that simple carelessness in giving advice is such a breach is a perversion of words' (at 362).
10   *Hospital Products Ltd v United States Surgical Corporation* [1983] 2 NSWLR 157, [84], per Mason J, citing with approval, *Phipps v Boardman* [1967] 2 AC 46, 123–125; *New Zealand Netherlands Society 'Oranje' Incorporated v Kuys* (1973) 1 WLR 1126, 1129–1130; *Canadian Aero Service Ltd v O'Malley* (1973) 40 DLR (3d) 371, 383 and 390.
11   *Hospital Products Ltd v United States Surgical Corporation* [1983] 2 NSWLR 157, [55], per Mason J; see also, *Tate v Williamson* (1866) 2 Ch App 55, 60–61.
12   SB Elliott, *Compensation Claims Against Trustees* (DPhil thesis, University of Oxford, 2002), 2.
13   PD Finn, *Fiduciary Obligations* (LBC, 1977).
14   *Corporations Act 2001* (Cth), s 180
15   *Corporations Act 2001* (Cth), s 181
16   Including, Canada and New Zealand.
17   See, *Breen v Williams* (1996) 186 CLR 71, 108; and *Chan v Zachariah* (1984)154 CLR 205, [24], per Deane J.

In contradistinction to the Australian approach, a series of judicial decisions in Commonwealth jurisdictions such as Canada seek to impart a greater degree of flexibility to the fiduciary obligation. For example, in the Supreme Court of Canada in *McIrney v MacDonald*, [18] a fiduciary was encumbered with the prescriptive duty of acting with 'the utmost good faith and loyalty' towards the beneficiary.[19] In this case, a doctor refused to give a patient access to medical records that were prepared by the patient's previous physicians. The Court first ruled that the relationship between a doctor and patient was fiduciary in nature as it was based on trust and confidence. Furthermore, it was held that providing access to medical records was incidental to the fiduciary duty imposed upon the doctor.[20]

Courts in Canada have donned the activist hat and endeavoured to include prescriptive duties within the spectrum of fiduciary duties.[21] Similar arguments have been made by legal scholars.[22]

In Australia, the fiduciary principle does not import the connotation of positive duties on the part of a fiduciary to the principal.[23] A better formulation may be 'relationships that give rise to fiduciary duties', rather than 'fiduciary relationships'.[24] The High Court of Australia has gone to some lengths to dispel any misconceptions that there might be some positive fiduciary duties in that jurisdiction. For example, the duties to exercise skill and care are not fiduciary.[25] These duties may be owed by persons who are properly described as fiduciaries, but the other duties are contractual or tortious – not fiduciary. If fiduciary duties properly only proscribe conduct then it will be wrong to treat every failure by a fiduciary as a breach of a fiduciary duty. For example, the duties on company directors to act in good faith for the benefit of the company or to exercise reasonable care and skill are tortious or contractual, rather than fiduciary duties[26] (even when owed

---

18 *McIrney v MacDonald* (1992) 93 DLR (4th) 415.

19 *McIrney v MacDonald* (1992) 93 DLR (4th) 415, 423 (La Forest J)

20 See also, D Ghosh, 'Fixing the Fiduciary Obligation: The Prescription-Proscription Dichotomy' (2012) 11(1) *Canberra Law Review* 24, 26.

21 J Brebner, '*Breen v Williams*: A Lost Opportunity or Welcome Conservatism?' (1996) 3 *Deakin Law Review* 237.

22 R Lee, 'Rethinking the Content of the Fiduciary Obligation' [2009] *Conveyancer and Property Lawyer* 236. See also, D Ghosh, 'Fixing the Fiduciary Obligation: The Prescription-Proscription Dichotomy' (2012) 11(1) *Canberra Law Review* 24, 25.

23 PD Finn, 'The Fiduciary Principle' in T Youdan (ed), *Equity, Fiduciaries and Trusts* (Carswell, 1989), 28.

24 GE Dal Pont, 'Conflicts of Interest, The Interplay Between Fiduciary and Confidentiality Law' (2002) 25 *Australian Mining and Petroleum Law Association Yearbook* 583, 584.

25 See *Breen v Williams* (1996) 186 CLR 71, 113, per Gaudron and McHugh JJ; and repeated by the High Court in *Pilmer v Duke Group Limited (In Liq)* (2001) 207 CLR 165, 180 (per McHugh, Hayne and Callinan JJ) and, 1092 (per Kirby J).

26 G Dempsey and A Greinke, 'Proscriptive Fiduciary Duties in Australia' (2004) 25 *Australian Bar Review* 1, 13.

by a fiduciary).[27] Furthermore, the duties owed by a particular fiduciary can vary from case to case.[28]

Whether or not fiduciary duties are prescriptive or proscriptive, it is important to note that their liability only fixes to third parties for their part in the wrong-doing if the particular wrong-doing is a breach of fiduciary duty (as understood in the relevant jurisdiction).

This is an area of the law that has developed in such a way that it can lead to difficult and complex disputes. Establishing with clarity the bases upon which third parties might be made liable for a breach of trust or a breach of fiduciary duty will ensure that the grounds for liability may be communicated in a way that is intelligible to all.[29] Although the law is dynamic and must be able to respond to social and commercial changes, it is also important to establish the key features of any legal obligation or liability, so that the community can commit to the rule of law.[30] While the practice of law precedes its description and systemisation, description and systemisation also has an effect on practice.[31]

Participants in digital economies may be the primary wrong-doers or third parties (including the wrong-doer's advisers and agents or government agencies). The wrong-doer may be a malicious stranger or other accessory, including those who are ostensibly innocent, but they can be fixed with liability if they orchestrated or knew of the wrong-doing (including turning a blind eye to the obvious); or if they were on notice of certain facts that would have put a reasonable person on notice of the wrong-doing.[32]

---

27 A Hudson, *Equity and Trusts* (6th edn, Routledge-Cavendish, 2009), 620. See also, *Breen v Williams* (1996) 186 CLR 71, 93 (per Dawson and Toohey JJ), 111 (per Gaudron and McHugh JJ); and G Dempsey and A Greinke, 'Proscriptive Fiduciary Duties in Australia' (2004) 25 *Australian Bar Review* 1, 37.

28 *News Limited v Australian Rugby Football League Ltd* (1996) 64 FCR 410, 539, per Burchett J; and *Hospital Products Ltd v United States Surgical Corporation* (1984) 156 CLR 41, 102 the court noted that the most that can be said is that whether or not the relationship between joint-venturers is fiduciary will depend upon 'the form which the particular joint venture takes and upon the content of the obligations which the parties to it have undertaken' (per Mason, Brennan and Deane JJ).

29 This argument for classifying and 'mapping' Equity is based on the arguments made by Birks in P Birks, 'Equity in the Modern Law, An Exercise in Taxonomy' (1996) 26 *University of Western Australia Law Review* 1, 7. See also, D Jensen, 'The Problem of Classification in Private Law' (2007) 31(2) *Melbourne University Law Review* 516, 516.

30 The rule of law is the idea that our society is controlled by legal rules, and those who exercise power within it (including the judges) are themselves bound by law, K Mason, 'The Rule of Law' in PD Finn (ed), *Essays on Law and Government, Principles and Values Vol 1* (Thomson Reuters, 1995), 117.

31 S Waddams, *Dimensions of Private Law, Categories and Concepts in Anglo-American Legal Reasoning* (Cambridge University Press, 2003), 225.

32 *Baden Delvaux & Lecuit v Societe General pour Favoriser le Developpement* [1992] 4 All ER 161; [1993] 1 WLR 509.

There are some existing and sometimes conflicting approaches to distinguishing different types of third party liability. For example, what has come to be known as 'the two limbs of *Barnes v Addy*' encompasses third party liability for knowingly receiving misapplied Trust property (knowing receipt) and knowingly assisting a Trustee in a dishonest and fraudulent design (knowing assistance). Over the past 140 years, Equity practitioners and judges have also cited *Barnes v Addy* as authority for knowingly dealing with misapplied Trust property, knowingly inducing or procuring a breach of Trust, and Trusteeship de son tort. The reason why these three additional types of liability are sometimes regarded as falling within the scope of *Barnes v Addy* is that they share a similar factual matrix, namely the participation or intermeddling of a third party or stranger in a breach of Trust. The term 'third party' connotes someone other than the Trustee or fiduciary who is an agent or advisor to the Trustee or fiduciary, while the word 'stranger' suggests that someone wholly unconnected to the impugned conduct has received some of the misapplied Trust property. For ease of reference, the terms 'accessory' and 'accessories' will be used to refer to both knowing assistants and knowing inducers (that is, non-recipient third parties to a breach).[33]

In *Barnes v Addy*, Lord Selborne set out what he saw as the bases upon which the Court would find a third party (in this case it was a solicitor) liable for their role in a breach by a Trustee. Lord Selborne held:

> Strangers to a trust may have extended to them the responsibility imposed by equity upon Trustees if they make themselves Trustees de son tort or are 'actually participating in any fraudulent conduct of the Trustee to the injury of the cestui que trust. ... Strangers are not to be made constructive Trustees ... unless [they] receive and become chargeable with some part of the trust property, or unless they assist with knowledge in a dishonest and fraudulent design on the part of the Trustees'.[34]

According to traditional formulation for 'the two limbs' of *Barnes v Addy*, third party liability is the liability of a third party to a Trust who receives misapplied Trust property ('the first limb') or assists in a breach of Trust ('the second limb'). Lord Selborne's judgment in *Barnes v Addy* also dealt with the liability of agents who receive and become chargeable with some or all of the Trust property; and the liability of agents who assist with knowledge in a dishonest and fraudulent design on the part of the Trustees. In *Jacobs' Law of*

---

33 However, the term 'accessory' has been applied to recipient and non-recipient third parties in *Barnes v Addy* claims. For example, Lord Nicholls' terminology in *Royal Brunei Airlines Sdn Bhd v Tan* [1995] 2 AC 378: 'Liability as an accessory is not dependent upon receipt of trust property. It arises even though no trust property has reached the hands of the accessory.' Further, in *Jacobs' Law of Trusts in Australia*, the authors use the term 'accessory' when referring to liability under the first (receipt) limb of *Barnes v Addy*; see JD Heydon and M Leeming, *Jacobs' Law of Trusts in Australia* (7th edn, Butterworths, 2006), [1334].

34 *Barnes v Addy* (1874) LR 9 Ch App 244, 251.

Trusts in Australia, [35] the learned authors note that in later cases it is clear that reference to Trustees in the second limb is to be read as including involvement of the third party in misconduct of fiduciaries who are not Trustees.[36]

Barnes v Addy liability is not limited to third parties who are the agents of Trustees. Strangers to a breach of Trust may also be made liable if they receive Trust property pursuant to a breach of Trust or breach of fiduciary duty.[37] *Barnes v Addy* is authority for additional grounds upon which a third party may be made liable as a constructive Trustee. For example, as well as the liability of agents, Lord Selborne refers to strangers who are not properly Trustees, but who by their misconduct in relation to trust property are made 'Trustees *de son tort*'.[38]

When a person, although not appointed a Trustee or a fiduciary, controls and administers Trust property and acts as a Trustee, they will be liable as a Trustee *de son tort*. Non-receipt liability must be distinguished from receipt liability, so that the obligations imposed upon non-recipient participants reflect the fact that no Trust property has passed into the hands of the defendant. The personal obligations that can attach to non-receipt liability reflect Equity's concern that a Trust gives rise to a special relationship between the Trustee and the beneficiaries of the Trust. Any errant agents of the Trustee or intermeddlers with the Trust must be made to account for any losses incurred as a result of their fraudulent interference with the Trust property.

It is possible (as was alleged in *Barnes v Addy*) that a third party's non-receipt participation in a breach of Trust can cause loss to a plaintiff. In such a case, there are no assets in the hands of the third party that the plaintiff claims were misdirected. If a third party has gained a benefit from their knowing assistance in a breach of Trust (without receiving any of the property misapplied pursuant to the breach) and they still have the unauthorised gains in their hands, then it is argued that the courts of Equity should have a discretion to impose a proprietary constructive Trust over those gains, in the same way that such a remedy might be applied to knowing recipients of non-

---

35   JD Heydon and M Leeming, *Jacobs' Law of Trusts in Australia* (7th edn, Butterworths, 2006).

36   See JD Heydon and M Leeming, *Jacobs' Law of Trusts in Australia* (7th edn, Butterworths, 2006), [1333]. See also notable cases that extend liability under the second limb to fiduciaries, *Consul Development Pty Ltd v DPC Estates Pty Ltd* (1975) 132 CLR 373, 397; *Hospital Products Ltd v United States Surgical Corporation* [1983] 2 NSWLR 157 and *Hospital Products Ltd v United States Surgical Corporation* (1984) 156 CLR 41.

37   There is authority in Australia for the classification of more than just two types of liability as falling within *Barnes v Addy*, see *Farah Constructions Pty Ltd v Say-Dee Pty Ltd* (2007) 230 CLR 89, [162]; and *Grimaldi v Chameleon Mining NL (No 2)* (2012) 200 FCR 296; (2012) 287 ALR 22; (2012) 87 ACSR 260; [2012] FCAFC 6, [141–142].

38   *Barnes v Addy* (1874) LR 9 Ch App 244, 251.

Trust property, where those misdirected funds are still traceable into the hands of the recipient.[39]

As well as imposing liability on a non-recipient for gains they make as a result of their participation in a breach of Trust, there may be good policy reasons why the law should hold the knowing assistant liable to compensate for losses caused by the Trustee, and might hold the knowing assistant liable for gains made by the Trustee.[40]

The key elements of third party liability include a clear expression of what must be proven to establish a breach of trust: that agents who act outside of the scope of their agency may not be able to plead that they were merely following the instructions of their principal; that knowledge of a breach of trust could fix third parties with personal liability for their participation in a breach of trust (whether or not they receive misdirected Trust property); that intermeddling in a trust without proper authority could fix the innocent (but wrongly appointed) third party with the obligations of an express trustee; and that fraudulent intermeddling of a Trustee *de son tort* could give rise to the imposition of a constructive trust.

The imposition of 'constructive trusteeship' will only arise from an equitable fraud (as opposed to fraud at common law). For the purposes of an action at law, fraud has to be established on the basis of a fraudulent misrepresentation that consists of a false statement of fact made by the defendant to the plaintiff, knowingly or without belief in its truth or a statement made recklessly, with the intent that it should be acted upon and when in fact it is acted upon by the plaintiff. In contrast fraud in Equity is formulated so as to include both actual and constructive fraud. It extends to any conduct which a court of Equity was prepared to designate as unfair, unconscionable and unjust. This appellation is readily used in many instances other than fraudulent misrepresentation.[41]

This characterisation of liability is important in any discussion of third party liability when the primary wrong-doer's misconduct can be characterised as equitable fraud. This could be misrepresentations to made by a fiduciary to their client, unconscionable conduct in operating a Ponzi scheme, trading while insolvent or knowingly facilitating misleading and deceptive business practices.

Statutory Liability of Fiduciaries in Digital Economies

In January 2017, the United Kingdom set a new tax evasion benchmark for businesses. The purpose of these reforms was to ensure that companies would

39 See, P Ridge, 'Constructive Trusts, Accessorial Liability and Judicial Discretion' in E Bant and M Bryan (eds) *Principles of Proprietary Remedies* (Thomson Reuters, 2013).

40 P Ridge 'Justifying the Remedies for Dishonest Assistance' (2008) 124 *Law Quarterly Review* 445, 457–460.

41 M Cope, 'The Constructive Trust as a Remedy for Mistake, Fraud, Duress and Undue Influence' (1987), 3 *Queensland Institute of Technology Law Journal* 111, 111.

know whether they have 'reasonable procedures' in place to prevent employees, contractors and others acting on their behalf from facilitating tax evasion.

Under sections 45 and 46 of the United Kingdom *Criminal Finances Act 2017*, directors may be made liable for their failure to prevent the facilitation of tax evasion. This innovative legislation created a new corporate offence that could make advisers and professionals liable if employees, or anyone else providing services for or on its behalf, assist a taxpayer in evading their tax liabilities. Penalties include unlimited fines.

Companies or partnerships doing business in, with or through the United Kingdom need to comply with a requirement that reasonable procedures are in place to prevent an employee, contractor or other 'associated person' from helping a third party evade either United Kingdom or foreign taxes. Under the new law, businesses must demonstrate that reasonable procedures are in place.

This new layer of legislation imposes on corporations the need for transparency and public scrutiny of tax administration and tax fraud. The new Corporate Criminal Offence (CCO) is a significant development in the United Kingdom's focus on tax evasion. Businesses convicted following a public prosecution could face an unlimited fine as determined by the court; a corporate criminal conviction (putting licences to operate at risk worldwide); exclusion from public procurement markets; and reputational damage. Compliance is put at risk in online trading environments. Sophisticated platforms for international trade may wittingly enable sellers to avoid paying import or export taxes, VAT or income tax on sales. If so, the business could be found guilty under the new regime, unless it can prove in court that it has taken reasonable preventive measures.

Commencing July 2020, the European Union is also introducing new requirements concerning tax planning, but these new laws are aimed specifically at advisors, accountants and lawyers. In March 2018, the European Council agreed on a proposal that requires tax advisors, accountants and lawyers to report tax planning schemes viewed as 'particularly aggressive.' EU Member States can automatically exchange key information through a centralised database that impose penalties on intermediaries who fail to comply with the new reporting requirements.[42]

Facilitating tax evasion includes, for example, being knowingly concerned in or taking steps with a view to another person's fraudulent tax evasion, or aiding, abetting, counselling or procuring the commission of a tax evasion offence.

Interestingly, under the UK law, it is a defence if the defendant had in place reasonable prevention procedures or it was not reasonable to expect the defendant to have any prevention procedures in place.[43] The Act stipulates that guidelines will be provided setting out the appropriate prevention

---

42   'Next Steps for CCO Compliance. Helping Financial Services Institutions Respond to the UK's New Corporate Criminal Offence', *EY* (2017) <https://www.ey.com/Publication/vwLUAssets/ey-next-steps-for-cco-compliance/%24FILE/ey-next-steps-for-cco-compliance.pdf>.

43   *Criminal Finances Act* 2017(UK) Section 45. <http://www.legislation.gov.uk/ukpga/2017/22/pdfs/ukpga_20170022_en.pdf>.

procedures.[44] The guidance provided by Her Majesty's Customs and Revenue mirrors the guiding principles in existing bribery legislation and focuses on:

i   Risk assessment – the relevant body should undertake a risk assessment to determine the nature and extent of its exposure to the risk that its employees/agents may engage in the facilitation of tax evasion. The assessment should focus on the opportunities and means by which employees/agents may engage in criminal activity and consider what prevention measures may mitigate such risks.

ii   Proportionality – prevention measures should be proportionate to the risk the relevant body faces and reflect the nature, scale and complexity of its activities.

iii   Top level commitment – senior management of the company/partnership should be committed to developing and implementing the prevention procedures.

iv   Due diligence – the relevant body should apply due diligence procedures to identify and respond to risks.

v   Communication – the prevention procedures should be adequately communicated, understood and embedded throughout the organisation.

vi   Monitoring and review – the prevention procedures should be monitored and reviewed regularly, and necessary improvements made.

A major challenge for operators of online financial advice and service platforms is how to ensure that these strategies are implemented and monitored effectively. A surge in registrations for Value Added Tax of existing businesses has proven that the threat of criminal liability has been an effective compliance tool.[45] Registration for tax is a simple and provable step to take for any business, but preventing an online platform from enabling tax avoidance by third parties is a more challenging proposition. For example, the 'know your client' and 'know your client's client' rules are much harder to obey when dealing with high volume business traffic or transacting via crypto-currencies.

Banks and financial advisers in the UK are required by law to comply with anti-money laundering (AML) laws and Know your Customer (KYC) requirements to prevent criminals and terrorists from using financial products or services to store and move around their money. If the customer is a corporate entity, then the identity of its controller will need to be proved.

In the case of crypto-currencies, like bitcoin, the pseudonymity with which users can buy and trade online makes identifying customers and clients almost

---

44   *Criminal Finances Act* 2017(UK) Section 47. <http://www.legislation.gov.uk/ukpga/2017/22/pdfs/ukpga_20170022_en.pdf>.

45   HM Revenue & Customs reported that 7,185 Internet retailers applied to register for VAT in the lead up to the commencement of the new laws, up from 695 in 2015. V Houlder, 'Online Sales Clampdown Nets VAT Registrations', *Financial Times* (21 December 2016) <https://www.ft.com/content/f037bd6c-c6d6-11e6-9043-7e34c07b46ef>.

impossible and philosophically contrary the intrinsic nature of the technology. Government officials in the many countries have signalled the challenges of balancing know-your-customer laws (to combat the money laundering problem and other nefarious activities) with the potentially valuable attributes of bitcoin (that is, its ability to add financial stability in developing countries, lower transaction costs and remove third-party intermediaries).[46]

This new legislation adds a layer of responsibility and potential liability for lawyers and financial advice professionals. Under the common law a solicitor would not be held liable just because his or her client has committed a breach of Trust, even in cases where the solicitor knew that there was a breach of Trust or other offending conduct. If this were the law, then it would become the duty of a solicitor to denounce his or her client whenever he or she determined the client to be acting in such a way. If the client has committed a fraud, it is likely they will try to conceal it from their lawyers. A solicitor cannot be tasked with conducting due diligence on all their client's transactions and affairs. If it were held that a person dealing with a client who is a Trustee or fiduciary has notice of everything relating to their obligations, and is bound to see that no breach is committed therein, even bankers, agents, solicitors, clerks or messengers when they have dealings with Trustees would have the duty imposed on them in every case to see to the due execution of those duties.[47] Such an obligation would be too onerous to impose upon business professionals.

In the case of this new legislation, and given the extraterritorial ramifications of the United Kingdom's *Criminal Finances Act 2017*, businesses in the United Kingdom, and those dealing with businesses in the United Kingdom, will need to address these challenges and their effects.[48] These extraterritorial ramifications are at their most acute for entities that conduct most or all of their business online. The government has recommended a 'risk-based and proportionate' approach to implementation of preventative procedures. This is especially applicable to those in the financial services and accountancy sectors, including branch offices, fiduciaries and Trustees, promoters and managers of investment products, and wealth managers.

Liability of Recipients in Digital Economies

The December 2008 collapse of the $50 billion Ponzi scheme masterminded by former NASDAQ chairman Bernard Madoff punctuated a miserable year for Wall Street. Revelations of the extent of Madoff's 40-year deception

---

46   Including the United States. See, NJ Ajello, 'Fitting a Square Peg in a Round Hole: Bitcoin, Money Laundering, and the Fifth Amendment Privilege against Self-Incrimination' (2015) 80 *Brooklyn Law Review* 435, 460.

47   *Fyler v Fyler* [1841] EngR 463; (1841) 3 Beav 550; 49 ER 216 at 559 (Beav).

48   T Corfield and J Schaefer, 'The Taxman Cometh: The Criminal Offences of Failure to Prevent Tax Evasion' (2017) 23(10) *Trusts & Trustees* 1030.

underscored, yet again, that savvy market-makers can harness arcane financial instruments as weapons of mass destruction.

In the 1970s, new regulation began to allow firms such as Madoff's to trade more prestigious blue-chip stocks and he began to gain market share in this area. As the decade progressed, Madoff developed a reputation for being a forward-thinker and his firm was one of the pioneers in electronic trading. His firm specialised in trading over-the-counter with retail brokers, bypassing the exchange specialists by using the new trading technology.

Electronic trading platforms typically stream live market prices on which users can trade and may provide additional trading tools, such as charting packages, news feeds and account management functions. Some platforms have been specifically designed to allow individuals to gain access to financial markets that could formerly only be accessed by specialist trading firms. They may also be designed to automatically trade specific strategies based on technical analysis or to enable high-frequency trading.

With the benefits of these trading technologies, Madoff became a big player on Wall Street and began working with important institutions. By 1990, Madoff executed around 9% of all trades on the New York Stock Exchange.

Just as it remains unclear when Madoff began managing client money, it also remains unclear whether it was ever a legitimate operation. Unsurprisingly, Madoff claims that it was legitimate and that the Ponzi scheme did not begin until 1992. But for the digitisation of the share market, it is arguable that the sheer scale of Madoff's deception would not have been possible.

He also claimed that he lost a significant amount of money trading in the early 1990s and – rather than coming clean to his investors – he manipulated the numbers, hoping that he would eventually recoup the losses. Seen in this light, the best that could be said for Madoff would be that he tried to trade his way out of trouble. Notable experts on Madoff, including *New York Times* reporter and author of *The Wizard of Lies* Diana B. Henriques, [49] believe that this story is fabricated and Madoff's Ponzi was more deliberate and had in fact begun long before.

Using money from new investors, Madoff paid old investors on false returns. Traditionally, Ponzi schemes collapse quite quickly under their own weight. However, Madoff was able to attract new investment and in the years leading up to the failure of his business, he was 'managing' more money than many of the largest institutions on Wall Street.

The December 2008 collapse of Madoff's Ponzi scheme caused the bankruptcy of many investors and was humiliating for the regulators. Madoff's methods had previously been investigated by the United States Securities Exchange Commission (SEC). In a 2005 email from Harry Markopoulos (a Boston money manager) to Meaghan Cheung at the SEC, the former warned: 'I spent some time over the weekend further improving my analysis on why Madoff Investment Securities, LLC is likely Ponzi Scheme (although there is a

---

49 D B Henriques, *The Wizard of Lies* (Times Books, 2011).

slight chance the returns are real but accrue from front-running customer order flow).'[50]

Markopoulos eventually helped to pull back the curtain on the scheme at Madoff Investment Securities. Prior to this correspondence, a 2001 article published by *Barrons* raised questions about his inscrutable strategies.[51] In his scathing 2005 report to the SEC, Markopoulos observed: 'A super-sized fraud of this magnitude was bound to happen given the lack of regulation of these off-shore entities.'[52]

But for investors pocketing windfalls, the lure of easy money outstripped suspicions raised by Madoff's shroud of secrecy. When that shroud was lifted, however, Madoff's investment fund stood revealed as a classic Ponzi scheme: a con game in which the illusion of solvency was created by paying off early investors with capital raised from later entrants. As long as new investment continued to come in the door, the earlier adopters reaped fat rewards; once markets tumbled and investors withdrew, however, the whole thing collapsed like a house of cards.

A key component of Madoff's Ponzi scheme was the facility to trade directly on a stock exchange. This is made possible via the use of Exchange Traded Funds (EFTs), which were introduced at the very end of the 1980s as an innovative product that was meant to be a proxy for the S&P 500 that also traded on an exchange like a stock. After being launched, this earliest ETF prototype was immediately targeted by lawyers of the Chicago Mercantile Exchange (CME) for illegally behaving like a futures contract. A lawsuit ensued, and a federal judge in Chicago ruled that they needed to be withdrawn. A year later, the first successful ETF was launched in Toronto, Canada. These investment units were instantly lauded for providing low-cost exposure to Canadian equities. Shortly afterwards, many more ETFs in Canada and the United States would follow suit.

ETF Trustees have a fiduciary duty to the ETF and serve to protect the interests of ETF shareholders. ETFs are subject to additional requirements, such as requirements imposed by the exchange on which the ETF's shares are traded and requirements imposed by the SEC's exemptive relief which permits the ETF to operate, as well as Board considerations regarding ETF-specific

---

50 Email from H Markopoulos to M Cheung (7 November 2005) *Madoff Exhibits – 04406*<https://www.sec.gov/news/studies/2009/oig-509/exhibit-0290.pdf>.

51 For example, *Barron's* Erin Arvedlund wrote 'Madoff's investors rave about his performance — even though they don't understand how he does it'. Arvellund quoted a 'very satisfied investor' as conceding, 'Even knowledgeable people can't really tell you what he's doing' – E Arvedlund 'Don't Ask Don't Tell: Bernie Madoff Attracts Skeptics in 2001', *Barrons* (7 May 2001) <https://www.barrons.com/articles/SB989019667829349012?tesla=y>.

52 'The World's Largest Hedge Fund Is a Fraud', *Madoff Exhibits – 04406* (7 November 2005) <https://www.sec.gov/news/studies/2009/oig-509/exhibit-0290.pdf>.

operational issues. The legal fallout of Madoff's arrest sounded both in criminal and civil law.

In the wake of the Madoff Ponzi scheme revelations and legal proceedings, the United States Justice Department has sought to liquidate seized assets from Madoff's empire and distribute those funds to his victims. Half of the $4 billion the Justice Department hopes to distribute to victims comes not only of Madoff and his family, but also from the wealthy investors who over the years who received dividends and profits that turned out to be fictions. The other half came from J.P. Morgan Chase, which was accused of ignoring red flags while it acted as Mr Madoff's bank.[53]

The government said it could return more than $4 billion to victims who lost their savings to Madoff and his investment firm. However, this number is still small compared with the imaginary profits the firm had promised investors and the real losses it incurred. The US Justice Department has approved more than 39,000 applications for compensation.

Under the common law, although agents of Trustees are not answerable to the beneficiaries before they intermeddle with the Trust, once they mix themselves up with a breach of Trust, they make themselves liable.[54] If then by any abuse of their powers as agents, they obtain possession of any of the Trust property, the beneficiary may proceed against them as Trustees *de son tort* or constructive Trustees.[55] In most jurisdictions, including the United States, this principle is found in legislation that grants power to government agencies to seize proceeds of crime.[56]

One of the first steps for any authority or regulator in the process of taking custody and control of the assets of a bankrupt or the proceeds of crime is to identify which of the assets can be received. For example, in the case of bankruptcy, money that does not form part of the bankrupt's ordinary income will likely be protected (including superannuation, inheritance money and compensation). Bankrupts and criminals could have numerous virtual wallets or they may have vested control over their crypto-assets with an exchange.

In 2009, a court-appointed trustee sued Madoff's brother, sons and niece for $198m in a suit accusing them of using the corrupt firm as a family piggy bank to finance lavish lifestyles. Irving Picard, the Trustee tasked with

---

53 K Benner, 'Victims of Bernard Madoff's Ponzi Scheme to Receive Millions More', *The New York Times* (12 April 2018) <https://www.nytimes.com/2018/04/12/business/madoff-ponzi-scheme-compensation.html>.

54 *Portlock v Gardner* [1842] EngR 827; (1842) 1 Hare 594; 66 ER 1168.

55 There needs to be a clear distinction between the liability that attaches to the fraudulent Trustee *de son tort* and the innocent *de facto* Trustee. See also JW Perry, *A Treatise on the Law of Trusts and Trustees* (2nd edn, Little Brown & Co, 1872), 538.

56 In 1970, criminal forfeiture was revived by the *Racketeer Influenced and Corrupt Organizations statute (RICO)*, 18 U.S.C. §§ 1961–1968 (1988 & Supp. IV 1992), and the *Continuing Criminal Enterprise (CCE) statute*, 21 U.S.C. § 848 (1988 & Supp. V 1993). See infra text accompanying notes 37–43. For examples of application of these and other forfeiture statutes.

recouping funds to reimburse victims of Madoff's Ponzi scheme, alleged that family members who worked at Madoff Investment Securities were 'completely derelict' in their professional duties.

The seizure of assets from recipients of the Madoff's fraud is made possible only if those ill-gotten gains were received as profits or gifts. If they were payments for legitimate services, then recipient liability would not apply. However, this is not the case. Madoff's sons (for example) spent 2008 shopping for multi-million dollar properties and spent thousands of dollars on skiing holidays using an Amex card funded by the firm.[57]

Even if they weren't aware of the scheme or its breadth, the Madoff sons, as licensed traders, should have understood that the basic numbers of their father's business could not be legitimate. Madoff promised (and delivered) 12 to 20% returns for his clients, no matter how the market was moving. In the words of hedge funder Suzanne Murphy, 'They had to know something funny was going on, because they weren't doing the trades'. The brothers had their own savings invested with their father's business: 'So presumably they were getting statements. And if they had looked at their statements, they would've said, "Wait a second"..[58]

It is not necessary that a recipient or accessory should have been aware of the precise nature of the fraud or even the identity of its victim. A person who consciously assists others by making arrangements that he or she knows are calculated to conceal what is happening from a third party, takes the risk that they are part of a fraud practised on that party.[59] If Madoff's sons were found to have wilfully and recklessly failed to make such enquiries as an honest and reasonable person would make about their father's business, then they would be made liable as constructive Trustees. The argument would run that in the particular positions they held and with their level of income from the business, they could not say that they made no inquires because they thought it was none of their business. Failing to make such enquiries would be morally obtuse and sufficient to make anyone in their position liable to account.[60] This approach is in line with the test for knowledge of a dishonest and fraudulent design. The nature of the design is not in dispute and the defendant has 'turned a blind eye' to these facts. In the only judgment rendered so far in relation to these allegations against Madoff's sons, a British judge in 2013 rejected the Trustee's case, affirming their 'honesty and integrity' and ruling that there was no evidence that they were involved in the crime.

---

57 K Menza, 'How Bernie Madoff Took His Family Down', *Town & Country* (19 May 2017) <https://www.townandcountrymag.com/society/money-and-p ower/a9656715/bernie-madoff-ponzi-scheme-scandal-story-and-aftermath/>.

58 B Ross, *The Madoff Chronicles: Inside the Secret World of Bernie and Ruth* (Disney Book Group, 2016).

59 *Agip (Africa) Limited v Jackson* [1990] Ch 265 at 294–295 (per Millet LJ).

60 A Berg, 'Accessory Liability for Breach of Trust' (1996) 59 *Modern Law Review* 443, 446.

It is remarkable that Madoff's Ponzi scheme operated for 30 years, amassing debts in the tens of billions of dollars and involving hundreds of immediate and thousands of secondary investors and yet no one but Bernie Madoff knew that it was a sham. It is arguable that but for the assistance of electronic trading and online bookkeeping, it would not have been possible. Madoff's clients were spread all over the world. They traded and communicated with and via his New York office using the power of the Internet and business technologies. This was a highly centralised organisation with little or no oversight beyond one man. A Ponzi scheme of this magnitude would not have been possible before the advent of digital technologies.

Liability of Accessories in Crypto-economies

After the hack and subsequent collapse of the Mt Gox bitcoin exchange, the operator of the exchange, Mark Karpeles, was placed under house arrest in Japan for a number of months for failing to secure the bitcoin and keep it safe from hackers. Karpeles apologised on Japanese television for the weakness in the system that left it exposed and vulnerable to attack. Although Karpeles claimed that the disappearance of the virtual currency stemmed from external attacks by hackers, many customers attributed the disaster to a combination of incompetence, lax security measures and deception.[61]

Mt Gox filed for bankruptcy in Japan on 28 February 2014 and then – shortly after – it filed for Chapter 15 bankruptcy in the United States. As well as the appointment of a Trustee in bankruptcy, a number of lawsuits followed in the wake of the collapse of Mt Gox. The class action suits brought filed in the Chicago federal court and the Ontario Superior Court of Justice against the Mizuho Financial Group alleged that (among other things) the bank knew of Mt Gox's fraud.[62]

Mizuho held non-Bitcoin currency on behalf of Tokyo-based Mt Gox and its customers. The class action complainant alleged that Mizuho directly benefited from the fraudulent and unfair conduct of Mt Gox. However, in January 2014, the bank had made efforts to close the exchange's account. According to a recorded conversation between Karpeles and a Mizuho Bank official, the financial institution told the Mt. Gox CEO to shut it down in late January. An unnamed Mizuho manager at Mizuho bank, in a recording leaked

---

61 JT Quigley, 'Japan's Mizuho Bank: The Latest Defendant in Mt. Gox Bitcoin Suit', *The Diplomat* (19 March 2014) <https://thediplomat.com/2014/03/japa ns-mizuho-bank-the-latest-defendant-in-mt-gox-bitcoin-suit/>. See also, T Hals and A Becker, 'Japan's Mizuho in U.S., Canada Suits Over Mt. Gox Bitcoin Losses', *Reuters* (16 March 2014) <https://www.reuters.com/article/us-bit coin-mtgox-mizuho/japans-mizuho-in-u-s-canada-suits-over-m t-gox-bitcoin-losses-idUSBREA2E01V20140316>.

62 Mizuho Financial Group is Japan's second largest bank by assets and third largest by market capitalization – *Mizuho Financial Group* <https://www.mizuho-fg. com/index.html>.

on the Internet, asks Karpeles to close his firm's account with the bank, citing compliance issues and moves by other banks to cut ties with the exchange.[63]

Mt Gox's troubles began in 2011, but 2013 was particularly fraught. On 22 February of that year, following the introduction of new anti-money laundering requirements by e-commerce and online payment system company, Dwolla, some of its accounts became temporarily restricted. As a result, transactions from Mt Gox to those accounts were cancelled by Dwolla.

In March 2013, the bitcoin transaction log temporarily 'forked' into two independent logs, with differing rules on how transactions could be accepted. Due to this, Mt Gox bitcoin briefly halted bitcoin deposits. So significant was Mt Gox's activity, that this temporary halt on trading caused bitcoin prices to dip briefly by 23%, before recovering to their previous level (approximately $48) in the following hours.

On 2 May 2013, CoinLab filed a $75 million lawsuit against Mt Gox, alleging a breach of contract. Then on 15 May 2013, the United States Department of Homeland Security issued a warrant to seize money from a Mt Gox account with Dwolla. The warrant asserted that the unlicensed subsidiary was operating as an unregistered money transmitter in the United States.

Mt Gox suspended withdrawals in US dollars on 20 June 2013. From then on, the Mizuho Bank branch in Tokyo pressured Karpeles to close its account. Despite its requests for Mt Gox to close its account, Mizuho is alleged to have continued to receive funds from customers, profiting from transaction fees associated with the deposits while limiting withdrawals. The most contentious aspect of this part of the dispute will turn on what the officers at Mizuho knew, when they found out and whether reasonable steps were taken to close the account.[64]

Whether or not a recipient knew of the Trust or Equitable fraud, a claimant has a proprietary right to claim any misapplied property that can be followed or traced into the recipient's hands.[65] The basis upon which Equity will permit such an enquiry into the defendant's assets is the breach of Trust or other fiduciary obligation. For example, in *Agip*,[66] the culprit was in a fiduciary position that give him the opportunity to misdirect his principal's money and

---

63 T Hals and A Becker, 'Japan's Mizuho in U.S., Canada Suits Over Mt. Gox Bitcoin Losses', *Reuters* (16 March 2014) <https://www.reuters.com/article/us-bit coin-mtgox-mizuho/japans-mizuho-in-u-s-canada-suits-over-m t-gox-bitcoin-losses-idUSBREA2E01V20140316>.

64 As at October 2018, an application had been filed in the suit against Mizuho seeking a stay of proceedings because the number of bitcoins recovered by the trustee in bankruptcy and their increased value meant it was possible that the plaintiffs would be able to recover their losses – D Aubin, 'Mizuho, Mt. Gox Customers Ask Court to Halt California Lawsuit', *Reuters* (3 October 2018) <http s://www.reuters.com/article/mizuho-mtgox-lawsuit/mizuho-mt-gox-custom ers-ask-court-to-halt-california-lawsuit-idUSL2N1WI1VJ>.

65 It is of course possible that trustees *de son tort* may also be fixed with proprietary or personal constructive trusteeship.

66 *Agip (Africa) Limited v Jackson* [1990] Ch 265.

that was enough to enable the court to invoke the doctrine of tracing.[67] Tracing facilitates a process of following the plaintiff's property so as to enable recovery from the defendant.[68] It is the means by which the plaintiff determines what has happened to their misapplied money or asset. Powerful remedies may therefore be available to a beneficiary, even one who has suffered no loss, acting as a strong deterrent to breaches of fiduciary duty.[69] As well as being able to trace misapplied property into the hands of an errant fiduciary, the plaintiff can also trace them into the hands of third parties.

The requirement that the defendant's receipt be of Trust property is satisfied simply where the property is misapplied from an express trust.[70] However, the scope for a knowing receipt claim is widened considerably by the fact that company assets are treated as Trust property in the hands of the company's directors.[71] This principle is extended to others in control of the company's assets if they owe fiduciary duties to the company.[72] The principle is not confined to company assets – it applies whenever property of the principal is under the fiduciary's control.[73]

There is an issue in the case law as to whether knowing receipt applies where a third party receives property from a Trustee or a non-Trustee fiduciary in breach of duty (the wider view); or *only* where property is received by the third party from a Trustee (the narrower view).[74] The preponderance of authority favours the view that liability for receiving misapplied funds or assets is capable of applying where property is received from either a Trustee or a non-Trustee

---

67 See Lord Millett, 'Recovering the Proceeds of Fraud' (1992) *Law Lectures for Practitioners* 25, 32 (retrieved from *Hong Kong Journals Online* on 18 February 2013 <http://hkjo.lib.hku.hk/archive/files/6f5ee9c9202127e01e89799e6f0d7a 2e.pdf>).

68 Where a successful claim is made to specific property (such as land or identifiable chattels) the plaintiff will in principle be entitled to its return. Conversion of a chattel into some other form will not bar recovery. However, 'fungible' property (for example, money and shares) is usually incapable of exact restoration. In such a case, a proprietary remedy entitles the plaintiff to a fund of money or shares rather than specific notes and coins. See, *Brady v Stapleton* (1952) 88 CLR 322; Dixon CJ and Fullagar J, 337–338 (money paid into a bank account); *Re Goode; Ex parte Mount* (1974) 24 FLR 61; R Goode, 'The Right to Trace and its Impact in Commercial Transactions' (1976) 92 *LQR* 360, 386–387, 529–530.

69 See *Phipps v Boardman* [1967] 2 AC 46; [1966] All ER 721; and *Warman International Ltd v Dwyer* (1995) 182 CLR 544.

70 J Dietrich and P Ridge, 'The Receipt of What? Questions Concerning Third Party Recipient Liability in Equity and Unjust Enrichment' (2007) 31(1) *Melbourne University Law Review* 47, 56.

71 *Belmont Finance Corporation Ltd v Williams Furniture Ltd (No 2)* [1980] 1 All ER 393, 405 (per Buckley LJ).

72 *Agip (Africa) Limited v Jackson* [1990] Ch 265, 290 (per Millett J).

73 *Foley v Hill* [1848] EngR 837; (1848) 2 HLC 28; 9 ER 1002 837, 46 (per Campbell LJ).

74 In *Rogers v Kabriel* [1999] NSWSC 368, [173], it was said that the first limb only applies to trust property in a 'strict sense'.

fiduciary in breach of their Trust or fiduciary duties.[75] In both cases, a knowing recipient of those funds can be made personally liable to the plaintiff.

There is a rich equitable history of authorities that underpin the way that the liability of accessories has developed. While the core elements that ground liability for breach have remained constant, the methods employed by errant Trustees and fiduciaries breach have changed dramatically since the end of the 20th century. Importantly, if the prime wrong-doer is insolvent, deceased or no longer within the jurisdiction, it may be difficult to recover any loss that has resulted from their breach. This is why the liability of third parties remains such a popular avenue for recovery. If the losses cannot be traced into the hands of the accessory, they can also be made personally liable as constructive Trustees. As the following examples show, professional advisers and banks are natural targets for knowing receipt and knowing assistance claims, because they are likely to have sufficient assets to satisfy the claim.

In *Lee v Sankey*, [76] the defendants were a firm of solicitors entrusted with a sum of money to hold pending final instructions from two Trustees. The solicitors received the Trust property as agents of the Trustees. No investment was made, but the defendants at various times repaid the money to one of the Trustees, supposing that he was authorised to act on behalf of both. He was not so authorised and the defendants were held liable. Bacon VC noted that the money had been placed in the defendants' hands by the two Trustees. By taking instructions from just one of the Trustees, the defendants were held to have dealt with it in a manner inconsistent with the Trust of which they were cognisant.[77] For this reason, the defendants were ordered to restore the misapplied funds to the plaintiffs.[78]

The decision of Bacon VC in *Lee v Sankey* [79] sets out the law in relation to the potential liability of a 'mere agent' who acts within the scope of the instruction of his principal – as compared with a third party who misapplies Trust funds with knowledge of the breach of Trust. Such liability is described by Bacon VC as 'clearly establishing' that a person who receives into his hands Trust moneys and who knowingly deals with them in a manner inconsistent with the performance of the Trusts is personally liable for the consequences which may ensue regarding the transaction.[80]

---

75 See, in particular, *DPC Estates Pty Ltd v Grey and Consul Development Pty Ltd* [1974] 1 NSWLR 443 at 459–460; *Belmont Finance Corporation Ltd v Williams Furniture Ltd (No 2)* [1980] 1 All ER 393, 405.

76 *Lee v Sankey* (1872–1873) 15 Eq 204.

77 In *Consul Development Pty Ltd v DPC Estates Pty Ltd* (1975) 132 CLR 373, Gibbs J (as he then was) cited *Lee v Sankey* (1872–1873) 15 Eq 204 in support of the proposition that although Lord Selborne (in *Barnes v Addy* (1874) LR 9 Ch App 244) speaks of dishonesty and fraud, it is clear that the principle extends to the case 'where a person received trust property and dealt with it in a manner inconsistent with trusts of which he was cognisant' (396).

78 *Lee v Sankey* (1872–73) Eq 204, 210.

79 *Lee v Sankey* (1872–73) Eq 204, 206.

80 *Lee v Sankey* (1872–73) Eq 204, 287.

The rationale for the decision in *Lee v Sankey* [81] follows the premise that a person who receives legal title to trust property becomes a Trustee of that property unless and until he is a *bona fide* purchaser for value without notice. It is difficult to establish the liability of an agent who receives misappropriated Trust property in the course of their agency. 'Receipt' in this context means receipt for the defendant's personal benefit. For this reason, *Lee v Sankey* falls with the discrete line of cases where the liability arises from knowingly dealing with the Trust property, even though the receipt of a personal benefit has not occurred (or been proved).[82] Therefore, a third party who deals with Trust monies with knowledge of the underlying Trust, could not get a good discharge from just paying the money to one Trustee. For this reason, they may be made personally liable for the consequences which may ensue upon his so dealing.

The plaintiffs in *Lee v Sankey*, [83] relied upon *The Attorney-General v The Corporation of Leicester*, [84] where an agent who was found to have assisted in a breach of Trust was held personally liable. In this case, a municipal corporation was the Trustee of a charity. The Corporation had allowed its town clerk to receive and retain the Trust monies, instead of making sure that they were applied for the purposes of the Trust. In making orders to restore the misapplied funds to the charity, the court noted that the town clerk (Mr Burbidge) was able to answer for only part of the full amount that was missing. The court ordered Burbidge to pay the full amount he had retained and the balance was to be repaid by the Corporation.[85] It is interesting to note that pursuant to the remedy fashioned by the court, only the amount traceable to Burbidge (plus any interest earned on that amount) was to be repaid by him. The Corporation was not insolvent and knew of its agent's misconduct, so an account was ordered of all misdirected funds so that the Corporation would be liable for the balance of the money that had been received by Burbidge, but that was no longer in his hands.

Applying this line of authority to the circumstances where a bank is accused of knowingly participating in and profiting from its customer's fraud, receipt of a profit or benefit is not necessary for liability to arise. Knowingly dealing with the proceeds of the fraud would be sufficient. As well as the authorities established by the early Equity cases, the relevant statutory provisions that regulate the conduct of banks would apply to the determination of liability for knowing receipt.

---

81 *Lee v Sankey* (1872–73) Eq 204.
82 Later cases that cite *Lee v Sankey* (1872–73) Eq 204 specifically in the context of knowing dealing include *Robb Evans of Robb Evans & Associates v European Bank Limited* [2004] 61 NSWLR 75, [177]–[181].
83 *Lee v Sankey* (1872–73) Eq 204, 208.
84 *Attorney-General v Corporation of Leicester* [1844] EngR 270; (1844) 7 Beav 176; 49 ER 1031.
85 *Attorney-General v Corporation of Leicester* [1844] EngR 270; (1844) 7 Beav 176; 49 ER 1031, 182 (Beav).

There are two interesting aspects to note about the relationship between Mt Gox and Mizuho. Firstly, as the customers of Mt Gox bought their bitcoin, their money was deposited directly into Mt Gox's bank account. The transaction activity through the account would have been very high in volume. We know this because by June 2013, Mt Gox was trading more bitcoin than any other exchange and it was managing 70% of all transactions. And while the price of bitcoin at that time was only about $48, the losses suffered by the collapse ran into the millions of dollars. This level of activity would not have been possible just 50 years ago. No bank in the world would have had enough staff to manage the transactions. The second interesting issue is the nature of the bitcoin and its popularity in its closed economy. Even though activity on a blockchain is published to all nodes in an open and transparent record, the identities of the wallet holders are kept secret. This is the first time in history that a currency or virtual asset has been developed in order to create a secret economy. Karpeles used the account with Mizuho to conduct financial transactions. Meanwhile, he had virtual wallets in cold storage in the vaults of several banks in Tokyo. It is ironic that the security of such a technologically sophisticated currency should call for the use of the least technical service a bank can offer: a safety deposit box.

Tracing Misapplied Crypto-currencies

'Tracing' is the process by which the plaintiff is able to identify and recover property held by the defendant. Descriptions of tracing emphasise its role as a technique for identifying property belonging to a plaintiff, as a preliminary step to recovering it from the defendant.[86] In Equity theory a plaintiff's proprietary claim to a traceable product is seen as a response to, and a vindication of, the plaintiff's proprietary right in the original asset.[87]

It is a reality of the modern banking landscape that in many countries including the United Kingdom, Australia, Canada, Germany and the United States, financial institutions are gradually becoming agents in the service of tax authorities. These financial institutions face increased governmental pressure to deliver information about account holders, to withhold taxes from earnings accumulating in financial accounts and to remit such taxes to taxing authorities around the world.[88] With great financial surveillance comes a loss in financial privacy. Bitcoin offers more than just privacy. It offers secrecy.

It is possible that some of the collapsed bitcoin exchanges and failed Ponzi schemes were orchestrated by the exchange's operator after transferring some or all of the corpus of the businesses operating account into their own secret

---

86 S Hepburn in P Parkinson and D Wright (eds), *The Laws of Australia* (LBC, 2010).
87 HAJ Ford and WA Lee, *Principles of the Law of Trusts* (2nd edn, LBC, 1990), [1716.1].
88 I Grinberg, 'The Battle over Taxing Offshore Accounts' (2012) 60 *UCLA Law Review* 304, 316–317.

virtual wallets. While blockchain technology is strong when it comes to revealing objective fraud (that is, fraudulent transactions), it is weak at identifying subject fraud (the identities of the contracting parties). If the operator of a bitcoin exchange does cause its collapse and steal the remaining bitcoin (for example) from the exchange, then – by virtue of the operator's breach of his or her fiduciary duty to the investors – the operator will hold the bitcoin on constructive trust for the exchange. A breach of fiduciary duty will entitle any investors whose bitcoin was held. The equitable doctrine of tracing is borne of Equity's concern for the protection of equitable estates and interests in property.[89]

Tracing is only possible, so long as the fund can be followed in a true sense (that is, so long as – whether mixed or unmixed – it can be located and identified). The way that bitcoin exchanges and asset trusts mingle assets into common funds will make tracing difficult, particularly as the assets are converted to substitutes. While bitcoin is simply a computer record on a ledger that can be stored and tracked, the transfer of funds is distributed, decentralised and encrypted. This makes it very difficult in theory and almost impossible in practice to trace the funds used in crypto-currency transactions. This applies to buyers and sellers of crypto-currency at both ends of the transaction.[90]

Tracing presupposes the continued existence of the money either as a separate fund or as part of a mixed fund as latent in property acquired by means of such a fund. If, on the facts of any individual case, such continued existence is not established, Equity is helpless. Thus tracing is impossible where an innocent volunteer spends the Trust money on a dinner or on an education or general living expenses.[91]

If an individual is running a crypto-currency exchange and it fails impacting their personal wealth, the operator may choose to declare bankruptcy. Because of the potential pseudonymity of the exchange's wallet holder or wallet holders, it may be difficult to ascertain whether the apparent failure of the exchange is caused by a deliberate scheme orchestrated by the operator. Using bankruptcy protection, the operator might have significant wealth in crypto-currency hidden from the Trustee in bankruptcy and thereby avoiding his or her creditors. Meanwhile, under bankruptcy and insolvency legislation in many jurisdictions,[92] Trustees can investigate and add to the pool any assets that the bankrupt transferred to a relative or spouse (that is, where the transfer was not at 'arms-length' and not in exchange for value or reasonable consideration) in the five years leading up to bankruptcy.

---

89 *Consul Development Pty Ltd v DPC Estates Pty Ltd* (1975) 132 CLR 373, 410.
90 E Engle, 'Is Bitcoin Rat Poison: Cryptocurrency, Crime, and Counterfeiting (CCC)' (2016) 16 *Journal on High Technology Law* 340.
91 P Pettit, *Equity and The Law of Trusts* (10th edn, Butterworths, 1993), 516.
92 For example, in Australia, Section 121 of the *Bankruptcy Act 1966* (Cth).

The risk for authorities and creditors is that crypto-assets can be hidden or kept secret more easily than fiat currency and traditional assets. For example, if a bankrupt dies leaving no record of their investment in bitcoin, it may be almost impossible for their Trustee in bankruptcy to learn of that parcel of wealth that could have otherwise been exchanged for Australian dollars and used to satisfy claims by the deceased bankrupt's creditors. There is also a further inherent risk to be borne in mind – that some users of crypto-assets have been attracted to a particular crypto-asset as a vehicle for storing or transferring value with the express (albeit secret) aim of hiding their income and wealth from creditors and regulators. Some argue that the bitcoin blockchain is now the biggest tax haven in the world.[93]

A further challenge arises from the way that crypto-assets may be held. They could be in a virtual wallet controlled by the bankrupt; or alternatively, they could be in the custody and control of an exchange. The anonymity or pseudonymity of bitcoin users makes tracing the virtual currency to criminal activity a difficult task.[94] For example, when Silk Road was decommissioned, one of the bitcoin exchange operators had records of more than one million transactions with customers.[95] However, authorities failed to track down any of his clients due to the difficulties faced by authorities in trying to decrypt the blockchain files.[96]

While bitcoin transactions can be tracked, if the virtual wallets in which they are recorded are kept secret is almost impossible to identify the owner of the bitcoins. This is an important point of distinction from traditional online transactions, which can usually be traced quite readily through named bank accounts.

93 O Marian, 'Are Cryptocurrencies Super Tax Havens' (2013–2014) 112 *Michigan Law Review First Impressions* 38.

94 J Lane, 'Bitcoin, Silk Road, and the Need for a New Approach to Virtual Currency Regulation' (2014) 8 *Charleston Law Review* 511, 541.

95 'Silk Road Drug Busts: 8 More Arrested', *USA Today* (8 October 2013) <http://perma.cc/T44K-6JW2>.

96 R White, 'CEO of Bitcoin Exchange Arrested', *Business Insider* (27 January 2014) <http://perma.cclYQ3M-RZJN>.

Part IV

Key Challenges and Conclusion

19 Closing the Tax Gap in Digital Economies

A tax gap is the difference between the amount of tax revenue that should be collected and the amount actually collected by tax regulators in each jurisdiction – for example, the United States Internal Revenue Service (IRS). There are tax gaps in every developed country in the world. This gap exists in large part due to the bank secrecy laws of tax havens and the shadow activities of the corrupt and other money-launderers. The gaps are driven by cultural and human factors, global forces, complexity in business and legal systems, those who take aggressive tax positions, and genuine errors.[1] Currently, the United States has an annual tax gap that exceeds US$400 billion.[2]

An important consideration in the creation and maintenance of trust in traditional and digital economies is the way that regulators respond to changing operating modes of particular marketplaces. The development of a digital economy enables companies to avoid tax through aggressive tax planning and complicated financial arrangements. For example, 'base erosion and profit shifting' (BEPS) is enabled by digital marketplaces. This is achieved by registering the place where profits are earned to a location that has a lower tax rate than the actual market in which the taxable transactions took place and where the profits were earned. Tax systems in countries around the world operate with the benefit of a consensus among nation states that each country should have the benefit of earning revenue on their own citizens and markets. In essence, BEPS can undermine the fairness and integrity of our tax systems, as they fundamentally distort competition, because businesses that engage in

---

1   'Australian Tax Gaps – Overview', *Australian Taxation Office* (26 October 2018) <https://www.ato.gov.au/About-ATO/Research-and-statistics/In-detail/Tax-gap/Australian-tax-gaps-overview/>.

2   According to the United States Internal Revenue Service, the average annual tax gap for 2008–2010 is estimated to be $458 billion, compared to $450 billion for tax year 2006. IRS enforcement activities and late payments resulted in an additional $52 billion in tax paid, reducing the net tax gap for the 2008–2010 period to $406 billion per year. The voluntary compliance rate is now estimated at 81.7% compared to the prior estimated rate of 83.1%. After accounting for enforcement and late payments, the net compliance rate is 83.7%. See, 'Tax Gap Estimates for Years 2008–2010', *United Stated Internal Revenue Service* (2017) <https://www.irs.gov/newsroom/the-tax-gap>.

cross-border strategies gain a competitive advantage compared with enterprises that operate mostly at the domestic level.[3]

Addressing BEPS is critical for countries and must be done in a timely manner, not least to prevent this existing consensus-based international tax framework from unravelling.[4] If there is a perception that nothing is being done to address this problem, then more markets will take advantage of the anonymity enabled by digital platforms and simply move their profits off-shore to hide it in tax havens.

Online transactions, increasing world trade, global mobility and crypto-enabled pseudonymity in finance and resourcing has challenged domestic and international tax laws.[5] Because digital processes have confidentiality and virtualisation features, it can be difficult for national taxation regulators to determine the true identity of taxpayers and the tax status of digital transactions.[6]

The cost borne globally of hiding money in digital economies is significant. Estimates run to the billions of dollars worldwide. According to the Organisation for Economic Co-operation and Development (OECD), the cost of corruption is more than 5% of global gross domestic product. Overall, corruption reduces efficiency, increases inequality and ultimately erodes trust in the institutions that are tasked with ensuring the distribution of services and infrastructure where it is needed most.[7] This is because the joint challenges of tax evasion and tax base erosion lie at the heart of the social contract.

National tax laws have not kept pace with the globalisation of corporations and the digital economy; accordingly, they have left significant legal gaps that can be exploited by multi-national corporations to artificially reduce their taxes.[8]

---

3   M van Rijmenam and P Ryan, *Blockchain: Transforming Your Business and Our World* (Routledge, 2019) Chapter 5. See also, remarks by A Gurría, Secretary-General of the OECD, *G20/OECD Action Plan on Base Erosion and Profit Shifting (BEPS) OECD, Closing the Tax Gap* (20 July 2013) <http://www.oecd.org/about/secretary-general/closing-the-tax-gap.htm>.

4   OECD, 'Addressing the Tax Challenges of the Digital Economy', OECD/G20 Base Erosion and Profit Shifting Project, *OECD Publishing* (2014) <http://dx.doi.org/10.1787/9789264218789-en>.

5   T Budak, 'The Transformation of International Tax Regime: Digital Economy' (2017) 8 *Inonu University Law Review* 297, 297.

6   The Organisation for Economic Co-operation and Development (OECD) has focused on issues of Base Erosion and Profit Shifting (BEPS), and also developed BEPS Action Plans to manage the issues of international taxation. The BEPS Action 1 specifically addresses the challenges that arise in the taxation of the digital economy. See, OECD, 'Addressing the Tax Challenges of the Digital Economy', OECD/G20 Base Erosion and Profit Shifting Project, *OECD Publishing* (2014) <http://dx.doi.org/10.1787/9789264218789-en>.

7   M van Rijmenam and P Ryan, *Blockchain: Transforming Your Business and Our World* (Routledge, 2019) – see Chapter 5.

8   OECD, 'Closing Tax Gaps – OECD Launches Action Plan on Base Erosion and Profit Shifting' (19 July 2013) <http://www.oecd.org/ctp/beps/closing-tax-gaps-oecd-launches-action-plan-on-base-erosion-and-profit-shifting.htm>

The OECD and its CleanGovBiz initiative[9] actively support governments and organisations to strengthen integrity, build trust and fight corruption. The OECD acknowledges that all citizens demand that the OECD and partners tackle offshore tax evasion by wealthy individuals and re-vamp the international tax system to prevent multinational enterprises from artificially shifting profits (in order to declare only very low taxes or even double non-taxation). It is these practices that erode the global tax base.[10]

In the wake of the stunning 'Panama papers' leak, governments around the world have begun cooperating to identify and bring to justice tax cheats and criminals who are hiding their untaxed or ill-gotten gains from authorities. It is important to keep in mind that while bitcoin travels on its road towards acceptance and legitimacy, its popularity as a tax haven is growing.[11]

As the darker side of bitcoin seems to be fading and a new era of legitimacy emerges, governments are now pondering how to treat bitcoin transactions for tax purposes. If bitcoin is ever to achieve the status of fiat currencies, this question needs to be resolved. The International Monetary Fund notes that on the global financial stage, bitcoin is a relatively minor player. In mid-2015, bitcoin accounted for about 90% of decentralised digital currency market value and had a small daily transaction volume compared to just one of the largest global credit card providers.[12]

Because the digital economy is increasingly becoming the economy itself, it would be difficult, if not impossible, to ring-fence the digital economy from the rest of the economy for tax purposes. Attempting to isolate the digital economy as a separate sector would inevitably require arbitrary lines to be drawn between what is digital and what is not. Although many digital economy business models have parallels in traditional business, modern advances in information and communications technologies have made it possible to conduct many types of business at substantially greater scale and over longer distances than was previously possible. These include several varieties of e-commerce, online payment services, app stores, online advertising, Cloud computing, participative networked platforms and high-speed trading.

9 The CleanGovBiz Initiative supports governments to reinforce their fight against corruption and engage with civil society and the private sector to promote real change towards integrity. See, CleanGovBiz <http://www.oecd.org/cleangovbiz/>

10 Remarks by Angel Gurría, Secretary-General of the OECD, G20/OECD Action Plan on Base Erosion and Profit Shifting (BEPS) OECD, 'Closing the Tax Gap' (20 July 2013) <http://www.oecd.org/about/secretary-general/closing-the-tax-gap.htm>.

11 D Meyer, 'Why a Swiss Tax Haven Is Embracing Bitcoin', *Fortune Magazine* (9 May 2016) <http://fortune.com/2016/05/09/zug-Bitcoin-services/>.

12 D He, K Harbermeier, R Leckow, V Haksar, et al., 'Virtual Currencies and Beyond: Initial Considerations' (January 2016) IMF Monetary and Capital Markets, Legal, and Strategy and Policy Review Departments, fn 15. See also, 'Market Cap' (11 January 2016). <http://coinmarketcap.com>.

Having said that, the digital economy is in a continuous state of evolution.[13]

Rapid changes in the economy, society and technology mean the issues driving tax gaps continue to evolve.[14] While technology can be used to hide wealth from regulators, it can also be used to detect and track taxable assets and transactions. For example, blockchain technology can help reduce the incidence of corruption, fraud, tax evasion and money laundering by securely managing identity in permissionless networks.

With many business and government records and transactions transitioning to online networks and storage systems, the adoption of blockchain technology to manage permissions, and ledgers, and report to regulators is the next logical step in the evolution of the Internet. These blockchain-based solutions are being explored by tax regulators around the world. This is an important endeavour, because making sure that everyone pays their fair share of tax is a problem in desperate need of a solution.

As Justice Oliver Wendell Holmes once said, 'Taxes are what we pay for civilised society'.[15] Any 'civilized society' is enormously expensive to operate. Raising these funds through a voluntary self-assessment tax system can only succeed if compliance is enforced. Maximum compliance can only be achieved if honest taxpayers are to have trust in the overall fairness of the system.[16]

13 OECD, 'Addressing the Tax Challenges of the Digital Economy', OECD/G20 Base Erosion and Profit Shifting Project, *OECD Publishing* (2014) <http://dx.doi. org/10.1787/9789264218789-en>.

14 'Australian Tax Gaps – Overview', *Australian Taxation Office* (26 October 2018) <https://www.ato.gov.au/About-ATO/Research-and-statistics/In-detail/Ta x-gap/Australian-tax-gaps-overview/>. See also, M van Rijmenam and P Ryan, *Blockchain: Transforming Your Business and Our World* (Routledge, 2019) Chapter 5.

15 See, *Compania General De Tabacos De Filipinas v Collector of Internal Revenue*, 275 US 87, 100 (1927) (Holmes, J).

16 NJ Hochman, 'Tax Defiers and the Tax Gap: Stopping Frivolous Squared Before It Spreads' (2009) 20 *Stanford Law and Policy Review* 69, 70.

20 Too Much Data?

The growing volume of data that is generated globally every day is not only shared, but much of it is accessible. It is the phenomenon of generation, sharing and availability that has given rise to the use of the language of neurosis to describe the psychological impact that this is having on individuals and work practices. While data is overwhelming us, there are entire industries built around the need to grab and to keep our attention.

'Attention economics' is an approach to the management of information that treats human attention as a scarce commodity and applies economic theory to solve various information management problems. Put simply, 'Attention is a resource – a person has only so much of it'.[1] However, constant distraction caused by attention to devices can become a risk for organisations that need to track the behaviour of their employees in order to defend decision-making.

The extreme conditions of dealing with big data sets are apparently causing 'infobesity',[2] 'device addiction'[3] and 'analysis paralysis'.[4] These apparent conditions are all symptomatic of our digital dependency in our personal and professional lives, This digital dependency is causing what is known as an 'information overload'. In the workplace, information overload occurs when it has become difficult to understand an issue and effectively make decisions

---

1   MB Crawford, 'Introduction, Attention as a Cultural Problem' in MB Crawford (ed), *The World Beyond Your Head: On Becoming an Individual in an Age of Distraction* (Farrar, Straus and Giroux, 2015), 11.

2   P Rogers, R Puryear and J Root, 'Infobesity: The Enemy of Good Decisions', *Bain & Co* (11 June 2013) <https://www.bain.com/insights/infobesity-the-enemy-of-good-decisions/>.

3   Professor Katina Michael, writing in *PC World* in 2017, said social problems associated with device addiction included 'sleep deprivation, anxiety, depression, diminished performance in either paid or academic work and issues with anger management'. See, K Michael, 'Facts and Figures: The Rise of Social Media Addiction', *PC World* (23 February 2017) <https://www.pcworld.idg.com.au/author/2147449222/katina-michael/articles>.

4   See, for example, T Hasan, 'Analysis Paralysis: When Big Data Gets Too Big', *Farber* (23 Jul 2018) <https://farbergroup.com/analysis-paralysis-big-data-gets-big/>.

because one has too much information about that issue. The paradox of big data and information overload is that one would assume that the more data that is available, the better informed a decision will be. However, research indicates that bigger spending on data analysis does not necessarily translate to an improved bottom line.[5]

Some businesses have adopted a tendency to collect more data than is needed just because it may be needed later and storage is cheap. However, collecting too much data can cause a compliance issue because some laws require entities to collect only the minimum amount of data necessary to achieve a stated purpose.[6] Also, as laws on data handling (particularly in relation to personal information) change, organisations need to be ready to evolve their handling practices in accordance with the rules set down by regulators. When it comes to directing the affairs of an organisation, big data and information overload can become a very real business risk.

Excessive data has also proved problematic in litigation. Both legal information management and e-Discovery are hampered when there are too many documents to process. The volume of data available to examine in legal disputes tests the historical rationale of discovery. Like affidavits and written submissions, discovery was designed to facilitate fact-finding, save time and reduce expense. However, the commercial realities of modern discovery in the context of possibly 'too much information' may represent a significant barrier to justice for many litigants, as well as amounting to a huge public cost. Most of the cost of litigation is not borne not by those who choose to litigate, but by the broader community (whose taxes fund the public services associated with the justice system). The cost and delay associated with discovery means that it may impede access to justice. Discovery is often the single largest cost in any corporate litigation, giving rise to concern about the scale of costs. Nonetheless, discovery remains an important feature of common law litigation in appropriate cases, ensuring that parties 'can proceed on an equal footing and without ambush, and that relevant materials are before the court'.[7]

When parties are under an obligation to disclose, they may need to consider using document analysis software. However, this is expensive and so arises a question of proportionality – weighing up what is at stake in the proceedings against the cost of e-Discovery. Of course, if a court has ordered the use of technology to manage a very large discovery, then the parties need to monitor

---

5   CF Mela and C Moorman, 'Why Marketing Analytics Hasn't Lived Up to Its Promise', *Harvard Business Review* (30 May 2018) <https://hbr.org/2018/05/why-marketing-analytics-hasnt-lived-up-to-its-promise>.

6   F Gilbert, 'Ten Privacy and Data Security Mistakes that Tech Start-ups Should Avoid' (2017) 63(5) *Practical Lawyer* 30.

7   Australian Government Solicitor, Submission DR 27, (11 February 2011). See also, 'Managing Discovery – Final Report – Discovery of Documents in Federal Courts', *Australian Law Reform Commission Report 115* (March 2011) <https://www.alrc.gov.au/sites/default/files/pdfs/publications/Whole%20ALRC%20115%20%2012%20APRIL-3.pdf>.

the processes they implement so as to ensure that they only disclose the relevant documents that are not privileged.[8] The failure of a lawyer, accountant or auditor to produce evidence that is against their client's or the firm's interests in litigation is regarded as professional misconduct and attracts severe penalties. Arthur Andersen was a prestigious international accounting firm that traced its history back to 1913. As the auditor of Enron Corporation, Arthur Andersen LLP was charged in March 2002 with obstructing justice by shredding Enron-related documents to impede a Securities and Exchange Commission investigation. When the trial started in May 2002, the break-up of the organisation was already under way with a mass exodus of Andersen partners and staff, as well as clients all over the world. The firm had disintegrated before the verdict was handed down by a grand jury at the Federal District Court in Houston on 15 June 2002.[9]

This event raised questions about failures and loopholes in the accounting firm's specific corporate governance operating process. Andersen's ability to enforce quality standards and internal procedures and to impose tougher controls to its regional offices was called into question. This deficiency in quality control was a governance problem and should not have arisen. The timing of these events is interesting, because the shredding of documents is almost a thing of the past.

Most modern litigation is conducted with documents that originated in digital form and have not been printed. On the face of it, deleting a file may seem easier than shredding paper. But this is not the case. When documents originate in digital form, they are shared electronically and backed up to external servers. This is why de-duplication is often the first process that passes through a discovery bundle. In fact, deleting a document with the hope of leaving no trace that it ever existed is actually quite difficult. In terms of the challenges of managing legal information and discovery, the multiplication of data as documents and attachments are shared amongst teams has multiplied exponentially the number of documents that need to be 'read' in order to decide which to produce in court. If too many documents are discovered, a judge might infer that the producing party is trying to over-burden their opponent, charge excessive costs to their client or conceal a smoking gun by hiding the needle in a haystack.

The rise of electronically stored information also poses a unique challenge to litigators. Even before the era of big data, litigation was increasing in complexity. The overwhelming amount of information also creates challenges for the lawyers who are trying to understand the facts. For example, an email train

8   A Hernandez, 'Common Problems with e-Discovery – and Their Solutions' (2016) 63 *Federal Law Review* 63; N Roberts, 'Electronic Disclosure – A Clear Way Forward' (2006) 27(4) *Business Law Review* 98.

9   C Sauviat, 'The Demise of Andersen: A Consequence of Corporate Governance Failure in the Context of Major Changes in the Accounting Profession and the Audit Market', in PH Dembinski, C Lager, A Cornford and JM Bonvin (eds) *Enron and World Finance – A Case Study in Ethics* (Palgrave, 2006), 143.

of one attachment could be forensically significant but almost impossible to prove. Even if it can be proven that a key officer knew an important fact on a certain date, it is understandable that the witness may struggle to remember whether they read the document, particularly in light of the number of emails and other pieces of digital communication that are sent and received each day.

The professional obligations that lawyers owe to the court mean that if there is a failure to produce a key document to the other party and that failure results in a less favourable outcome for the party that was denied access to that evidence, then courts can impose costs orders and make the lawyers liable for the loss suffered due to their conduct (including if the failure was inadvertent). As Arthur Anderson shows, the financial and reputational consequences of such an order could be devastating for a firm.

Discerning the facts and dealing with expert testimony is challenging for everyone in the courtroom, including the bench.[10] As we know, a wealth of information creates a poverty of attention.[11] The production of electronically stored information and trial presentation can disrupt the attention economy of the judicial system, resulting in judges placing limits on the use of e-Discovery.

With these challenges in mind, it is easy to sympathise with judges who demand five page summaries of the case before them, including a short list of the key documents. Skeleton arguments are now required in the United Kingdom courts on all civil appeals, all administrative court proceedings, at trial in civil cases (opening and closing speeches) and for interlocutory applications. They are often required as a result of orders made at directions hearings, even in criminal cases. Failure to comply with the order to produce such a document can result in costs orders made personally against the practitioner.[12] Judicial intervention to case manage trials has been justified in mega-litigation on the basis that it presents the courts with apparently 'intractable difficulties'. As Justice Sackville bemoaned extra-judicially in his reflections of his own experience with mega-litigation,

> Not only do the parties incur vast costs, often utterly disproportionate to the subject of the dispute, but mega-litigation imposes great burdens on the judicial system and on individual judges unfortunate enough to be allocated such cases.[13]

---

10 J Savage and E Kimball, 'ESI in Environmental Enforcement: Less Is More' (2014) 45 *Trends* 17.

11 HA Simon, 'Designing Organizations for an Information-Rich World', Speech at the Johns Hopkins University and Brookings Institution Symposium, in *Computers, Communication and the Public Interest* 37 (Martin Greenberger ed, 1971), 40.

12 In *Haggis v DPP* [2003] EWHC 2481; [2004] 2 All ER 382, Brooke LJ threatened to make 'disagreeable orders as to costs' for non-compliance with an order to produce a skeleton argument.

13 Justice R Sackville, 'Mega-litigation: Towards a New Approach' (FCA) [2007] *Federal Judicial Scholarship* 13.

Sackville J's proposed solution requires a re-evaluation of some fundamental tenets of the judicial process. The particular 're-evaluation' that Sackville J suggested was a more proactive role in managing to the way the evidence is presented in court. Skeleton arguments are an example of this measure. Identifying the key documents and presenting them to the bench early in the proceedings is also regarded as an important strategy in managing large cases.[14] However, the pressure to summarise facts, to present less information and to tender fewer documents in court can of itself lead to procedural and substantive injustice. For example, it may be during the trial process (including cross examination) that the significance of a document or a class of documents becomes apparent. Furthermore, some cases are factually complex and require longer than usual time to explain.

This tension between big data discoveries in mega-litigation and the need to know what is in the data set to be discovered has given rise to an industry in computer assisted review or predictive analysis. Predictive analytics is a discipline that has grown alongside the exponential growth of data in the digital world. The legal industry is making use of this type of analysis to improve overall efficiency and accuracy. Software comes with language-based technologies that scan, read and synthesise written documents. The analysis applies statistical techniques to glean patterns from data mining, predictive modelling and machine learning. In 2012, New York magistrate Judge Andrew Peck became the first federal judge to order litigants to use predictive analytics in case. In a class action complaint, the judge ordered the use of software to identify the relevant documents for discovery.[15] Since that landmark moment in the history of civil litigation, there have been other examples of predictive analysis orders in other jurisdictions.[16] It seems that one set of technologies created a problem that is now being solved by another, even more sophisticate technology.

On reviewing the decision of Judge Peck, Judge Andrew L Carter observed that there simply is no review tool that guarantees perfection. The parties and the judge had acknowledged that there are risks inherent in any method of reviewing electronic documents. Manual review with keyword searches is costly, though appropriate in certain situations. However, even if all parties here were willing to entertain the notion of manually reviewing the documents, such review is prone to human error and marred with inconsistencies

---

14 'Managing Discovery – Final Report – Discovery of Documents in Federal Courts', *ALRC Report 115* (March 2011) <https://www.alrc.gov.au/sites/default/files/p dfs/publications/Whole%20ALRC%20115%20%2012%20APRIL-3.pdf>.

15 *Da Silva Moore v Publicis Groupe et al.,* No. 1:2011cv01279 - Document 175 (S. D.N.Y. 2012).

16 For example, the United Kingdom in *Pyrrho Investments Ltd v MWB Property Ltd* [2016] EWHC 256 (Ch); in Ireland, in *Irish Bank Resolution Corporation Ltd & Ors v Quinn & Ors* [2015] IEHC 175 (03 March 2015); in Australia in, *McConnell Dowell Constructors (Aust) Pty Ltd v Santam Ltd & Ors (No 1)* [2016] VSC 734 (2 December 2016).

from the various attorneys' determinations of whether a document is relevant or responsive.[17]

An irony of 'too much data' is that an entire layer of data may mask the information that sits inside the data. Importantly, data is often not causal. Big data can be effective in revealing patterns of behaviour, but will not necessarily explain why the behaviour occurs in the first place. Often it is small data that reveals causal links and explains outcomes. If businesses and analysts do not know what causes behaviour, then they will not know how to influence or persuade their customers. If government sees only trends, but not what causes them, it is difficult to plan fiscal measures and public spending. If there is too much data to make sense of the inputs, then it will be difficult to trust the conclusions that are being drawn from their analysis. Decisions based on those conclusions will in turn be unreliable and not necessarily result in the expected outcomes. It is therefore very likely that too much data can be as bad as too little.[18]

The problem with excessive data and big data's failure to identify causal links between inputs and outcomes is why Google Flu Trends stopped predicting who will get sick.[19] Google Flu Trends was a web-based service operated by Google between 2008 and 2014. It provided estimates of influenza cases for more than 25 countries. It did this by aggregating Google search queries in an attempt to make accurate predictions about flu activity. In what was described as an act of 'big data hubris', Google was accused of placing too much weight on their capacity to analyse large data sets and to form accurate predictions: data sets that were eventually proven to be inherently flawed. According to researchers at Northeastern University and Harvard University, Google's Flu Trends prediction system overestimated the number of influenza cases in the United States for 100 out of 108 weeks.[20]

In addition to this breach of the privacy of individual users, Google committed an even bigger breach of the public's trust. Google has expanded researchers' ability to examine our search queries and has given them a motive to focus in particular on some of the most sensitive information about us: our medical symptoms.[21] This sort of research is usually the domain of respected medical research institutions with an established track record of respecting

---

17 *Da Silva Moore v Publicis Groupe et al.*, No. 1:2011cv01279 – Document 175 (S. D.N.Y. 2012).

18 G Dunne, 'Regulation Z: Turn of the Tide' (1977) 94(2) *Banking Law Journal* 99, 99.

19 C Arthur, 'Google Flu Trends Is No Longer Good at Predicting Flu, Scientists Find', *The Guardian* (27 March 2017) <https://www.theguardian.com/technol ogy/2014/mar/27/google-flu-trends-predicting-flu>.

20 C Arthur, 'Google Flu Trends Is No Longer Good at Predicting Flu, Scientists Find', *The Guardian* (27 March 2017) <https://www.theguardian.com/technol ogy/2014/mar/27/google-flu-trends-predicting-flu>.

21 P Ohm, 'The Underwhelming Benefits of Big Data' (2012) 161 *University of Pennsylvania Law Review* 339, 342.

personal privacy and that conduct human research subject to ethics approvals.[22]

If tech giants like Google can gather our online search terms to guess what medical symptoms we might have, it may be lucrative for big pharmaceutical companies to purchase that raw data and conduct their own research – free of the usual constraints imposed by regulators and obligations to get informed consent. In the future, if big data is to be the basis of medical research and if its outcomes are to be trusted, then it should be done within the ambit of responsible research; conducted by trained researchers; with consent; and subject to controls and monitoring of trust protocols.

Of course, if Google has asked users if they want to help avoid pandemics and save lives, then most would probably agree to such use. However, the privacy debate about this project was not held openly with users, regulators and experts. Instead, Google pressed ahead with the project without seeking anyone's permission.

Clearly big data analytics can still be plagued by the same sample errors, biases and methodological hurdles of traditional information gathering. Notwithstanding Google's massive data capture capability and its vast warehousing of international data from 25 countries, it turned out a more accurate prediction model for the forthcoming week was the relatively humble and more manageable number of cases recorded by the United States Center for Disease Control in the previous week.

---

22 See also, Professor Schwartz's examples of beneficial analytics focus largely on health researchers who, presumably, undergo scrutiny by institutional review boards, in PM Schwartz, 'Information Privacy in the Cloud' (2013) 161 *University of Pennsylvania Law Review* 1623, 1631–32.

21 The End of Ownership in Digital Economies?

One of the most tangible effects of digital economies is the form of the content that we purchase. Before the advent of Kindle, iTunes and AppleTV, books, music and films were purchased as paperbacks, records and CDs (compact discs) or 'DVDs ('digital video discs' or 'digital versatile discs'). In these physical formats, we could create libraries that we owned in such a complete sense that we could lend or bequeath these titles to friends and family. In digital economies, retailers and copyright holders argue that we do not own such purchases. We merely license them. That means e-book vendors (for example) can delete the book from our device without warning or explanation. This fact has surprised some purchasers of digital content in recent years.

This tenuous relationship between purchasers of content and content providers was made apparent in a dramatic and prosaically ironic way when – in 2009 – Amazon deleted copies of George Orwell's dystopian novel *1984* from hundreds of their customers' Kindles. An Amazon spokesman said at the time that the books were added to the Kindle store by a company that did not have rights to them (using an Amazon self-service function). When Amazon was notified of this by the holder of the rights to *1984*, Amazon moved to remove the illegal copies from their systems and from customers' devices. The customers were refunded when the content was unilaterally removed.[1]

In 2012, Hollywood actor Bruce Willis attempted to create a testamentary trust to preserve his music collection for his children after his death. However, his lawyer informed him that the licence he has purchased gives him the right to listen to content, but does not create a right or a type of ownership that can be conveyed or transferred to someone else (including under his will). It is understandable that Mr Willis might assume he had purchased the content outright. Apple's media services agreement provides that through Apple's services, consumers can 'buy, get, license, rent or subscribe to media, apps ("Apps"), and other in-app services ("Content")'. The inclusion of the word 'buy' in this clause seems to confer outright ownership when purchased.

---

1   B Stone, 'Amazon Erases Orwell Books from Kindle', *New York Times* (17 July 2009) <https://www.nytimes.com/2009/07/18/technology/companies/18ama zon.html>.

However, it is in the detail of the usage rules for each type of content that the limitations become apparent. For example, the word 'license' appears 57 times in the Agreement conditions. However, the word 'own' is found just three times and in relation to the ownership of the device on which the content can be played or viewed. Other clauses stipulate that rentals via iTunes are viewable for just 48 hours and music purchases can only be burned to CD up to seven times. Family sharing is allowed on numerous devices, but the original agreement remains connected to the Apple ID of the original purchaser. The purchaser's Apple ID is required to manage and maintain the service. It seems that Mr Willis could bequeath his iPods to his children and they could then listen to the music on those devices. However, this is merely a technical work-around and not a legal right that is conferred by the gift of the device. The content remains subject to the conditions set by Apple and has limitations on life cycle and support, which attach to the purchaser's ID only.[2]

The assertion by digital content providers that their products are provided subject to a licence only is a declaration that is at odds with both established consumer expectations and marketing claims by retailers. For example, when consumers download from iTunes, the link to click reads: *Buy now on iTunes.* [3] Purchasers could be forgiven for assuming that the word 'buy' means that they will own the content outright. This can be distinguished from the words 'Rent now' or 'License now'. Within the iTunes app, there is an option to *Gift this song.* The law has long been settled that a 'gift is complete upon delivery'. The purchaser of the gift might in this case imagine themselves to be a donor of a song to the donee, who will receive the gift and own it outright. However, this is not the case. The gift is the purchase of a licence for the donee to enjoy the song. However, the original purchaser is not the licensee. This creates complexity about how the song or other gifted content can be controlled by the donee in the future that is all covered in the lengthy terms and conditions of the vendor. This is a graphic example of the problem that arises when users experience in the online marketplace creates a different expectation to the reality that is only discoverable if the purchaser reads the vendors' terms and conditions. The sale of items in the physical world tends towards using these terms in a way that aligns with expectations. For example, real estate websites have buttons for users to select to indicate whether they are looking for a property to buy or to rent.

Notions of ownership have shifted in the digital marketplace, and make an argument for the benefits of personal property.[4] While ebooks, Cloud storage, streaming and other digital goods offer users convenience and flexibility, consumers should be aware of the trade-offs involving user constraints, permanence, and privacy.

2   Apple Media Services Terms and Conditions <https://www.apple.com/ca/legal/internet-services/itunes/ca/terms.html>.
3   iTunes Charts <https://www.apple.com/au/itunes/charts/movies/>.
4   A Perzanowski and J Schultz, *The End of Ownership* (The MIT Press, 2016).

For this reason, introducing aspects of private property and ownership into the digital marketplace would offer both legal and economic benefits. Our relationship with physical files in a drawer is very different to how we regard and relate to a file in the Cloud. This shift is happening just as dramatically with respect to testamentary requests for the deletion of files.

During our lifetimes we have the right to access, modify and delete our data. However, these rights attach to us personally and do not continue after we die. Unlike inheritance law, which recognises heirs as the continuation of the deceased person, in regard to digital matters the heirs have no right to stop the use of processed data or recover data if the deceased person expressed no last wishes. As we know from Bruce Willis' experience, even if the deceased has expressed last wishes about the use of their content, the rights of the beneficiaries and the powers of executors may not accord with the wishes of the deceased.

Article 40 of the United States Data Protection Act deals with the data of deceased persons, and provides that 'the heirs of a deceased person, providing proof of their identity, may ... require the data controller to take the death into account and update the data accordingly'. Under the European Union's General Data Protection Regulation, personal data must be erased immediately where the data are no longer needed for the original processing purpose, or the data subject has withdrawn his consent and there is no other legal ground for storing or processing the data.[5]

Furthermore, when a person dies, friends and relatives must decide whether to delete all the deceased's data or to ensure the digital survival of the deceased. A huge amount of data and information is collected about people during their lifetimes, and the growth of professional and personal social networks is only increasing this phenomenon. Of course, if the deceased left instructions about what to do with their social media accounts (for example), this would be an easier decision-making process.

The right to be forgotten is not unreservedly guaranteed. It is limited, particularly if it conflicts with the right of freedom of expression and information. Other exceptions are if the processing of data which is subject to an erasure request is necessary to comply with legal obligations, for archiving purposes in the public interest, scientific or historical research purposes, statistical purposes or for the defence of legal claims.

It will be interesting to test in court a beneficiary's objection to the deletion of the deceased's online content or 'property' on the grounds that the request is against good policy, capricious or vindictive. In the physical world, requests made by testators to have property and assets destroyed as part of their legacy can be stopped by the courts.[6] A testator cannot require their successor to do something that is capricious or against good policy.

---

5   Art. 17 General Data Protection Regulation Right to erasure ('right to be forgotten') (2018) <https://gdpr-info.eu/art-17-gdpr/>.
6   A Perzanowski, 'You Buy It, You Break It: A Comment on Dispersing the Cloud', (2017) 74 *Washington & Lee Law Review* 527, 531.

There are many examples of the courts refusing requests by testators to destroy their property after their death. In the early English case of *Egerton v Brownlow*, [7] it is stated:

> The owner of an estate may himself do many things which he could not (by a condition) compel his successor to do. One example is sufficient. He may leave his land uncultivated, but he cannot by a condition compel his successor to do so.

In the case of *In re Scott's Will, Board of Commissioners of Rice County v. Scott et al/*, [8] the Supreme Court of Minnesota was invited to rule on a direction to an executor to destroy money belonging to the estate. In *Brown v Burdett*, [9] the testatrix devised her house with directions that the doors and windows be boarded, shuttered, bricked and sealed, to be held by the trustees in this wasteful manner for twenty years. In both cases, the courts struck down the offending clauses in the wills on the basis that they were included vindictively and were against public policy. In *Eyerman v Mercantile Trust Co*, [10] a testator's sought the destruction of her house. Louise Woodruff Johnston was the owner of the property in question. She died in January 1973, and by her will directed the executor 'to cause our home at 4 Kingsbury Place to be razed and to sell the land upon which it is located and to transfer the proceeds of the sale to the residue of my estate'. The Plaintiffs asserted that razing the home would adversely affect their property rights, violate the terms of the subdivision trust indenture for Kingsbury Place, as well as produce an actionable private nuisance and be contrary to public policy. The court found that demolition of the dwelling would indeed result in an unwarranted loss to this estate, the plaintiffs and the public.

These cases reveal an interesting split in the way that the courts regard on our treatment of property while we are alive and after death. Courts have long expressed the greatest scepticism of the right to destroy when it comes to real property. Property owners have a lot of control over their physical property while they are alive, but not after death. This shift is also evidence in the digital world. However, it may become problematic as testators make requests for their digital content to be destroyed.[11]

There is likely to be a difference in approach depending on whether the content that a testator seeks to destroy was created by the testator or not; and whether there are third party intellectual property or copyright interests

---

7   *Egerton v Brownlow* (1853) 10 Eng Rep 359, 417.
8   *In re Scott's Will, Board of Commissioners of Rice County v. Scott et al.*, 88 Minn. 386, 93 N.W. 109 (1903).
9   *Brown v Burdett* (1882) 21 Ch Div 667.
10 *Eyerman v Mercantile Trust Co* (1975) 524 S.W.2d 210.
11 See D Martin, 'Dispersing the Cloud: Reaffirming the Right to Destroy in a New Era of Digital Property' (2017) 74 *Washington & Lee Law Review* 467, 510–11 (2017) (noting terms and conditions of various Cloud providers).

attached to that content. For example, a social media post, email or messenger communication would not usually create third party rights. However, digital music or art work might have licensing arrangements that limit the capacity to delete freely or destroy the content. One proposed solution could be the creation of a digital asset trust. The Trust's ownership of the assets can survive death. Moreover, Trusts can be amended more easily than wills, a useful mechanism for both ownership of the assets and recording of information so that others can access them. A Trustee of digital assets is able to secure and manage valuable property as well as user IDs and passwords.

The way we protect our digital assets and personal information is usually managed with password and identification numbers. Protecting these after our death is a critical step in ensuring the security of our assets that are the subject of our wishes as expressed in our wills. A deceased may want their financial, health and employment information deleted by service-providers. The reason for wanting this personal information deleted could be to protect privacy or assets. In a time where identity theft of both the living and the deceased is rife, the rights of deceased whose personal data security has been breached will be fertile ground for future litigation. Consumers and users need to trust digital platforms. Trust is created and supported when we feel in control of our digital assets, personal data and online communications, both while we are alive and after we die.

22 Conclusion

The advent of the Internet has had a significant impact on commerce and human interaction, and that impact has further accelerated since the advent of mobile computing. However, technological change has caused uncertainty and legal problems. The next step in this evolution seems to demand a reduction in the friction that causes uncertainty and litigation. The technologies that are available to help address these problems includes messaging applications, voice controlled devices and advances in artificial intelligence (specifically machine learning, natural language processing) and natural language understanding. The next wave of e-commerce will feature automated contracts and chat bots.

In order to address the crisis of trust in social relationships as well as legal and democratic institutions, it is necessary to identify the root cause of its erosion. Strategic challenges that countries face regarding cyberspace and the fight against cybercrime are being addressed through the coordination of effort between government agencies and international standards organisations.[1] These include in particular strengthening law enforcement cooperation on a global and at regional levels; implementing a 'multi-stakeholder approach' by strengthening cooperation with the economy, academia and civil society; developing a legal framework for the exchange of information among businesses as well as between public authorities and the private sector; and, finally, by strengthening digital economies at the national in order to foster governments', economies' and citizens' trust in digital products and services.[2]

The key question for the maintenance of trust is determining where machines can replace humans and where they cannot. This is important in many areas of human endeavour, but of particular significance in the way we do business. While assessing the behaviour and trustworthiness of automated systems, it is important to keep in mind that competent humans are capable of

---

1 For example, the Institute of Electrical and Electronics Engineers (IEEE, founded 1884) and the International Standards Organisation (ISO, founded 1949) develop standards for new technologies that promote and support interoperability, reliability, and trust in systems See, IEEE.org <https://www.ieee.org/about/corporate/governance/p7-8.html>; and ISO.org <https://www.iso.org/>.
2 M Plachta, 'New Measures on Counter-terrorism and Cybersecurity Proposed by the European Union' (2015) 31(5) *International Enforcement Law Reporter* 176, 177.

making mistakes,[3] unfairly discriminating[4] and acting dishonestly.[5] The implementation and regulation of automation needs to aim explicitly at reducing errors, eliminating bias and behaving honestly. Systems are also needed to automate auditing, reporting and transparency, while protecting data and personal privacy. Such a framework will enable and support both human and automated trust in digital economies.

Societies benefit from high levels of social trust, and while we are now communicating quicker and in a greater variety of ways than ever before, it is not immediately obvious whether the many forms of digital technology and their rapidly evolving natures have a positive or negative impact on the social trust within a society.[6] Trust becomes a particularly important concept when we look beyond the traditional focus on voluntary relations among persons who are more or less equals.[7]

In an era of 'technology-driven capitalism' the frameworks of democracy, the free market and fair trade remain as valuable and as venerated as ever. However, the more important institutions of stable family, harmonious community, mutual respect and social trust cannot be legislated into existence.[8]

When we think about the design of online systems that will power digital economies, we must ask how we will design new systems to enable certain norms. This is a significant interaction in the context of trust because we live in a time when we rely on code that has been programmed into our online environment to substitute for 'trust'.[9]

A number of studies have identified a lack of trust as one of the main possible constraints on e-commerce, particularly in terms of consumer protection.[10] The

3   See, LT Kohn et al., eds, 'To Err is Human: Building a Safer Health System – Comment on Quality of Health Care in America' (2000) *Institute of Medicine* 63.

4   See generally Sendhil Mullainathan et al., *The Market for Financial Advice: An Audit Study* (Nat'l Bureau Econ. Research, Working Paper No. 17929, 2012) (noting that financial advisers tend not to de-bias their clients and instead often reinforce biases that are in their interests).

5   See, N Mazar et al., 'The Dishonesty of Honest People: A Theory of Self-Concept Maintenance' (2008) 45 *Journal of Marketing Research* 633, 642.

6   P McBride, 'Digital Technologies and the Erosion of Social Trust', in *Essays* (8 November 2017) <https://paulmcbride.me/2017/11/08/essay-digital-technology-and-the-erosion-of-social-trust/>.

7   D Koehn, 'Should We Trust in Trust?' (1996) 34 *American Business Law Journal* 183, 187.

8   F Fukuyama, *Trust: The Social Virtues and the Creation of Prosperity* (Free Press Paperbacks, 1995), 4.

9   L Lawrence, 'Preface to a Conference on Trust' (2001) 81 *Boston University Law Review* 329, 300.

10 For example, A Ben-Ner and L Putterman, 'Trust in the New Economy', HRRI Working Paper 11–02 Industrial Relations Centre, University of Minnesota (June 2002) <https://pdfs.semanticscholar.org/c7b4/b844243d9fb4428e59073727 d2352104e97b.pdf>. In this report, the survey findings in 2001 reveal that 60% of adults who go online in the United States do not do business on the Internet due to privacy and security concerns, and 86% of those who do business have concerns

potential for difficulties in establishing the authenticity of the identity of a consumer or online business is one of the characteristics that distinguishes trust issues in electronic environments from most other contexts. At a broad level, the degree of trust that prevails among parties to economic transactions depends on a number of factors. Significantly, it has been suggested that high-trust cultures enjoy better economic results because they can execute more transactions at lower cost.[11] De Filippi and Wright argue that legal entities deploying blockchain technology can decrease uncertainty among shareholders and investors by reducing the risk that parties will act in conflict with their own self-interest. Blockchain's transparency and cryptographic validation of transactions can foster trust within and between organisations. This in turn may result in competitive advantages and the production of more wealth.[12]

The value of trust for a particular purpose is obviously, and plainly, contingent upon a pile of factors that cannot be known in the abstract. Fukuyama's claim that 'trust makes relationships efficient'[13] may be true given a certain combination of technologies. For example, contracts allow strangers with no basis for trust to work with one another, but the process works far more efficiently when the trust exists. However, with another combination of technologies, there may evolve a more efficient way to support institutions of trust.[14] The Internet is the ultimate emergent phenomenon: a platform for untold forms of economic, social and personal connectivity and interaction. The challenge will be to find a way to build trust into these interactions.

We can subject these mechanisms to legal regulation, but then we will need regulators to regulate the regulators. If we are to avoid an endless regress, we will have to trust persons at some point to look after our interests. We cannot specify every relevant circumstance or condition of every human interaction even if we wanted to do so. At some point we are simply driven to trust other persons.[15]

The extent of trust is a function of both characteristics of A and B and of characteristics of the situation. Among these characteristics is B's degree of trustworthiness, an attribute that is determined by the costs and benefits associated with building and maintaining a reputation, the cost and ability to deceive, the agent's preferences and values regarding acceptable modes of

about giving out personal information. See also, 'IBM-Harris Multi-National Consumer Privacy Survey', *Privacy & American Business* (January 2000).

11 F Fukuyama, *Trust: The Social Virtues and the Creation of Prosperity* (Free Press Paperbacks, 1995), 149.

12 See, P De Filippi and A Wright, *Blockchain and the Law: The Rule of Code* (Harvard University Press, 2018).

13 F Fukuyama, *Trust: The Social Virtues and the Creation of Prosperity* (Free Press Paperbacks, 1995), 150.

14 L Lawrence, 'Preface to a Conference on Trust' (2001) 81 *Boston University Law Review* 329, 300.

15 D Koehn, 'Should We Trust in Trust?' (1996) 34 *American Business Law Journal* 183, 187

behaviour, and the anticipated actions of other parties that bear on the costs of engaging in prohibited behaviour.

Greater social trust enables both greater levels of economic growth as well as more stable and reliable political institutions. In this way, social trust performs many of the same functions as the rule of law and thus can be seen as a valuable complement to the rule of law in building healthy societies and economies.[16] The rule of law is a precondition for both economic growth and the achievement of human capabilities such as literacy, health and other amenities of life.[17] This is because economic activities are regulated by a legal system and social norms. If these rules and systems cannot be relied upon, all that remains is chaos. Chaos is unpredictable and nothing can be trusted in a chaotic system.

Trust in digital economies is still a gamble that relies upon people and systems, as well as the digital environment in which the relevant business, service or enterprise functions. Trust in government is also crucial for ensuring financial inclusion, regulatory compliance as well as securing investment, and therefore digital opportunity. Indeed, research conducted at the Chinese University of Hong Kong reveals that a higher level of trust can facilitate coordination in a firm or across firms by encouraging innovators to share ideas and knowledge which can potentially boost innovation. Innovation as a channel through which trust affects economic growth.[18] A higher level of trust can provide a greater tolerance for failure by allowing innovators to take actions without fear of the adverse consequences. While appropriate skills and good faith are fundamental requirements in commercial trust, innovative businesses have greater investment opportunities. When the intangible essentials are present and manifestly so, investors will be more willing provide external equity finance. A higher level of trust can reduce investor concerns, lower firms' financial constraints and allow them to pursue long-term investment.

The predominantly positive societal outcomes of generalised social trust results from one important quality of trust: it facilitates co-operation between people and among groups of people. High levels of social trust lead to more economic growth. Economic growth leads to greater levels of social trust.[19] As this book has demonstrated, both legal and technology systems can serve the vital purpose of instilling trust and cooperation into relations between strangers, so that they will feel as comfortable doing business online as they would face-to-face. Only with trust can our digital economies thrive.

16 TJ Zywicki, 'The Rule of Law, Freedom, and Prosperity' (2003) 10 *Supreme Court Economic Review* 1, 26.
17 MC Nussbaum, 'Martha C. Nussbaum's Jefferson Lecture: Powerlessness and the Politics of Blame', University of Chicago Law School (12 July 2017) <https://www.law.uchicago.edu/news/martha-c-nussbaums-jefferson-lecture-powerlessness-and-politics-blame>.
18 W Zhang et al., 'China Business Knowledge', *CUHK* (2017) <https://cbk.bschool.cuhk.edu.hk/>.
19 TJ Zywicki, 'Bankruptcy Law as Social Legislation' (2001) 5(2) *Texas Review of Law & Politics* 393.

Index